The Enforcement of Securities

Wenming Xu

The Enforcement of Securities Law in China

A Law and Economics Assessment

 Springer

Wenming Xu
School of Law and Economics
China University of Political Science
and Law
Beijing, China

This book is financially supported by the Fundamental Research Funds for the Central Universities, Fok Ying Tung Education Foundation for Junior Faculties in the Higher-Education Institutions, and Interdisciplinary Nurturing Program of China University of Political Science and Law.

ISBN 978-981-19-0906-1   ISBN 978-981-19-0904-7   (eBook)
https://doi.org/10.1007/978-981-19-0904-7

This Springer imprint is published by the registered company Springer Nature Singapore Pte Ltd.
The registered company address is: 152 Beach Road, #21-01/04 Gateway East, Singapore 189721, Singapore

Contents

1 **Introduction**   1
   References   7

2 **Law, Enforcement and Securities Market Development**   9
  2.1 Legal Determinants of Securities Market Development   9
  2.2 The Rise of "Enforcement Matters Hypothesis" 11
      2.2.1 Theoretical Discussions Concerning Securities Law
            Enforcement 11
      2.2.2 Case Study: American Private Enforcement Regime 13
      2.2.3 Case Study: American Public Enforcement Regime 15
  2.3 The Law and Finance of Securities Law Enforcement in China 17
      2.3.1 Public Enforcement of Securities Law in China 17
      2.3.2 Private Enforcement of Securities Law in China 18
      2.3.3 Preliminary Reflections on the Securities Law
            Enforcement in China 20
   References 21

3 **China's Securities Market and Anti-Securities-Fraud "Law
on the Book"** 25
  3.1 The Establishment of National Stock Exchanges
      and the Quota Regulation 25
  3.2 Securities Law of 1998 and the Merit Regulation 28
  3.3 Securities Law of 2005 and the Split Share Reform 30
  3.4 The Registration Reform and Securities Law of 2019 32
  3.5 Securities Law of 2019 and Anti-Securities-Fraud Rules 36
      3.5.1 Disclosure Obligation and the Liability
            for Misrepresentations 36
      3.5.2 The Prohibition of Insider Trading and the Liability
            of Inside Traders 41
      3.5.3 The Prohibition of Market Manipulation
            and the Liability of Manipulators 44
   References 46

**4 Public Enforcement Initiated by the CSRC and Its Regional
    Offices** 49
　　4.1 CSRC and Its Enforcement Proceedings 49
　　4.2 Enforcement Inputs of the CSRC 55
　　4.3 Enforcement Outputs of the CSRC 58
　　　　4.3.1 Enforcement Outputs at Commission Level 58
　　　　4.3.2 Enforcement Outputs at the Regional Office Level 61
　　4.4 Is CSRC's Enforcement Action Biased? 65
　　　　4.4.1 Hypotheses and Sample 65
　　　　4.4.2 Empirical Findings 66
　　4.5 Is CSRC's Enforcement Action "Toothless"? 71
　　　　4.5.1 Hypothesis Development 71
　　　　4.5.2 Sample Description 72
　　　　4.5.3 Stock Market Reactions to Enforcement Actions 73
　　References 78

5 Complementary Public Enforcement Proceedings 81
　　5.1 Alternative Enforcement Proceedings Administered
　　　　by the CSRC 81
　　　　5.1.1 Prioritized Compensation Scheme 81
　　　　5.1.2 Administrative Settlement Regime 83
　　5.2 Enforcement Efforts of the Stock Exchanges 86
　　5.3 Enforcement Efforts of the Securities Association of China 89
　　5.4 Enforcement Efforts of the Ministry of Finance 90
　　5.5 Criminal Enforcement Proceedings 90
　　5.6 Is Public Enforcement of the CSRC and Stock Exchanges
　　　　Responsive? 92
　　　　5.6.1 The Categorical Analysis of the Enforcement Outputs 93
　　　　5.6.2 The Tested Hypotheses 94
　　　　5.6.3 Empirical Findings 95
　　References 99

**6 SPC's 2003 Provisions and the Collective Action Problem
    of Securities Litigation** 101
　　6.1 Institutional Background 101
　　6.2 The Enforcement Outputs of Securities Litigation 105
　　6.3 The Calculation of the Tortious Compensation 110
　　6.4 Collective Action Hypothesis, Sample and Identification 113
　　6.5 Empirical Findings 116
　　References 118

**7 Securities Law of 2019 and the Enhanced Private Enforcement
    Regime** 121
　　7.1 Securities Law of 2019 and Multidimensional Securities
　　　　Litigation System 121
　　7.2 Regular Representative Litigation: Wuyang Case 126

7.2.1   The Corporate Bond Sector and Wu Yang
Misrepresentation Case 126
7.2.2   The Debatable Elements About the Compensation
Awarded 127
7.3   Special Representative Litigation 131
7.3.1   China Securities Investor Services Centre 131
7.3.2   The Specialized Financial Court 133
7.3.3   Kangmei Case 134
7.4   Stock Market Reactions to the Private Enforcement Reform 137
7.4.1   The Hypothesis, Identification Strategy and Sample 137
7.4.2   Market Responses to SPC's 2020 Provisions 139
7.4.3   Market Responses to Wuyang Case and Kangmei Case 140
7.5   Alternative Dispute Resolution for Securities Fraudulent
Misconducts 141
References 144

8   **Conclusion** 145

About the Author

Wenming Xu is Associate Professor and Associate Dean of School of Law and Economics at China University of Political Science and Law (CUPL). He obtained his BA in Economics and Master of Law from CUPL and Ph.D. in Law and Economics from University of Bologna. Wenming's research interests mainly include law and economics, securities law and regulation, and empirical legal studies, and he teaches Law and Economics, Law and Finance, and Empirical Methods in Legal Studies at both undergraduate and postgraduate levels. Wenming has served as Visiting Scholar at University of Oxford, University of Chicago, Northwestern University, National University of Singapore, and Max Planck Institute for Comparative and International Private Law. He has received multiple research grants and published extensively in both international and Chinese peer-reviewed journals, including *International Review of Law and Economics*, *European Business Organization Law Review*, *European Journal of Law and Economics*, and *Economics of Governance*.

Chapter 1
Introduction

The law and economics scholarship has a long tradition in studying law enforcement, as least dating back to the Nobel Laureate Gary Becker. In his seminal paper, the author argues that criminals are rational actors, and they will compare expected benefits and costs in their decision-making process.[1] Both law and enforcement will contribute to the deterrence of potential criminal behaviors. Securities law enforcement discussed in this book is defined as the procedures through which legal liabilities are imposed on those committing securities misconduct, which mainly include misrepresentation, insider trading and market manipulation. It can be further divided into two broad categories, i.e., private enforcement and public enforcement, based on the identity of the entities initiating the enforcement proceedings.[2] Private enforcement is primarily initiated by private entities through civil litigation, arbitration or mediation proceedings.[3] In contrast, public enforcement is initiated by public agencies, mainly through administrative and criminal proceedings.

A rich body of literature has already analyzed the advantages and disadvantages of public and private enforcement. The advantage of private enforcement is obvious: the costs and benefits derived from the enforcement proceeds will be enjoyed by the enforcers, and their incentives are compatible with the promotion of enforcement proceedings.[4] Hence, they act like "bounty hunters" and have strong incentives to advance enforcement actions.[5] In addition, private enforcement has an informational advantage in dealing with certain misconducts, particularly those directly infringing on private benefits. Finally, private parties have incentives to innovate during enforcement proceedings, which might reduce social enforcement costs.

At the same time, private enforcement also suffers from certain disadvantages. In situations where private benefits from enforcement proceedings are smaller than

---

[1] Becker [1].

[2] Polinsky and Shavell [2].

[3] Landes and Posner [3].

[4] Polinsky [4].

[5] Coffee [5].

W. Xu, *The Enforcement of Securities Law in China*,
https://doi.org/10.1007/978-981-19-0904-7_1

private costs, even though the social benefits might be extremely large, private entities are unlikely to initiate enforcement proceedings due to collective action problems.[6] This phenomenon is most noticeable in "mass tort" cases, such as those relating to environmental pollution and securities fraud, in which a large number of victims suffer small personal damages.[7] In addition, the risks of frivolous and strike suits are significant.[8] Private parties tend to enforce excessively in situations where private costs are smaller than social costs and, hence, cause negative externalities. Finally, private enforcement might disturb public enforcement instead of cooperating with it.[9] Public agencies often maintain a cooperative relationship with the regulated agencies and offer lenient sanctions in exchange for future compliance. Private enforcement could undermine the long-term relationship between these parties.[10]

The advantages of public enforcement mainly concentrate on its professionalism and economies of scale. On the one hand, the staffs of public agencies are trained specialists and repeatedly deal with similar cases. They will accumulate much higher human resources than private parties, which significantly reduces the average enforcement costs. On the other hand, public enforcers enjoy a noticeable economy of scale in dealing with cases that have a large number of victims. In the case of private enforcement, the victims have to repeatedly assume the enforcement costs, whereas public enforcers can pool the cases together and only have to pay once for the enforcement action. Furthermore, public enforcers have an informational advantage in dealing with certain misconducts, particularly in situations where private parties have no information about the violators or the misconduct, such as insider trading.[11]

The disadvantage of public enforcement is mainly related to incentive problems. Public agents normally receive fixed compensation, which is uncorrelated with the number of enforcement actions initiated, but the costs of public enforcement are, instead, partly borne by public agents.[12] Hence, they lack sufficient incentives to pursue cases that mostly benefit private victims. In addition, public enforcement is subject to the risk of selective enforcement. On the one hand, violators have strong incentives to pursue rent-seeking activities and try to reduce the sanctions imposed.[13] As the size of the penalties increase, the corruption risks also surge accordingly because violators are willing to pay more to public agents. On the other hand, public enforcement tends to stick to political preferences, avoiding enforcing, or enforcing lightly, against certain entities.[14]

Securities law enforcement has drawn far and wide academic attention from empiricists since the early 2000s. The empirical law and finance movement claims

---

[6] Choi [6].

[7] Faure and Weber [7].

[8] Van den Bergh [8].

[9] Hay and Shleifer [9].

[10] Rose [10].

[11] Shavell [11].

[12] Schantl and Wagenhofer [12].

[13] Becker and Stigler [13].

[14] Lemos and Minzner [14].

that investor protections on the books determine the cross-country differences in securities market development.[15] However, these arguments attracted a tidal wave of criticism from legal scholars. Alternative institutions, such as financial intermediaries and stock exchanges, could perform a similar function to protect investors' interests.[16] One major counterargument against the "Law matters" scholarship is the "Enforcement matters". It is found that the effects of law enforcement dominate the "law on the books" in cross-jurisdiction regressions.[17] Furthermore, the case study also shows that law enforcement is the major determinant for the exceptionally developed American securities market.[18]

Currently, a mixed enforcement regime has become the dominant model across the world, and different jurisdictions vary in their reliance on public or private enforcement of securities law.[19] Even in the U.S., where securities class actions are highly active, public enforcement still plays a crucial role. For example, private enforcement tends to free-ride the enforcement efforts of public regulators to increase its success rate.[20] In contrast, in Germany, where procedural law failed to provide tailored rules for mass litigation, the Capital Markets Model Case Act still specifies "model case proceedings" to reduce the litigation costs of private enforcers.[21] Seldom does a jurisdiction rely solely on either private enforcement or public enforcement to protect its investors.

In addition to academic value, the securities law enforcement regime is also of significant practical importance to emerging economies such as China.[22] The Chinese securities market was only established in the early 1990s, and most securities laws and regulations are transplanted from jurisdictions with sophisticated markets, such as the U.S. and the UK. At its early development stage, law enforcement was rarely on the radar of financial regulators, who were busy figuring out the literal text of statute securities law. As the market continues to grow broadly and deeply, investor protection has become of both economic and political importance. Due to the path-dependent effect, securities law enforcement follows a centralized regime in which public enforcement plays a dominant role and private enforcement is repressed. Since the early 2000s, securities law enforcement has been blamed for being weak and for failing to adequately protect investors.[23]

It is much more difficult to build a modern and efficient enforcement regime from scratch than to transplant legal rules. A systematic reform on securities law enforcement was partly driven by the need to rebalance the national financial structure in China. After the subprime mortgage crisis of 2007, China launched the "4 Trillion

---

[15] Pagano and Volpin [15].

[16] Cheffins [16].

[17] Jackson and Roe [17].

[18] Coffee [18].

[19] Gelter [19, p. 104].

[20] Johnson et al. [20].

[21] Verse [21, pp. 400–401].

[22] Berglof and Claessens [22].

[23] Allen [23].

Stimulus Plan" (Henceforth "Stimulus Plan") in November 2008 to mitigate the negative shock brought about by plunging exports.[24] The Stimulus Plan was designed to upgrade national infrastructure, and local governments were required to partly finance these projects.[25] Unfortunately, local governments have insufficient budgets for such large investments, and bank loans are channeled to support these projects through the shadow banking sector.[26] The side effects of the Stimulus Plan are an overreliance on the loans provided by commercial banks, which leads to a highly leveraged economy.[27]

The solution to the systemic risk of a banking crisis is to increase the amount of direct finance provided by financial markets. The Third Plenary Session of the 18th CPC Central Committee issued the Decision on the Major Issues concerning Comprehensively Deepening Reform in November 2013,[28] which, for the first time, explicitly proposed increasing the percentage of direct finance and accelerating the IPO registration reform in party policy. The deregulation of entry into the securities market is the unquestioned central part of the IPO registration reform. However, entry deregulation reduces *ex ante* efforts to screen out low-quality issuers, and reform also requires increasing the intensity of ongoing monitoring and *ex post* enforcement, which will counteract the negative effects on investor protection.

Hence, the China Securities Regulatory Commission (CSRC) launched a pilot project to delegate the authority to impose administrative sanctions on Regional Offices (ROs) in Shanghai, Guangdong and Shenzhen.[29] In October 2013, it further expanded the scope of the delegation, and all ROs obtained authority.[30] The CSRC issued the Opinions on Further Strengthening Securities Law Inspection and Enforcement[31] to streamline the enforcement proceeding and explicitly ranked law enforcement among the top policy priorities. According to the Provisions of the ROs to Impose Administrative Sanction,[32] the Commission-level enforcement department

---

[24] Hachem and Song [23].

[25] Chen et al. [24].

[26] Guo and Xia [25].

[27] Bai et al. [26].

[28] See Zhonggong Zhongyang Guanyu Quanmian Shenhua Gaige Ruogan Zhongda Wenti De Jueding, available at http://www.beijingreview.com.cn/2009news/wenujian/2014-01/24/content_5 92979.htm (Last accessed 31 October, 2021).

[29] See The CSRC Delegated Administrative Sanction Authority to ROs in Shanghai, Guangdong and Shenzhen in Pilot Project, available at http://news.hexun.com/2010-11-02/125372590.html (Last accessed 31 October, 2021).

[30] See The CSRC Delegated Administrative Sanction Authority Comprehensively, available at http://finance.people.com.cn/stock/n/2013/0930/c67815-23082442.html (Last accessed 31 October, 2021).

[31] See Guanyu Jinyibu Jiaqiang Jicha Zhifa Gongzuo De Yijian (promulgated on 19 August 2013), available at http://www.csrc.gov.cn/pub/newsite/zjhxwfb/xwdd/201308/t20130819_232829.html (Last accessed 31 October, 2021).

[32] See Paichu Jigou Xingzheng Chufa Gongzuo De Guiding (promulgated on 27 September 2013), available at http://www.csrc.gov.cn/pub/newsite/zjhxwfb/xwdd/201309/t20130927_235486.html (Last accessed 31 October, 2021).

is only responsible for investigating and sanctioning major cases, and ROs are responsible for cases within their jurisdictions.

The governance structure of China's public enforcement of securities law mimics its authoritarian political regime, which is also called a "regionally decentralized authoritarian (RDA) model".[33] The RDA model combines the attributes of centralization and decentralization. On the one hand, the Chinese political and personnel governance structure has been highly centralized, and subnational government officials have been appointed and promoted from above. On the other hand, substantial powers are delegated to subnational governments. They have general responsibility for initiating and coordinating reforms, providing public services, and making and enforcing laws within their jurisdictions. Hence, local governmental officials compete with each other in key indicators established by their superiors in their efforts to strive for political promotion.[34]

The relationship between the CSRC and its local agencies duplicates the relationship between China's central and local governments. On the one hand, local agencies are subject to the CSRC's orders (particularly its personnel power), which means that authority is highly centralized. On the other hand, local agencies have been granted considerable power to regulate listed companies, leading to a certain degree of decentralization. The RDA regime significantly increases public enforcement outputs for the following reasons. First, the incentive mechanism of ROs is aligned with the goal of increasing enforcement intensity.[35] Officials in local agencies are incentivized to compete with each other on performance indicators, such as sanctions issued or fines collected each year, and therefore become aggressive in law enforcement. Moreover, an RDA-like governance structure helps to improve the performance of China's public enforcement in securities law by taking advantage of the territorial proximity between local agencies and targeted listed companies.[36] Finally, an RDA-like structure distances the CSRC itself from blame-generating situations in which local agencies fail to enforce securities law effectively. In other words, local agencies act as 'buffer zones' that protect the CSRC from social dissatisfaction and cushion the CSRC from potential crises.

The reform in securities private enforcement reform was deferred until the Securities Law was revised in 2019. The Supreme People's Court of China (SPC) issued the Provisions Concerning the Adjudication of Civil Compensation Securities Cases Based upon Misrepresentation of 2003 (Henceforth "SPC's 2003 Provisions")[37] to govern private litigations and adopted an "opt-in" design, which only allows investors

---

[33] Xu [27].

[34] Li and Zhou [28].

[35] Zhu [29].

[36] Xu et al. [30].

[37] See Zuigao Renmin Fayuan Guanyu Shenli Zhengquan Shichang Yin Xujia Chenshu Yinfa De Minshi Peichang Anjian De Ruogan Guiding (promulgated on.9 January 2003), see http://www.csrc.gov.cn/pub/tianjin/tjfzyd/tjjflfg/tjsfjs/201210/t20121015_215783.htm (Last accessed 31 October, 2021).

to initiate individual or joint suits. Harmed investors are, therefore, poorly compensated because of collective action problems. Investor protection and compensation are major problems addressed in the process of IPO registration reform. The revised draft of the Securities Law was first submitted to the Standing Committee of the National People's Congress for review in April 2015. However, the stock market later suffered from a severe crisis, in which the major stock market indices fell by nearly two-thirds. Market fluctuations slowed down legislative progress, and the newly revised version, which appeared to be more conservative, was submitted for a second review in April 2017. Finally, the third review of the revised draft was only carried out in April 2019, and the revised Securities Law was enacted at the end of 2019. The Securities Law of 2019 stipulates a multilayered securities private litigation regime. The most radical innovation is the Chinese-style class action, which adopts the American "opt-out" design and assigns the lead plaintiff role to nonprofit investor protection agencies.

Such legislative choice is a balance between the costs of frivolous suits and the benefits of investor compensation. On the one hand, the "opt-out" design maximizes the number of plaintiffs that could participate in litigation and partly solves the collective action problem. It significantly decreases the average costs for harmed investors to obtain judiciary relief. On the other hand, the court trial is not controlled by self-interested private parties but by investor protection agencies, which do not have strong incentives to pursue frivolous suits or to sacrifice the interests of investor groups for their own interests.[38] However, investor protection agencies work similarly to governmental entities, which might compromise their role in pursuing the maximization of investor compensation. Based on the limited number of cases adjudicated following the Securities Law of 2019, the damages paid by those found culpable have increased significantly.

Due to the aforementioned academic and policy value, this book tries to examine the securities law enforcement regime in China and is arranged as follows. Chapter Two reviews the related literature on the relationship between securities law enforcement and the theoretical advantages and disadvantages of public and private enforcement. Chapter Three reviews the evolution of securities regulatory regimes and discusses the substantive rules regulating securities misconduct, including misrepresentation, insider trading and market manipulation, and administrative and criminal liabilities against the background of the Securities Law of 2019. Chapter Four provides an in-depth empirical analysis of the enforcement proceedings initiated and administered by the CSRC and its ROs. Chapter Five examines the enforcement efforts of other public agencies and empirically tests whether the enforcement proceedings of the CSRC and the stock exchanges are responsive to the behavior of regulatees. Chapter Six empirically analyses the collective action problem of harmed investors under the "opt-in" design. Chapter Seven examines the outputs of securities litigation and compares the case outcomes before and after the enactment of the Securities Law of 2019. Chapter Eight concludes the book.

---

[38] Lin and Xiang [31].

References

1. Becker, G. S. (1968). Crime and punishment: An economic approach. *Journal of Political Economy, 76*(2), 169–217.
2. Polinsky, M., & Shavell, S. (2000). The economic theory of public enforcement of law. *Journal of Economic Literature, 38*, 45–76.
3. Landes, W. M., & Posner, R. A. (1975). The private enforcement of law. *Journal of Legal Studies, 4*(1), 1–46.
4. Polinsky, M. (1980). Private versus public enforcement of fines. *The Journal of Legal Studies, 9*(1), 105–127.
5. Coffee, J. (1983). Rescuing the private attorney general: Why the model of the lawyer as bounty hunter is not working. *Maryland Law Review, 42*, 215–288.
6. Choi, S. J. (2004). The evidence on securities class actions. *Vanderbilt Law Review, 57*, 1465–1526.
7. Faure, M., & Weber, F. (2016). Potential and limits of out-of-court rapid claims settlement: A law and economics analysis. *Journal of Environmental Law, 28*(1), 125–150.
8. Van den Bergh, R. (2013). Private enforcement of European competition law and the persisting collective action problem. *Maastricht Journal of European and Comparative Law, 20*(1), 12–34.
9. Hay, J. R., & Shleifer, A. (1998). Private enforcement of public laws: A theory of legal reform. *American Economic Review, 88*(2), 398–403.
10. Shavell, S. (1993). The optimal structure of law enforcement. *The Journal of Law and Economics, 36*(1), 255–287.
11. Schantl, S. F., & Wagenhofer, F. (2020). Deterrence of financial misreporting when public and private enforcement strategically interact. *Journal of Accounting and Economics, 70*(1), 101311.
12. Becker, G., & Stigler, G. (1974). Law enforcement, malfeasance, and compensation of enforcers. *Journal of Legal Studies, 3*, 1–18.
13. Lemos, M. H., & Minzner, M. (2006). For-profit public enforcement. *Harvard Law Review, 127*, 853–913.
14. Pagano, M., & Volpin, P. (2006). Shareholder protection, stock market development, and politics. *Journal of the European Economic Association, 4*(2–3), 315–341.
15. Cheffins, B. R. (2001). Does law matter? The separation of ownership and control in the United Kingdom. *The Journal of Legal Studies, 30*(2), 459–484.
16. Jackson, H. E., & Roe, M. J. (2009). Public and private enforcement of securities laws: Resource-based evidence. *Journal of Financial Economics, 93*, 207–238.
17. Coffee, J. C. (2007). Law and the market: The impact of enforcement. *University of Pennsylvania Law Review, 156*(2), 229–311.
18. Gelter, M. (2019). Global securities litigation and enforcement. In P.-H. Conac & M. Gelter (Eds.), *Global securities litigation and enforcement* (pp. 3–108). Cambridge University Press.
19. Johnson, M. F., Nelson, K. K., & Pritchard, A. C. (2007). Do the merits matter more? The impact of the private securities litigation reform act. *Journal of Law, Economics, and Organization, 23*, 627–652.
20. Verse, D. A. (2019). Germany: Liability for incorrect capital market information. In P.-H. Conac & M. Gelter (Eds.), *Global securities litigation and enforcement* (pp. 363–411). Cambridge University Press.
21. Berglof, E., & Claessens, S. (2006). Enforcement and good corporate governance in developing countries and transition economies. *World Bank Research Observer, 21*, 123–150.
22. Allen, F., Qian, J., & Qian, M. (2005). Law, finance, and economic growth in China. *Journal of Financial Economics, 77*(1), 57–116.
23. Hachem, K., & Song, Z. (2021). Liquidity rules and credit booms. *Journal of Political Economy, 129*(10), 2721–2765.
24. Chen, Z., He, Z., & Liu, C. (2020). The financing of local government in China: Stimulus loan wanes and shadow banking waxes. *Journal of Financial Economics, 137*, 42–71.

25. Guo, L., & Xia, D. (2014). In search of a place in the sun: The shadow banking system with Chinese characteristics. *European Business Organization Law Review, 15*, 387–418.
26. Bai, C., Hsieh, C., & Song, Z. M. (2016). The long shadow of a fiscal expansion. *Brookings Papers Economic Activity, 60*, 309–327.
27. Xu, C. (2011). The fundamental institutions of China's reforms and development. *Journal of Economic Literature, 49*(4), 1076–1151.
28. Li, H., & Zhou, L. (2005). Political turnover and economic performance: the incentive role of personnel control in China. *Journal of Public Economics, 89*(9–10), 1743–1762.
29. Zhu, X. (2012). Understanding China's growth: Past, present, and future. *Journal of Economic Perspectives, 26*(4), 103–124.
30. Xu, W., Chen, J., & Xu, G. (2017). An empirical analysis of the public enforcement of securities law in China: Finding the missing piece of the puzzle. *European Business Organization Law Review, 18*(2), 367–389.
31. Lin, Y.-H. L., & Xiang, Y. (2022). The rise of non-profit organizations in global securities class action: A new hybrid model in China. *Columbia Journal of Transnational Law, 60* (Forthcoming).

Chapter 2
Law, Enforcement and Securities Market Development

2.1 Legal Determinants of Securities Market Development

It is widely recognized that the securities market development is positively related to the intensity of external investors protection. Early theoretical discussions on stock market development mainly focus on product competition, and pay no attention to legal institutions. It is argued that product competition will discipline issuers, because those who exploit external investors will have higher production costs due to increased costs for external finance.[1] Consequently, it is important to maintain a competitive product market, instead of imposing securities laws and regulations, which will eventually increase the production costs.

However, both the product and securities markets are far from perfect competition in real world, and legal protection for investors is valuable from a principal-agent perspective.[2] Legal institutions facilitate stock market development because they curb agency costs, which could be broadly grouped into the following three types: The one between professional managers and shareholders in firms with dispersed ownership structures; the one between controlling shareholders and minority shareholders in firms with dominant shareholders; and the one between shareholders and other corporate constituencies, such as creditors in the vicinity of insolvency.[3] Poor investor protection increases the agency costs, and hence the required rate of return for external investors.[4]

The empirical law and finance literature has devoted significant efforts in proving the relationship between investor protection law and securities market development. Since the late 1990s, the "legal origin theory", which is defined as "a style of social control of economic life (and maybe of other aspects of life as well)", has gained both academic and political popularity. In the seminal paper coauthored by La Porta,

---

[1] Stigler [1].

[2] Shleifer and Vishny [2].

[3] Kraakman et al. [3].

[4] Shleifer and Wolfenzon [4].

© The Author(s), under exclusive license to Springer Nature Singapore Pte Ltd. 2022
W. Xu, *The Enforcement of Securities Law in China*,
https://doi.org/10.1007/978-981-19-0904-7_2

Lopez-de-Silanes, Shleifer and Vishny, the authors argue that laws in most countries are transplanted from a small number of legal traditions through conquest, colonization, and imitation, which results in two main legal traditions: common law, which is English in origin, and civil law, which derives from Roman law and can be further classified into French, German, and Scandinavian law.[5] Common law countries are found to better protect investors (shareholders and creditors) than civil law countries, and on-the-book securities law, as measured by the "antidirector rights index" and "creditor rights index", is shown to be empirically correlated with the securities market development in the cross-jurisdiction study.[6]

The scholarship inspires a series of studies examining the effects of investor protection on securities market outcomes. La Porta et al. compare the effects of *de jure* rights of public and private enforcers on stock market development using data from 49 countries and concludes that private enforcement, which are proxied by those rules increasing information disclosure and the rights of private litigants, dominates public enforcement in facilitating stock market development.[7] Djankov et al. later construct the "anti-self-dealing index" measuring the legal protection of minority shareholders against the exploitation from corporate insiders, and also find that the index is positively correlated with stock market development.[8] Cumming et al. look into the anti-fraud listing rules of 42 stock exchanges and find that the stock exchange liquidity as measured by velocity, volatility, and bid-ask spread is highly correlated with the quality of trading rules concerning insider trading and market manipulation.[9] The underlying rationale for the aforementioned studies is straightforward: because the external protection of minority investors is strong, their interests are less likely to be exploited by corporate insiders. Hence, investors will require a smaller discounting factor and are willing to put their money in securities market, which leads to a higher percentage of external finance and developed market.

Another strand of literature follows the law and finance nexus in the transitional and emerging economies, which is featured with state-owned enterprises and controlled listed companies. Considering that the securities laws in these jurisdictions are drafted with general terms and highly incomplete, the enforcement regime should be a much more important determinant for their stock markets development.[10] The empirical findings concerning the law and securities market development in this group of jurisdictions are mixed. For example, Pistor et al. construct revised shareholder protection indices and find that only the quality of securities market regulation matters for stock market development using data from 22 transition economies.[11] One explanation for the observed diverged effects of legal rules is the transplant

---

[5] La Porta et al. [5].
[6] La Porta et al. [6].
[7] La Porta et al. [7].
[8] Djankov et al. [8].
[9] Cumming et al. [9].
[10] Pistor and Xu [10].
[11] Pistor et al. [11].

effect, which argues that the transplanting process will influence the legality of the transplanted rules, and consequently the economic outcomes of the transition countries.[12]

The first generation of "Law matters" scholarship suffers from several caveats in the research design, though their conclusions are attractive.[13] The identification assumption that legal origins are valid instruments for endogenous institutional variables is rejected because the assumption violates the exclusion restrictions.[14] Without valid instruments, it is highly likely that the empirical conclusion that "Law matters" suffers from the omitted variable bias, model specification bias and reverse causality bias.[15] Meanwhile, the popular indices, such as the "antidirector rights index" and "anti-self-dealing index", are constructed with home-country bias, which employs the American criteria as the yardsticks for measuring the quality of corporate governance in other countries. Finally, studies conducted from time-series perspectives negate the "Law matters" argument. Panel data analysis finds no significant correlation between legal institutions and proxies for stock market development.[16] Countries with weak shareholder protection, for example, those with French legal origins, have in recent years been found to converge with the best practices in *de jure* corporate governance institutions.[17]

2.2 The Rise of "Enforcement Matters Hypothesis"

2.2.1 Theoretical Discussions Concerning Securities Law Enforcement

Besides the aforementioned caveats, the "Law matters" hypothesis faces strong competition from the "Enforcement matters hypothesis". The seminal paper by Nobel Laureate Gary S. Becker proposes that rational violators will consider the expected benefits and costs of criminal behavior. Given that the expected benefits are exogenous, the expected costs will be determined by the *de jure* punishment and the intensity of enforcement.[18] Globally, most jurisdictions adopt a mix of both public and private enforcement, but are varied in their preferences of the enforcement instruments.[19] Cross-country empirical studies generally confirm the "Enforcement matters hypothesis". Bhattacharya and Daouk present an empirical study using a

---

[12] Berkowitz et al. [12].

[13] La Porta et al. [13].

[14] Bazzi and Clemens [14].

[15] Xu [15].

[16] Armour [16].

[17] Martynova and Renneboog [17].

[18] Becker [18].

[19] Gelter [19].

sample of 103 jurisdictions and find that the enforcement of insider trading laws, instead of the introduction of such laws, significantly reduces the costs of equity finance.[20] Furthermore, Jackson and Roe use the staffing number and annual budget as the proxies for the intensity of public enforcement, and find that these indicators are more powerful in explaining the stock market outcomes than *de jure* rules.[21]

In addition to the "Enforcement matters hypothesis", the law and society school develops the "Responsive Enforcement Theory", which focuses on constructing the optimal enforcement strategy responding to the behaviors of regulatees. It is argued that market participants are heterogenous in complying with legal rules, and could be divided into three broad categories[22]: First, the virtuous actors are self-motivated to comply with laws and regulations, because they are morally driven to pursue the civic virtue. Hence, the enforcement regime should not employ punishments to deter their criminal behavior, but adopt instruments to encourage their compliance. Second, the rational actors are "Becker-type" and carry out cost–benefit analysis on criminal behaviors. Law enforcement should consider the usage of optimal publishment to deter their misconducts. Third, the irrational actors, who nevertheless will conduct infringe the legal rules, without calculating potential personal costs and benefits. The best enforcement strategy is to exclude this group from the securities market. Consequently, the deterrence-oriented enforcement strategy overlooks the different incentives for complying the law, and hence might result in distorted incentives. The "Responsive Enforcement Theory" promotes a pyramidal enforcement strategy, which starts with a lenient sanction and escalates punishments if the offender chooses not to cooperate.[23] It further develops into "smart enforcement" emphasizing the cooperation between self-regulation and co-regulation to enforce legal rules, which will bring additional resources to secure the law enforcement.[24]

The optimal securities law enforcement regime is a mix between public and private enforcement, and is local and determined by the historical, cultural, economic and political conditions of a given jurisdiction.[25] The most prominent case identified in the literature for the "Enforcement matters hypothesis" is the American securities enforcement regime, which adopts a decentralized model.[26] Public enforcers including Securities and Exchange Commission (SEC), Financial Industry Regulatory Authority, Department of Justice and state regulators, together with private parties could independently initiate enforcement proceedings.[27] Both the public and private enforcement are highly developed in the U.S., and the high enforcement

---

[20] Bhattacharya and Daouk [20].

[21] Jackson and Roe [21].

[22] Ayres and John Braithwaite [22].

[23] Braithwaite [23].

[24] Gunningham et al. [24].

[25] Gelter [19].

[26] The majority of enforcers cite Section 11 of 1933 Securities Act against misrepresentation in the registration documents and the Section 10(b) of the 1934 Securities Exchange Act and Rule 10b-5 to combat with secondary market fraudulent behaviors.

[27] Rose [25].

intensity assures the deterrence to securities misconducts and the compensation to harmed investors.

2.2.2   Case Study: American Private Enforcement Regime

The private enforcement, as represented by securities class action, is highly active and regarded as a "failsafe" for public enforcement in the U.S.[28] The "entrepreneurial litigation", which is characterized as the one financed and managed by risk-taking attorneys representing a large number of claimants holding small stakes, is even regarded as the "American exceptionalism".[29] Securities fraud is a typical mass tort case, which involves a large number of small harmed investors mainly holding negative value claims.[30] Hence, those investors will suffer from collective action problem and be passive to initiate private litigation to protect their own interests, if there is no special procedure for group representation.[31] American securities class action provides strong incentives to securities attorneys, who are also called "private attorney general" and act as a principal instead of agent, to promote securities litigation.[32]

Instead of requiring investors to opt into the securities litigation individually, American class action adopts an "opt-out" design, which stipulates that harmed investors are deemed to join the plaintiff class unless they explicitly express to quit the class. The design aggregates the claims of harmed investors and maximizes the class size. By taking the advantage of economy of scale, the class action minimizes the average private enforcement costs for obtaining the damages. In addition to the "opt-out" design, three other institutional arrangements facilitate the development of American class action.[33] The first one is the contingent attorney fee agreement. Comparing to the fix fee arrangement, it provides strong incentives for plaintiff's attorneys to maximize the damages and aligns the interests of the two parties. In addition, plaintiffs are exempted from the "loser-pays-fee" rule. There is a special "American rule" on fee shifting for plaintiffs, who will only have to bear its own attorney fee even if they lose the case. The rule minimizes the potential loss for entrepreneurial attorneys. Third, the attorney fee is paid from the recovered damages. According to the legal doctrine of unjust enrichment, it is possible to pay plaintiff's attorneys out of the realized damage, instead of from certain plaintiffs. The cost-sharing mechanism solves the problem relating to the litigation funding, and encourages the securities lawyers to prepaid for the costs to obtain judiciary reliefs.

---

[28] Coffee [26].

[29] Coffee [27].

[30] Such claims are negative in value because the litigation costs are much higher than the expected recovery, though the case is meritorious, see Coffee [27].

[31] Xu [28].

[32] Rubenstein [29].

[33] Coffee [30].

The outputs of securities class action in the U.S. are significantly higher than those in other jurisdictions.[34] There were 427 cases filed in the federal and state courts in 2019, though the number decreased to 334 in 2020 due to the world-wide pandemic.[35] In 2019, about 8.9% of listed companies in NYSE and Nasdaq serve as the defendant in securities class filings, and the litigation risks have been rising for 8 consecutive years since 2012.[36] In about 87% of the cases, the plaintiffs alleges that the defendants beak the Rule 10b-5, at the same time, in 98% of cases the defendant are alleged to conduct misrepresentation in financial documents.[37] An interesting phenomenon of the securities class action is the filing outcomes. In 2019, only about 1% of the cases filed between 1997 and 2018 reached a trial verdict, and about 49% and 43% of cases are settled and dismissed, respectively.

However, such high-powered private enforcement also brings significant costs to American securities market. On one hand, it is criticized that the frivolous suits and strike suits are costing American listed companies too much, and the American securities markets are losing its competitive advantages.[38] On the other, the investors in general are not satisfactorily compensated, because a significant proportion of covered damages are paid to securities attorneys. The aforementioned two caveats are due to the agency costs, which is ascribed to the fact that the U.S. entrepreneur litigations are dominate by attorneys. First, it is shown that the plaintiff's attorneys are overbilling the clients to boost the attorney fee, which significantly reduces the amount distributed to harmed investors.[39] Second, because the securities class actions are *de facto* financed and controlled by securities attorneys, and the decision to settle the case is mainly made by these attorneys subjecting to weak client and control and court oversight, it is shown that settlements fail to maximize the welfare of the plaintiff class.

The U.S. Congress passed the Private Securities Litigation Reform Act (PSLRA) of 1995, National Securities Markets Improvement Act of 1996 and Securities Litigation Uniform Standards Act of 1998 to reform the private enforcement regime. The effects of these legislations on securities class action found in empirical studies are mixed.[40] For example, PSLRA reforms the rule for lead plaintiff and regards the plaintiffs with the most stakes to be the adequate lead plaintiff, rather than assign it to those who bring the case first. The change aims at reducing the influence of the professional plaintiffs and encouraging the harmed institutional investors to control the litigation. However, empirical studies show that institutional investors seem to

---

[34] Gevurtz [31].

[35] Cornerstone Research [32, p. 1].

[36] Cornerstone Research [33, p. 11].

[37] Cornerstone Research [33, p. 10].

[38] Doidge et al. [34].

[39] Choi et al. [35].

[40] Choi [36].

be apathetic to the participation of the litigation,[41] and lawyers increase their political donations to those official with control over the institutional shareholders, in
exchange for be appointed as the plaintiff's representative.[42]

2.2.3 Case Study: American Public Enforcement Regime

The public enforcement of securities law in the U.S. is also of high intensity. SEC,
being an independent regulatory agency, is delegated with the authority to administer
the Securities Act of 1933 and Securities Exchange Act of 1934.[43] The organizational
structure of SEC includes five divisions, 23 offices and 11 regional offices, among
which the Division of Enforcement and regional offices are mainly responsible for
enforcing securities law.[44] According to its annual report, SEC maintained over 4,500
staff and its annual budget was around 2.6 billion dollars in 2020.[45] The budget of
SEC experiences significant cyclical feature, which tends to increase significantly
after major financial scandal.[46]

The public enforcement intensity, as measured by enforcement outputs, is
increasing during the last two decades.[47] Most recently, the annual average outputs
of SEC between 2016 and 2020 are around 808 enforcement proceedings,[48] of
which around 10% are against public companies and their subsidiaries.[49] According
to a recent empirical research, the most frequent misconducts targeted by SEC
enforcement proceedings are Broker-Dealer, Delinquent Filing, Investment Advi-
sors/Investment Companies, Issuer Reporting and Securities Offering.[50] In addition,
SEC imposes billions of monetary penalties through the enforcement proceedings,
for example, in total 4.68 billion dollars are ordered in 2019, of which 3.6 billion
dollars are disgorgement of ill-gotten gains and 1.1 billion dollars are penalties.[51] It
is worthy noted that the size of monetary damages collected by SEC is only around

---

[41] Cox and Thomas [37].

[42] Choi et al. [38].

[43] Choi and Pritchard [39].

[44] Atkins and Bondi [40].

[45] SEC [41].

[46] Lohse and Thomann [42].

[47] SEC's enforcement proceedings could be further divided into primary enforcement action, follow-
on action and secondary enforcement action. If the latter two types of actions, which require
fewer regulatory inputs are excluded, the growth rate of the public enforcement is much lower,
see Velikonja [43].

[48] SEC Enforcement Division [44, p. 16].

[49] Choi [45].

[50] SEC Enforcement Division [44, p. 17].

[51] SEC Enforcement Division [44, p. 17].

half of that ordered.[52] Such monetary penalties are then used to compensate harmed investors by way of fair funds, which distribute about 14.5 billion dollars between 2002 and 2013.[53]

The public enforcement also brings other significant indirect costs. Notably, firms sanctioned by SEC on average suffer from about −25.24% decrease in their market capitalization,[54] and about 93% and 28% of individuals sanctioned lose their jobs and face criminal sanctions, respectively.[55] But a very recent empirical study finds only mild decline of −2.73% in market capitalization for sanctioned firms, which suggests that the magnitudes of the impacts of public enforcement on stock price are uncertain.[56] In addition, public enforcement might indirectly influence the future business of sanctioned intermediaries. For example, if financial intermediaries are sanctioned by SEC, not only they will lose its future market share, but also those listed companies served by these intermediaries will suffer from stock price decline.[57]

The SEC's enforcement actions also face some controversies. First, it takes the advantages of the authorized prosecutorial discretion, and undertakes forum-shopping to move the cases from federal and district courts to its Administrative Law Judges.[58] Such movement is most obvious after the Dodd-Frank Act of 2010 authorizing SEC to impose civil penalties through the Administrative Law Judges.[59] Empirical research shows that SEC has brought complex and weaker cases to its administrative proceedings to achieve a settlement with the defendants and maximize its monetary penalties.[60] Second, the majority of these enforcement proceedings are settled, instead of reaching a verdict. Furthermore, defendants with such settlements are allowed to neither admit or deny the allegations, which is favorable to those involved entities in the sense that their reputational capital is maintained and damages will be paid by insurance companies.[61] The major incentives for SEC to settle are two folds. On one hand, SEC is limited in resources and needs to make tradeoff between cases.[62] Settlement will save valuable resources, which could be used in other enforcement actions. On the other, the enforcement proceedings of SEC face significant failure risk, because the results of a trial are uncertain. To minimize the probability of failure, SEC could achieve part of policy goals without risking the enforcement actions by settling with the defendants.

---

[52] Velikonja [43].

[53] Velikonja [46].

[54] Karpoff et al. [47].

[55] Karpoff et al. [48].

[56] Choi [45].

[57] For an empirical study on securities underwriter, see Beatty et al. [49].

[58] Jones [50].

[59] Velikonja [51].

[60] Choi and Prichard [52].

[61] Slaughter [53].

[62] Thomsen [51].

2.3 The Law and Finance of Securities Law Enforcement in China

Due to the effects of path dependence, China adopts a centralized enforcement model, in which the public enforcement led by the CSRC, plays a dominant role, and private enforcement is overlooked. Law enforcement in China has long been blamed to be weak, which even compromises the effectiveness of the strong "on-the-book" rules.[63] It is regarded as the counterexample to the "Law-and-Finance Nexus" that claims an efficient law enforcement system is a prerequisite for financial market development.[64] However, a static and "black-or-white" view could not reflect the dynamics of China's securities enforcement regime. This subsector reviews the literature in this field.

2.3.1 Public Enforcement of Securities Law in China

Public enforcement mainly serves the deterrence function but fails to compensate harmed investors.[65] On one hand, empirical studies show that the frequency of and direct costs due to the enforcement actions of the CSRC in the early twentieth century are relatively low. Before 2011, the CSRC initiated very few enforcement proceedings against listed companies, and the monetary penalties are of small scale, which are partly due to the statutory limits on the maximum monetary fines.[66] During the early years of the stock market development, the enforcement actions were not disclosed by the CSRC, but the sanctioned firms themselves, which significantly delayed the timeliness of information disclosure and the dissemination of valuable information to market participants.[67]

In addition, the public enforcement action also leads to significant indirect costs. It is shown that those sanctioned firms generally experience between -1 and -2% decrease in their market capitalization.[68] Furthermore, public enforcement also increases the costs of debt for sanctioned firms.[69] Both indirect costs are argued to be mainly ascribed to the reputational loss, because their contractual counterparts will reassess the potential risks of the sanctioned listed companies. Another source of indirect costs is the forced turnover of incumbent insiders. The enforcement actions against fraudulent misconducts committed by listed companies increases the propensity of its CEO turnover. But the effects are also dependent on the ownership structure of the listed companies, for example, the effects are generally compromised in the

---

[63] Humphery-Jenner [55].

[64] Allen et al. [56].

[65] Xu et al. [57].

[66] Zhou [58].

[67] Firth et al. [59].

[68] Chen et al. [60].

[69] Gong et al. [61].

subsample of state-owned listed companies.[70] And the final indirect costs of public enforcement are the decrease in their competitive advantage in the product market, and sanctioned firms on average suffer from about -11.9 to -17.1% decline in sales revenue and -2.4 to -2.8% in the gross profit margin.[71]

The enforcement of the two stock exchanges, the major self-regulatory agencies, also attracts a lot of academic attention. An early study finds that those firms publicly criticized by the Shanghai Stock Exchange and Shenzhen Stock Exchanges between 2001 and 2006 experienced between -1% and -2% over the 3-day event window.[72] A more recent study on the "letters of concern" issued by the two stock exchanges in the situation where listed companies try to amend their charters and add takeover defense, shows that those amendments significantly decreasing shareholder value are stopped due to such "soft law" approach that encourage listed companies to self-regulate.[73]

Another strand of literature studies the enforcement proceedings against particular type of fraudulent behavior. For example, in examining the public enforcement against insider trading cases, it is found that the CSRC deviated from the theory of fiduciary duty and misappropriation as required by the Securities Law and adopted an equal access theory in identifying the insider trading misconducts.[74] It is also documented that the number of enforcement proceedings against insider trading was extremely low before 2011, and increased significantly thereafter. Between 2011 and 2016, the CSRC completed 212 enforcement actions against insider trading, which is about 6 times of the number between 1991 and 2010.[75]

2.3.2 Private Enforcement of Securities Law in China

China's securities private enforcement has long been depressed due to its preference for public enforcement, and the compensation for harmed investors has been overlooked.[76] The doctrinal studies focus on the relevant legal institutions, and their resultant effects. Though it is explicitly said in the Securities Law that harmed investors are entitled to pursue tortious damages, Chinese courts were reluctant to hear such cases. SPC temporarily suspended the acceptance of private securities litigations in September 2001, because it thought that Chinese courts were not equipped with the

---

[70] Chen et al. [62].

[71] Xin et al. [63].

[72] Liebman and Milhaupt [64].

[73] Zeng [65].

[74] Howson [66].

[75] Huang [67].

[76] Xu [28].

expertise to hear such cases.[77] Such judiciary standings received overwhelming criticisms. SPC quickly changed its attitude and ordered the lower courts to hear such cases in January 2002.[78] Later, SPC issued a follow-on measure about the substance and procedural requirements of the civil litigations concerning securities fraud in April 2003, and the SPC's 2003 Provisions became the primary judiciary guidance since then.

However, SPC's 2003 Provisions is unfriendly to harmed investors and imposes significant substantive and procedural hurdles.[79] First, it adopts an "opt-in" design, which requires investors to bring individual or joint suits and actively participate in the litigation.[80] This arrangement is in sharp contrast to the "opt-out" design of the American class action, which allows harmed investors to free-ride and get compensated. Second, harmed investors face several procedural obstacles to obtain judiciary relief. Firstly, it limits civil compensations only to those investors harmed by securities misrepresentation, and excludes those harmed by insider trading and market manipulation.[81] Secondly, those investors harmed by securities misrepresentation had to satisfy the administrative prerequisites so that Chinese courts would hear their cases. The prerequisites include administrative sanctions issued by governmental agencies and criminal judgments delivered by Chinese courts. Thirdly, the jurisdictional rules are not friendly to investors, because the intermediate courts in the defendant's residence have the authority over such cases. Considering that listed companies are either SOEs or large and established private enterprises, which are important to regional development, local protectionism is highly likely to drive intermediate courts to favor defendants. Because of both the substantive and procedural hurdles against private litigation, it is even argued that private enforcement should not be emphasized considering the political environment at that time.[82]

The complexity of securities law enforcement in China is manifested by the discussions of administrative prerequisites. The doctrinal analysis accuses that such arrangements significantly limit the ability of investors to access the judiciary protection, and result uneven protection of investors.[83] But several recent studies show a different picture. An empirical study collects the disclosed securities fraud cases adjudicated between 2002 and 2013, and finds that there are in total 65 cases, which

---

[77] See 2001 Notice Concerning Temporarily Not Accepting Civil Compensation Cases Related to Securities (SPC's 2001 Notice) (Zuigao Renmin Fayuan Guanyu She Zhengquan Minshi Peichang Anjian Zan Buyu Shouli De Tongzhi), available at http://www.csrc.gov.cn/pub/newsite/flb/flfg/sfjs_8249/200802/t20080227_191599.html (Last accessed 31 October, 2021).

[78] See 2002 Notice Regarding Accepting Tort Cases Arising from Stock Market False Disclosure (henceforth, SPC's 2002 Notice) (Zuigao Renmin Fayuan Guanyu Shouli Zhengquan Shichang Yin Xujia Chenshu Yinfa De Minshi Qinquan Jiufen Anjian Youguan Wenti De Tongzhi), available at http://www.csrc.gov.cn/pub/newsite/flb/flfg/sfjs_8249/200802/t20080227_191599.html (Last accessed 31 October, 2021).

[79] Lu [68].

[80] Wang and Chen [69].

[81] Lu [68].

[82] Layton [70].

[83] Wang and Chen [69].

is much fewer than those sanctioned by the CSRC.[84] It is hence concluded that the major obstacle to investor compensation is not administrative prerequisites, because a large percentage of qualified cases are not brought to Chinese courts. For those satisfying the administrative prerequisites, the qualified investors are waived with the trouble of proving that the defendants committed misrepresentation and their behaviors satisfy the standard of materiality. In analyzing the first securities fraud cases trialed by Chinese courts, i.e. *Chen Lihua et al. vs Daqing Lianyi Ltd & Shenyin Securities Ltd*,[85] it is shown that the court found the defendants guilty mainly based on the administrative sanctions issued by the CSRC.[86]

2.3.3 Preliminary Reflections on the Securities Law Enforcement in China

The securities law enforcement regime in China has attracted an increasing level of academic attention. The existing literature on this topic have generated valuable knowledge about this topic. Unquestionably, the securities law enforcement outputs in China are limited as compared to that in the U.S. However, the view is subject to two qualifications. On one hand, the high enforcement outputs in the U.S. seem to be an exception rather than the global average level. Even those common law jurisdictions lag far behind in securities law enforcement outputs. On the other, the enforcement of securities law in China should be viewed dynamically, as it has changed rapidly during the last decade. Those observations in the early twenty-first century might not be able to reflect the situation nowadays. A dynamic review about the relationship between financial market development and securities law enforcement is also conformant to the relevant theories. As the market becomes mature, the protection of the investors' interests gains both economic and political support, which will in turn facilitate the future market growth.[87] Hence, a systematic analysis of the most recent legislature and those judiciary and regulatory enforcement efforts will deliver an updated picture.

Second, there lacks sufficient empirical studies, which systemically examine the enforcement regime of securities law in China, particularly those employing large-sample data and sophisticated econometric methods. The data generated by enforcement actions are increasing compared to a decade ago. First, specialized financial data companies provide datasets for information about both public and private enforcement related to listed companies. In addition, the website of China Judgments

---

[84] Huang [71].

[85] The decision of First Instance was delivered on 19 August 2004 by the Intermediate People's Court of Harbin Municipality (Heilongjiang Province), and the decision of Second Instance by the Higher People's Court of Heilongjiang Province on 21 December 2004.

[86] Guo and Ong [72].

[87] Zhang [73].

Online,[88] which is a valuable improvement of the recent judiciary reform, discloses most judgments of the securities fraud cases. Using the new information from the two resources, this book contributes the literature by systemically analyzing the enforcement outcomes in a dynamic perspective, and tries to provide readers with a more complete picture about the underlying rationale of the securities law enforcement regime in China.

References

1. Stigler, G. J. (1958). The economies of scale. *Journal of Law and Economics, 1*(1), 54–71.
2. Shleifer, A., & Vishny, R. W. (1997). A survey of corporate governance. *Journal of Finance, 52*(2), 737–783.
3. Kraakman, R., Armour, J., Davies, P., Enriques, L., Hansmann, H., Hertig, G., Hopt, K., Kanda, H., Pargendler, M., Ringe, W.-G., & Rock, E. (2017). *The anatomy of corporate law: A comparative and functional approach* (3rd ed.). Oxford University Press.
4. Shleifer, A., & Wolfenzon, D. (2002). Investor protection and equity markets. *Journal of Financial Economics, 66*(1), 3–27.
5. La Porta, R., Lopez-De-Silanes, F., Shleifer, A., & Vishny, R. W. (1998). Law and finance. *Journal of Political Economy, 106*(6), 1113–1155.
6. La Porta, R., Lopez-De-Silanes, F., Shleifer, A., & Vishny, R. W. (1997). Legal determinants of external finance. *Journal of Finance, 52*(3), 1131–1150.
7. La Porta, R., Lopez-De-Silanes, F., & Shleifer, A. (2006). What works in securities laws? *Journal of Finance, 61*(1), 1–32.
8. Djankov, S., La Porta, R., Lopez-De-Silanes, F., & Shleifer, A. (2008). The law and economics of self-dealing. *Journal of Financial Economics, 88*(3), 430–465.
9. Cumming, D., Johan, S., & Li, D. (2011). Exchange trading rules and stock market liquidity. *Journal of Financial Economics, 99*(3), 651–671.
10. Pistor, K., & Xu, C. (2003). Incomplete law. *N.Y.U. Journal of International Law and Politics, 35*, 931–1013.
11. Pistor, K., Raiser, M., & Gelfer, S. (2000). Law and finance in transition economies. *Economics of Transition, 8*(2), 325–368.
12. Berkowitz, D., Pistor, K., & Richard, J.-F. (2003). Economic development, legality, and the transplant effect. *European Economic Review, 47*(1), 165–195.
13. La Porta, R., Lopez-De-Silanes, F., & Shleifer, A. (2008). The economic consequences of legal origins. *Journal of Economic Literature, 46*(2), 285–332.
14. Bazzi, S., & Clemens, M. A. (2013). Blunt instruments: Avoiding common pitfalls in identifying the causes of economic growth. *American Economic Journal: Macroeconomics, 5*(2), 152–186.
15. Xu, W. (2014). Law Matters? A Bayesian analysis of the cross-country relationship between anti-self-dealing rules and stock market outcomes. *Applied Economics Letters, 21*(5), 366–371.
16. Armour, J., Deakin, S., Sarkar, P., Siems, M., & Singh, A. (2009). Shareholder protection and stock market development: An empirical test of the legal origins hypothesis. *Journal of Empirical Legal Studies, 6*(2), 343–380.
17. Martynova, M., & Renneboog, L. (2011). Evidence on the international evolution and convergence of corporate governance regulations. *Journal of Corporate Finance, 17*(5), 1531–1557.
18. Becker, G. S. (1968). Crime and punishment: An economic approach. *Journal of Political Economy, 76*(2), 169–217.

---

[88] The website is available at https://wenshu.court.gov.cn/ (Last accessed 31 October, 2021).

19. Gelter, M. (2019). Global securities litigation and enforcement. In P.-H. Conac & M. Gelter (Eds.), *Global securities litigation and enforcement* (pp. 3–108). Cambridge University Press.
20. Bhattacharya, U., & Daouk, H. (2002). The world price of insider trading. *Journal of Finance, 57*(1), 75–108.
21. Jackson, H. E., & Roe, M. J. (2009). Public and private enforcement of securities laws: Resource-based evidence. *Journal of Financial Economics, 93*, 207–238.
22. Ayres, I., & Braithwaite, J. (1992). *Responsive regulation: Transcending the deregulation debate.* Oxford University Press.
23. Braithwaite, J. (2011). The essence of responsive regulation. *UBC Law Review, 44*(3), 475–520.
24. Gunningham, N., Grabosky, P., & Sinclair, D. (1998). *Smart regulation: Designing environmental policy.* Oxford University Press.
25. Rose, A. M. (2009). Multienforcer approach to securities fraud deterrence: A critical analysis. *University of Pennsylvania Law Review, 158*, 2173–2231.
26. Coffee, J. C. (2016). *Entrepreneurial litigation: Its rise, fall, and future.* Harvard University Press.
27. Coffee, J. C. (2007). Law and the market: The impact of enforcement. *University of Pennsylvania Law Review, 156*(2), 229–311.
28. Xu, W. (2016). Reforming private securities litigation in China: The stock market has already cast its vote. *International Review of Law and Economics, 45*, 23–32.
29. Rubenstein, W. B. (2004). On what a private attorney general is and why it matters. *Vanderbilt Law Review, 57*, 2129–2173.
30. Coffee, J. C. (2017). The globalization of entrepreneurial litigation: Law, culture, and incentives. *University of Pennsylvania Law Review, 165*, 1895–1925.
31. Gevurtz, F. A. (2019). United States: The protection of minority investors and compensation of their losses. In P.-H. Conac & M. Gelter (Eds.), *Global securities litigation and enforcement* (pp. 109–142). Cambridge University Press.
32. Cornerstone Research. (2020). *Securities class action filings: 2020 year in review.*
33. Cornerstone Research. (2019). *Securities class action filings: 2019 year in review.*
34. Doidge, C., Karolyi, A., & Stulz, R. M. (2010). Why do foreign firms leave U.S. equity markets? *Journal of Finance, 65*, 1507–1553.
35. Choi, S. J., Erickson, J., & Pritchard, A. C. (2020). Working hard or making work? Plaintiffs' attorney fees in securities fraud class actions. *Journal of Empirical Legal Studies, 17*(3), 438–465.
36. Choi, S. J. (2004). The evidence on securities class actions. *Vanderbilt Law Review, 57*, 1465–1525.
37. Cox, J. D., & Thomas, R. S. (2002). Leaving money on the table: Do institutional investors fail to file claims in securities class action? *Washington University Law Quarterly, 80*, 855–865.
38. Choi, S. J., Fisch, J. E., & Pritchard, A. C. (2005). Do institutions matter: The impact of the lead plaintiff provision of the private securities litigation reform act. *Washington University Law Quarterly, 83*, 869–906.
39. Choi, S. J., & Pritchard, A. C. (2019). *Securities regulation: Cases and analysis* (5th ed., pp. 857–937). Foundation Press.
40. Atkins, P., & Bondi, B. (2008). Evaluating the mission: A critical review of the history and evolution of the SEC enforcement program. *Fordham Journal of Corporate & Financial Law, 13*, 367–417.
41. SEC. (2020). *Agency financial report: Fiscal year 2020.* Available at https://www.sec.gov/reports-and-publications/annual-reports/sec-2020-agency-financial-report. Last accessed 31 Oct 2021
42. Lohse, T., & Thomann, C. (2015). Are bad times good news for the securities and exchange commission? *European Journal of Law and Economics, 40*, 33–47.
43. Velikonja, U. (2016). Reporting agency performance: Behind the SEC's enforcement statistics. *Cornell Law Review, 101*, 901–980.
44. SEC Enforcement Division. (2020). *Enforcement division 2020 annual report.* Available at https://www.sec.gov/files/enforcement-annual-report-2020.pdf. Last accessed 31 Oct 2021

45. Choi, S. J. (2020). Measuring the impact of SEC enforcement decisions. *Fordham Law Review, 89*(2), 385–408.
46. Velikonja, U. (2015). Public compensation for private harm: Evidence from the SEC's fair fund distributions. *Stanford Law Review, 67*, 331–395.
47. Karpoff, J. M., Lee, S., & Martin, G. (2008). The consequences to managers for cooking the books. *Journal of Financial Economics, 88*, 193–215.
48. Karpoff, J. M., Lee, S., & Martin, G. (2008). The cost to firms of cooking the books. *Journal of Financial and Quantitative Analysis, 43*, 581–612.
49. Beatty, R. P., Bunsis, H., & Hand, J. R. (1998). The indirect economic penalties in SEC investigations of underwriters. *Journal of Financial Economics, 50*, 151–186.
50. Jones, R. (2015). The fight over home court: An analysis of the SEC's increased use of administrative proceedings. *S.M.U. Law Review, 68*, 507–536.
51. Velikonja, U. (2017). Are the SEC's administrative law judges biased? An empirical investigation. *Washington Law Review, 92*, 315–370.
52. Choi, S. J., & Prichard, A. C. (2017). The SEC's shift to administrative proceedings: An empirical assessment. *Yale Journal on Regulation, 34*, 1–32.
53. Slaughter, S. R. (1988). Statutory and non-statutory responses to the director and officer liability insurance crisis. *Indiana Law Journal, 63*, 181–200.
54. Thomsen, L. (2009). *Testimony of Linda Chatman Thomsen before the United States Senate Committee on Banking, Housing and Urban Affairs Concerning Investigations and Examinations by the Securities and Exchange Commission and Issues Raised by the Bernard L. Madoff Investment Securities Matter.* Available at https://www.securitiesdocket.com/2009/01/27/testimony-of-secs-linda-thomsen-before-senate-banking-committee-madoff-matter/. Last accessed 31 Oct 2021
55. Humphery-Jenner, M. (2013). Strong financial laws without strong enforcement: Is good law always better than no law? *Journal of Empirical Legal Studies, 10*(2), 288–324.
56. Allen, F., Qian, J., & Qian, M. (2005). Law, finance, and economic growth in China. *Journal of Financial Economics, 77*(1), 57–116.
57. Xu, W., Chen, J., & Xu, G. (2017). An empirical analysis of the public enforcement of securities law in China: Finding the missing piece to the puzzle. *European Business Organization Law Review, 18*(2), 367–389.
58. Zhou, T. (2015). Is the CSRC protecting a "level playing field" in china's capital markets: Public enforcement, fragmented authoritarianism and corporatism. *Journal of Corporate Law Studies, 15*(2), 377–406.
59. Firth, M., Rui, O. M., & Wu, X. (2009). The Timeliness and Consequences of Disseminating Public Information by Regulators. *Journal of Accounting and Public Policy, 28*, 118–132.
60. Chen, G., Firth, M., Gao, D. N., & Rui, O. M. (2005). Is China's securities regulatory agency a toothless tiger? Evidence from enforcement actions. *Journal of Accounting and Public Policy, 24*, 451–488.
61. Gong, G., Huang, X., Wu, S., Tian, H., &·Li, W. (2021). Punishment by securities regulators, corporate social responsibility and the cost of debt. *Journal of Business Ethics, 171*(2), 337–356.
62. Chen, J., Cumming, D., Hou, W., & Lee, E. (2016). CEO accountability for corporate fraud: Evidence from the split share structure reform in China. *Journal of Business Ethics, 138*(4), 787–806.
63. Xin, Q., Zhou, J., & Hu, F. (2018). The economic consequences of financial fraud: Evidence from the product market in China. *China Journal of Accounting Studies, 6*(1), 1–23.
64. Liebman, B. L., & Milhaupt, C. J. (2008). Reputational sanctions in China's securities market. *Columbia Law Review, 108*, 929–983.
65. Zeng, S. J. (2019). Regulating Draconian takeover defenses with soft law: empirical evidence from event studies in China. *European Business Organization Law Review, 20*, 823–854.
66. Howson, N. C. (2012). Enforcement without foundation? Insider trading and China's administrative law crisis. *American Journal of Comparative Law, 60*, 955–1002.
67. Huang, R.H. (2002). Enforcement of Chinese insider trading law: An empirical and comparative perspective. *American Journal of Comparative Law, 68*(3), 517–575.

68. Lu, G. (2003). Private enforcement of securities fraud law in China: A critique of the Supreme People's Court 2003 provisions concerning private securities litigation. *Pacific Rim Law & Policy Journal, 12,* 781–805.
69. Wang, W.-Y., & Chen, J. (2008). Reforming China's securities civil actions: Lessons from PSLRA reform in the U.S. and government-sanctioned non-profit enforcement in Taiwan. *Columbia Journal of Asian Law, 21*(2), 115–160.
70. Layton, M. A. (2008). Is private securities litigation essential for the development of China's stock markets? *New York University Law Review, 83,* 1948–1978.
71. Huang, R. H. (2013). Private enforcement of securities law in China: A ten-year retrospective and empirical assessment. *American Journal of Comparative Law, 61*(4), 757–798.
72. Guo, L., & Ong, A. (2009). The fledgling securities fraud litigation in China. *Hong Kong Law Journal, 39,* 697–718.
73. Zhang, Z. (2016). Law and finance: The case of stock market development in China. *Boston College International and Comparative Law Review, 39*(2), 283–360.

Chapter 3
China's Securities Market and Anti-Securities-Fraud "Law on the Book"

By the end of September 2021, China had more than 4500 listed companies in its two stock exchanges, and the market capitalization reached nearly 87 trillion RMB and ranked the second in the world.[1] Considering that stock exchanges were only established in the early 1990s, i.e., the Shanghai Stock Exchange in 1990 and Shenzhen Stock Exchange in 1991, the achievements in the last thirty years are impressive. Figure 3.1 shows the annual number of newly listed companies between 1991 and 2020. The number of newly listed companies has maintained a relatively high level. In contrast to more mature markets, Chinese securities regulations prefer entry regulations, which have gone through three stages, i.e., the quota regulatory system, the merit regulatory system and the registration regulatory system. Accordingly, in the first two stages, securities law enforcement is not a primary concern, but in the registration system, ongoing monitoring and *ex post* enforcement have been repeatedly emphasized as the foundations for the healthy development of the securities market.[2] This chapter discusses the aforementioned changes and the major anti-securities-fraud rules following the Securities Law of 2019.

3.1 The Establishment of National Stock Exchanges and the Quota Regulation

The development of China's securities market is mainly driven by its gradual economic reform, and the governance of the securities market was deeply embedded in the indigenous circumstances created by the transition from a planned economy to a socialist market economy. The Chinese government adopted the Reform and

---

[1] The data is obtained from the Choice Information.

[2] See The President of the CSRC, Huiman Yi, Proposes to Increase Costs of Misconducts, Sanction Informational Misconducts and IPO fraud, available at https://www.jiemian.com/article/3213058.html (Last accessed 31 October, 2021).

W. Xu, *The Enforcement of Securities Law in China*,
https://doi.org/10.1007/978-981-19-0904-7_3

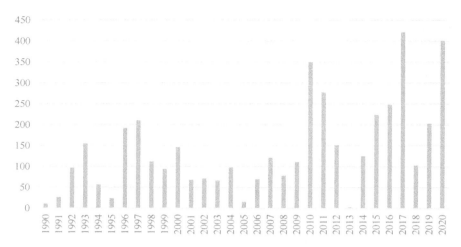

Fig. 3.1 The annual number of newly listed companies in China. *Source* Choice Information

Opening-up Policy in 1978. The state-corporate sector was inefficient in making profits and mainly relied on bank loans to survive, which also brought significant risks of nonperformance loans to the commercial bank sector.[3] State-owned enterprises (SOEs) were encouraged to diversify their financial sources in the 1980s, and the first joint-stock company was established in 1984. At that time, the concept of the securities market was seen as the primary feature of capitalism and was subject to heated debate. Eventually, a pragmatic view was adopted that the securities market is merely an instrument to facilitate economic development. The Shanghai Stock Exchange and Shenzhen Stock Exchange were established in 1990 and 1991, respectively, to cater to the financial needs of SOEs.[4] Both exchanges were established first as regional markets, subject to the supervision of local government. They had been operating without the Securities Law for nearly ten years. Market development consequently followed the principle of "crossing the river by feeling the stones", and mainly SOEs undertook IPOs to raise external equity and mitigate their financial difficulties.

For decades, the PBoC was the sole financial regulator in China and served as the first financial regulator for the Chinese securities market.[5] In the early stage, stock issuance was regulated in a decentralized fashion. Public stock issuances were required to obtain permissions from the local branches of the PBoC, and private placements to employees and other enterprises did not even need to obtain such permissions.[6] The PBoC tightened regulations in 1990 by depriving its local branches of

---

[3] See Huang [1].

[4] Walter and Howie [2].

[5] See Article 5 of the Interim Regulations on the Administration of Banks (Yinhang Guanli Zanxing Tiaoli, promulgated on 7 January 1986), available at http://fgcx.bjcourt.gov.cn:4601/law?fn=chl013 s087.txt&dbt=chl (Last accessed 31 October, 2021).

[6] Fang [3].

the authority to approve public stock issuances.[7] However, due to concerns about increasing regulatory specialization, the State Council established the Securities Policy Committee and the CSRC in October 1992. The major regulatory authority over the securities market was transferred from the PBoC to the Securities Policy Committee, which further delegated such authority to the CSRC. CSRC now supervised enforcement actions. The regulation of the securities market has been centralized ever since. It was an interesting arrangement in which the CSRC was established as an unofficial organization without administrative rank, mainly playing the role of implementing the decisions made by the Securities Policy Committee. During this period, the securities market was governed according to the Interim Regulations on the Administration of Stock Issuance and Trading of 1993 issued by the State Council. The Securities Policy Committee was dissolved in March 1998, after the first Securities Law was promulgated.

The entry regulations were regarded by the financial regulator as the key to safeguarding the development of the securities market and the interests of retail investors. However, the selection of high-quality listed companies was not an easy task. Between 1993 and 2000, the governance of the securities market mainly relied on the quota regulatory system, which was designed to mitigate the information asymmetry between issuers and external stakeholders, including financial regulators and investors.[8] Each year, the total number of shares issued was fixed, and ministerial-level governmental agencies needed to compete for the allocation of issuance quotas. Simply speaking, the financial regulatory rules set mandatory merit and disclosure requirements and invited ministerial-level agencies to recommend candidate firms.[9] It allocated the IPO quota among these agencies based on the performance of their previously recommended listed companies. The quota system provided incentives to regional governments to collect local information and select strong local SOEs to list on the market.[10] It was a compromise with regard to China's local conditions and supporting institutions. The GDP per capita was merely approximately 300 dollars, and the market-oriented reform was only in its initial stage. In addition, the private sectors were small in size, and candidate firms were mostly SOEs. Finally, the societal and political understanding of the securities market was still developing, and specialized human resources were limited. Taken together, a pure market-based governance system was regarded as unlikely to function well for Chinese securities markets.

Building a modern law enforcement regime was neither a prominent policy goal nor a pragmatic project in the short term. Private enforcement was not initiated in this period due to the tradition of repressing private litigation, whereas public

---

[7] See Notice of PBoC about Strictly Controlling Share Issues and Transfers (Zhongguo Rennin Yinhang Guanyu Yan'ge Kongzhi Gupiao Faxing He Zhuanrangde Tongzhi, promulgated on 4 December 1990), available at http://www.law-lib.com/law/law_view1.asp?id=52576 (Last accessed 31 October, 2021).

[8] Pistor and Xu [4].

[9] Fang [3].

[10] Xu and Zhuang [5].

enforcement, including administrative and criminal enforcement proceedings, was occasionally initiated in cases of securities misconduct, particularly those related to fraudulent IPOs. Because of the high rents related to the IPO quota, the officials positioned in the selection process were exposed to fierce rent-seeking activities.[11] Several high-profile scandals reveal that low-valued candidate firms cooked their books and successfully issued their shares to the general public.[12] The corruption costs due to quota systems became unbearable and impeded the healthy development of the securities market. As a result, financial regulation was pushed toward a more market-oriented model.

3.2 Securities Law of 1998 and the Merit Regulation

The first Securities Law, promulgated in 1998, delegated to the CSRC the authority to regulate the securities market. Entering the twenty-first century, one major motivation for developing the securities market in China was entry into the WTO in 2001. The commitments obliged the government to promote market-oriented reform measures. The Report of the 16th CPC National Congress explicitly emphasized the advancement of the reform and opening up of the securities market.[13] Eventually, the CSRC promulgated the CSRC Approval Procedures of Stock Issuance[14] in March 2000 to abolish the quota "on the books" and institute IPO merit-based regulations. Instead of allocating IPO quotas to ministerial-level governmental agencies, the CSRC assigned quotas to securities firms, which acted as the lead underwriters and prepared the required materials. Merit regulation based on securities firms did not last long and was replaced by the IPO sponsor regulation in 2004, which borrowed from the regulation adopted by the British securities market. In contrast to the previous regulatory regime, the sponsor system increases its reliance on market-based mechanisms, and securities firms are responsible for underwriting securities and continuously assisting issuers in complying with the listing rules. They, together with other financial intermediaries, are tasked with the gatekeeper function and assume the risks associated with not fulfilling their duties.

Candidate firms had to receive counsel from these intermediaries for one year prior to the submission of application materials. The CSRC would conduct a preliminary review about the completeness of the materials and consult the State Development Planning Commission and State Economic and Trade Commission to verify that the

---

[11] Du and Xu [6].

[12] For example, the Kang Sai case, the Hua Gufen case and Xingfu Shiye case, see Chen [7].

[13] See The Party Has Guided the Stock Market Development, available at http://www.xinhua net.com/fortune/2021-07/01/c_1127614846.htm#:~:text=2002%E5%B9%B411%E6%9C%88,%E6%94%BE%E5%92%8C%E7%A8%B3%E5%AE%9A%E5%8F%91%E5%B1%95%E2%80%9D%E3%80%82 (Last accessed 31 October, 2021).

[14] See Zhongguo Zhengjianhui Gupiao Faxing Hezhun Chengxu, available at http://www.csrc.gov.cn/shenzhen/xxfw/tzzsyd/ssgs/scgkfx/scfz/200902/t20090226_95445.htm (Last accessed 31 October, 2021).

applicant firms satisfied the national industrial policy. After the preliminary review, the application was transferred to the Issuance Examination Commission for the final vote. The CSRC then decided whether to grant the issuer permission based on the voting outcomes of the Issuance Examination Commission. In this process, the substantive review is conducted over the merits of the candidate companies, in particular their ability to make profits.

The enforcement of securities law was improved during this period, partly due to the frequent outbreak of high-profile scandals. One well-known economist commented that the stock market in China was worse than a casino,[15] which apparently was repeatedly cited, becoming a stereotype for the Chinese securities market. As revealed by the case file of Daqing Lianyi, the books were cooked by the applicant firm, the financial intermediaries and the local government together when they prepared for the IPO application.[16] Daqing Lianyi was a local SOE in the petrochemical industry and started corporatization reform in 1996. Because the Interim Regulations on the Administration of Stock Issuance and Trading of 1993 required that a qualified applicant company should make profits for three consecutive years, it cooperated with the Commission for Structural Reforms of Daqing Municipality to falsify financial statements and show that it had increased its profit by over 162 million RMB. The underwriter, Shenyin Wanguo Securities Corporation, together with law firms and accounting firms, knowingly assisted the issuer in obtaining the IPO quota. After the case was revealed, the violators received both administrative and criminal penalties. One unsolved problem was compensation for the harmed investors. After nearly five years of a court trial, 381 harmed investors in Daqing Lianyi cases finally obtained damages of approximately 9 million in December 2006.[17]

The public enforcement regime was gradually established after the enactment of the Securities Law of 1998. In September 2000, the CSRC first set up 9 regional enforcement units, based on which it further established provincial regional offices (ROs) in 2004. Since then, the ROs started to assume the regulatory authority over the securities activities within its jurisdiction and investigative responsibilities against securities misconduct, which is regarded as the most important reform for public enforcement regimes.[18] The private enforcement regime also welcomed important judiciary opinions.

Although the Securities Law of 1998 granted harmed investors the right to civil compensation, there was a lack of detailed substantive and procedural rules for adjudicating such cases. A primary concern about promoting civil compensation for harmed investors was related to the ownership structure of Chinese listed companies. According to an empirical analysis on the identities of the ultimate controllers

---

[15] The comment by Proessor Wu Jinglian was first released when he received an interview by an official channel in January 2001, available at http://finance.sina.com.cn/stock/stocktalk/20101210/15269087941.shtml (Last accessed 31 October, 2021).

[16] Xi [8].

[17] See The Case of Daqing Lianyi Settled, available at http://futures.money.hexun.com/1945598.shtml (Last accessed 31 October, 2021).

[18] Walter and Howie [2].

of the listed companies, approximately 84% of the listed companies are under state control.[19] It is highly likely that SOEs pay for private investor damage in securities fraud cases, which will further aggravate the balance sheets of troubled SOEs. Learning that a number of harmed investors brought individual claims against Hongguang Shiye, which conducted a fraudulent IPO in 1997 and was sanctioned by the CSRC in 1998, the SPC first issued the 2001 notice to temporarily stop local courts from hearing such cases. The disclosed reasons for this decision were that local courts lacked expertise and that the relevant rules were incomplete.

However, it quickly reversed its position and admitted securities litigation in the SPC's 2002 notice due to strong reactions from financial regulators, academics and practitioners. Finally, the SPC's 2003 Provisions were issued and laid down relatively detailed guidance on private enforcement, which is the primary rule governing private securities litigations even after the Securities Law was revised in 2019. The concerns for maintaining the interests of SOEs were gradually diminished for the following two reasons. First, several high-profile fraudulent IPO cases caused sizable damage to a massive number of investors, which significantly reduced the reputational capital of the Chinese stock market. The national government valued its strategic importance to the national economy and wanted to develop a healthy and mild bull market. The CSRC, as the market regulator, also suffered from significant political pressure and wanted to censure violators to compensate defrauded investors. Second, after nearly one decade of development, the number of investors participating in the securities market had increased exponentially, and their interests were no longer ignored by the national government, which regarded a stable society as the primary policy goal.[20]

3.3   Securities Law of 2005 and the Split Share Reform

The Securities Law of 1998, which was drafted against the backdrop of the Asian Financial Crisis and written in a way to prevent and contain financial risks, was revised significantly in 2005 to tailor the needs for the rapidly developing stock market. The Securities Law of 2005 improved both the on-the-book anti-fraud rules and the enforcement toolkit of regulatory agencies.[21] On the one hand, it provided a more detailed *de jure* regulation of typical financially fraudulent behaviors, such as insider trading and market manipulation. On the other hand, the enforcement instruments of both the CSRC and the stock exchanges were strengthened. The CSRC obtained the authority to prohibit guilty parties from entering the market; to access and copy the records of asset registrars, bank accounts and personal contacts related to the investigated cases; to freeze and seal bank accounts and evidence; and to restrict the trading of potential violators. Furthermore, stock exchanges were

---

[19] Liu and Sun [9].

[20] Chen [10].

[21] See The Innovation of the New Securities Law, available at http://www.gov.cn/ztzl/2005-10/31/content_87585.htm (Last accessed 31 October, 2021).

delegated with a variety of self-regulatory enforcement instruments, including the authority to suspend trading of suspicious accounts.[22]

After the promulgation of the Securities Law of 2005, the split share reform, which aimed to solve the problems related to the dual-share structure and move the development of the stock market to a market-based path, was launched. At the beginning of reforming the corporate sector, the State Council issued the Standard Opinion for Companies Limited by Shares[23] in 1992 to safeguard the potential risks of state asset erosion in the process of corporatization, which divided the common A-shares of listed companies into tradeable classes and nontradable classes.[24] The latter were further classified into state shares and legal person shares. When the SOEs are applying for the listing quota, they are required to be restructured to the corporate form, with one-third of the total shareholdings being state shares and one-third being legal person shares. Consequently, there were two types of A-shares for an issuer before 2005: floating shares and nonfloating shares. The former are normally held by retail investors, and the latter are held by institutional investors and governmental entities. According to an empirical study, only five listed companies have not obtained any nontradable state and legal person shares.[25]

The dual-class share structure was then regarded as the major impediment to the healthy development of the stock market because it distorted the market price and incentive structure. First, because the majority of the shares are nontradable, listed companies are not subject to the market for corporate control.[26] Second, the interests of the two shareholder groups are heterogeneous, and the listed companies are controlled by shareholders holding nonfloating shares.[27] Those shareholders holding tradable shares are, consequently, not well protected because the companies are not managed in a way to maximize shareholder wealth but rather to tunnel assets to controllers.[28] Third, the share is mispriced because a large proportion of the total share issued does not float, which is an unattractive feature and discourages international investors from participating in the domestic market.[29]

A consensus about unifying the share categories gradually formed. The State Council issued the Opinions on Promoting the Reform and Opening Up of the Securities Market and its Stable Development in 2005, which served as the guideline for the reform. Then, a Commission comprising the CSRC, the State-owned Assets Supervision and Administration Commission, the Ministry of Finance, and PBoC

---

[22] See An Analysis of the Major Revisions of the Securities Law, available at http://www.csrc.gov. cn/pub/newsite/flb/lfzl/jnlfssyzn/yjyd/200701/t20070108_77314.html (Last accessed 31 October, 2021).

[23] See Gufen Gongsi Guifan Yijian, available at http://www.csrc.gov.cn/pub/newsite/gjb/gzdt/199 703/t19970324_79368.html (Last accessed 31 October, 2021).

[24] Clarke [11].

[25] Guo et al. [12].

[26] Fan [13].

[27] Joyce [14].

[28] Jiang [15].

[29] Beltratti et al. [16].

launched the reform. The CSRC subsequently issued the Measures for Adminis-tration of Split Share Structure Reform of Listed Companies[30] and stipulated the negotiation process and disclosure rule for transferring nontradable shares to trad-able shares. The Split Share Reform was finally completed at the end of 2011, when approximately 98.79% of the listed companies had completed the unification of the three types of shares. Empirical studies on the performance of listed SOEs after the reform show that their production, profitability and employment all increased following the reform.[31]

During this period, the public enforcement regime underwent the most funda-mental reform. The basic principle separating the function of investigation and review was established. The CSRC systemically streamlined the enforcement function in 2007, which comprised the Inspection Team, Enforcement Bureau, and Adminis-trative Penalty Committee at the Commission level and the enforcement division at the Regional Office level. The Enforcement Bureau was responsible for case register and case closure, the Inspection Team and Regional Office were responsible for the investigation, and the Administrative Penalty Committee and Administrative Review Committee were responsible for case trial and decision review, respectively. The reform has to some extent improved the enforcement outcomes. Between 2002 and 2010, the CSRC initiated 1462 investigations and transferred 156 cases to the policy department.[32]

3.4   The Registration Reform and Securities Law of 2019

The Chinese government has always been aware of the adverse impacts of merit regu-lations and the consequence of inefficient securities markets on economic develop-ment. However, strong economic growth temporarily masked the urgency of radical market-based reform. Market-based reform was accelerated by the need to rebal-ance the national financial structure in China. After the Subprime Mortgage Crisis, China launched the "4 Trillion Stimulus Plan" to update its infrastructure in 2009 and counteract the economic slowdown brought about by plunging exports.[33] However, local governments lacked enough capital to finance these projects and had to rely on bank loans channeled through the shadow banking sector. The Stimulus Plan had a significant side effect in weakening the balance sheet of the banking sector and increasing the level of national leverage.[34] According to the statistics released by the PBoC, bank loans accounted for approximately 58.3% of the total external finance

---

[30] See Shangshi Gongsi Guquan Fenzhi Gaige Banfa, available at http://www.csrc.gov.cn/pub/new site/flb/flfg/bmgf/ssgs/gqfz/201012/t20101231_189887.html (Last accessed 31 October, 2021).

[31] Liao et al. [17].

[32] China Securities Regulatory Commission [18, p. 346].

[33] Hachem [19].

[34] Liang [20].

obtained by market participants at the end of 2011.[35] The shadow of a bank crisis also compelled the Chinese government to speed up securities market reform and increase the percentage of market-based finance.[36] The solution to the potential banking crisis and economic slowdown was to increase the amount of direct finance provided by financial markets. The merit regulation was lengthy and stipulated restrictive financial requirements, which is an inefficient way of allocating credit to issuers needing external finance.

In addition, industrial innovation was placed at the top of the policy priorities by the Chinese government and was regarded as the key to climbing up the supply chain and further improving national welfare.[37] Unfortunately, the bank-dominated financial system was not compatible with entrepreneurial activities because start-ups and innovative firms were of relatively high risk and lacked physical assets as collateral for bank loans. The venture capital funds specializing in financing start-ups gained favorable policy support.[38] The private equity sector has maintained a high growth rate since 2013 and reached 13.74 trillion RMB by the end of 2019.[39] A vibrant venture capital sector needs an efficient capital market for investment exit.[40] The private equity sector also became a strong lobbying interest group for the IPO registration reform.

The Third Plenary Session of the 18th CPC Central Committee released the Decision on the Major Issues concerning Comprehensively Deepening Reform[41] in November 2013, which for the first time explicitly proposed registration reform in party policy. It emphasized the increase of market-based finance and an efficient multilayered securities market to facilitate the development of the real economy. In 2015, the Central Government Work Report of 2015[42] also listed the registration reform in the annual targets to achieve, and subsequently, a draft of the revised Securities Law was submitted to the National People's Congress for the first review. This draft explicitly abolished the IPO Issuance Examination Commission, which was regarded as a primary feature for Chinese merit securities regulation, and delegated

---

[35] See Statistical Report on the Size of Total Social Finance, available at https://www.chinabond. com.cn/Info/12382979#:~:text=%E5%88%9D%E6%AD%A5%E7%BB%9F%E8%AE%A1% EF%BC%8C201,1.11%E4%B8%87%E4%BA%BF%E5%85%83%E3%80%82 (Last accessed 31 October, 2021).

[36] Allen and Gu [21].

[37] See The Outlines for the National Strategy of the Innovation Driven Development, available at http://www.scio.gov.cn/xwfbh/xwbfbh/wqfbh/33978/34585/xgzc34591/Document/ 1478339/1478339_1.htm (Last accessed 31 October, 2021).

[38] Gompers and Lerner [22].

[39] See CSRC Annual Report of 2019, available at http://www.csrc.gov.cn/pub/newsite/zjhjs/zjhnb2 020/202008/P020200825360018516101.pdf (Last accessed 31 October, 2021).

[40] Black and Gilson [23].

[41] See Zhonggong Zhongyang Guanyu Quanmian Shenhua Gaige Ruogan Zhongda Wenti De Jueding, available at https://www.chinacourt.org/index.php/article/detail/2013/11/id/1146036. shtml (Last accessed 31 October, 2021).

[42] See 2015 Nian Zhengfu Gongzuo Baogao, available at http://www.china.com.cn/lianghui/news/ 2018-02/27/content_50484688.shtml (Last accessed 31 October, 2021).

the authorities to examine the completeness, consistency and readability of application materials to the stock exchanges. Because of the high volume of shadow margin lending, the Chinese stock market had been increasing in value since the middle of 2014. Realizing the potential risks, the CSRC started to deal with leveraged buyers, which partly led to the market crash in June 2015. The market index fell by more than 50%; the financial catastrophe alerted the Chinese government to the devastating impacts of a financial crisis, which temporarily stopped legislative progress. Not until the end of 2017 was the revised draft of the Securities Law, which was more conservative than the previous version, submitted to the National People's Congress for the second review.

It seemed extremely difficult to reach a consensus on the registration reform among the governmental agencies, and the revision process was again paused after the second review. The debate was mainly concerned with the nature of such a reform. The radical proposal argued that securities regulators should mainly perform the function of a record registrar, which only examines the completeness of the application materials. The issuers should ensure that the required information is disclosed in the prospectus and investors should make decisions based on the principle of caveat emptor. A more rational attitude, in contrast, proposed that the registration reform should mainly streamline the application process and reduce arbitrary administrative interventions in the IPO process. Issuers should maintain the quality of information disclosure, and stock exchanges should play a gatekeeper role and screen out fraudulent issuers.

On November 5, 2018, President Xi announced the establishment of the Science and Technology Innovation Board at the Shanghai Stock Exchange and launched the pilot project for IPO registration reform.[43] The revision of the Securities Law consequently had to accommodate the Science and Technology Innovation Board. The more rational plan was adopted, the third revision of the Securities Law was submitted for review in April 2019, and the revised Securities Law was promulgated in December 2019. The Securities Law of 2019 explicitly specified that the IPO entry regulation adopted a registration regime and delegated the authority of reviewing the suitability of IPOs to the stock exchanges. The CSRC only maintained the authority to register securities. In contrast to previous merit regulations, which made substantive judgements about the business model of issuers at the stage of market entry, the Securities Law of 2019 emphasized market mechanisms relying on complete information disclosure and investor protection. It added two chapters, "Information Disclosure" and "Investor Protection", and revised 166 articles of a total of 226 articles.

At the same time that the entry regulations were being relaxed, the CSRC also started to improve ongoing monitoring and *ex post* enforcement. It summarized the

---

[43] See Establishing the Science and Technology Innovation Board at Shanghai Stock Exchange and Launching the Pilot Project for IPO Registration, available at http://shanghai.xinmin.cn/xmsz/2018/11/05/31450279.html (Last accessed 31 October, 2021).

new governance strategy in three key words, i.e., "institution building, nonintervention and zero tolerance",[44] which separately represent the efforts for lawmaking, the reliance on market mechanisms and high-intensity enforcement. The Securities Law of 2019 made an important institutional innovation for investor protection and established a multidimensional securities private litigation regime comprising individual lawsuits, opt-in representative lawsuits and opt-out special representative lawsuits, which are the most radical institutional innovations and are called Chinese-style class actions. The opt-out special representative lawsuit adopts the opt-out design of the American class action to minimize the burden of obtaining judiciary relief for investors but assigns the governmental investor protection agency to the role of lead plaintiff.

From a political point of view, protecting the legitimate interests of external investors is increasingly aligned with the policy priorities promoted by the Chinese Communist Party. First, the number of individual securities market investors reached 177.8 million by the end of 2020.[45] The interests of retail investors, which are no longer a small percentage of wealthy people, belong to the general public interest stressed in the policy documents. It is important to maintain a stable societal and political environment to provide everyday citizens with efficient judiciary relief. Second, in contrast to the early days of stock market development when SOEs were the target issuers of the securities market, private firms now account for approximately two-thirds of the total Chinese listed companies. Private enforcement was no longer about private investors suing the SOEs, and the central government had no incentives to protect those private violators. Third, institutional investors, particularly social security funds and pension funds, hold a nontrivial stake in the securities market. According to a recent report, they held more than fifty percent of the floating market capitalization by the end of 2019.[46] It is crucial for China's social and economic stability to protect their interests. Finally, the Chinese government promoted the internationalization of the securities market to attract international capital inflows. It would be extremely detrimental to the confidence of foreign investors if their losses due to securities fraud could not be compensated efficiently by a court trial.

---

[44] See Jianzhidu, Buganyu, Lingrongren, Tuidong Zibenshichang Gaozhiliang Fazhan, available at http://www.chinadevelopment.com.cn/news/zj/2021/06/1729595.shtml (Last accessed 31 October, 2021).

[45] See China Securities Depository and Clearing Corporation Statistical Yearbook 2020, available at http://www.chinaclear.cn/zdjs/editor_file/20210820191941632.pdf (Last accessed 31 October, 2021).

[46] Wu and Fang [24].

3.5   Securities Law of 2019 and Anti-Securities-Fraud Rules

Anti-securities-fraud rules were first instituted in the Provisional Measures on Prohibition of Securities Fraud of 1993,[47] which prohibited the securities misconduct of insider trading, market manipulation, misrepresentation and defrauding customers. Later, the CSRC Notice on Strictly Prohibiting Securities Market Manipulation was released in October 1996[48] and further tightened the regulation of manipulative behaviors, which were deemed the source of the soaring stock price causing the instability of the stock market. These rules are mainly used in administrative proceedings, and the enforcement actions are of low intensity and quality. The Securities Law of 1998 codified the aforementioned rules and laid down the basic framework of the on-the-book rules against securities fraud. However, such rules are not suited for the securities market twenty years later, and the Securities Law of 2019 significantly revised the anti-fraud rules and increased the legal liabilities of securities misconduct.[49] Generally, the Securities Law of 2019 explicitly grants harmed investors the private right to pursue tortious damages from infringers in civil litigation. It furthermore stipulates various types of administrative liabilities for violators. Finally, the Criminal Law of 2020 also updates the criminal liabilities for securities misconduct.

3.5.1   Disclosure Obligation and the Liability for Misrepresentations

Section 5 of the Securities Law of 2019 systemically defines the information disclosure for obligors, which can be divided into standards and detailed rules. The standards are principles for information disclosure and mainly stipulated by Article 19 and Article 78, requiring that the issuers and other obligors be specified by the law and regulations to fully disclose the information relevant for investors' valuation and investment decision-making and ensure the truth, accuracy and completeness of the information disclosure.[50] Section 2 of Article 78 further sets the principle of conciseness and accessibility of the information disclosed. For issuers cross-listing at overseas exchanges, Section 3 of Article 78 requires that information disclosure be conducted simultaneously.

The detailed rules list the specific disclosure requirements for the obligors. For example, Article 80 and Article 81 list a total of 12 and 10 categories of major

---

[47] See Jinzhi Zhengquan Qizha Xingwei Zanxing Banfa, available at http://www.csrc.gov.cn/pub/newsite/ssb/ssflfg/bmgzjwj/ybgd/200911/t20091110_167675.html (Last accessed 31 October, 2021).

[48] See Guanyu Yange Jinzhi Caozhong Zhengquan Shichang Xingwei De Tongzhi, available at https://www.pkulaw.com/chl/460b55fa3c55de45bdfb.html (Last accessed 31 October, 2021).

[49] The monetary liability set by securities law is not adjusted according to the inflation rate, and hence the amount set decades ago used to be blamed for its failure to deter securities misconducts.

[50] Article 19 of Securities Law of 2019.

events for stock issuers and debt issuers, respectively. For stock issuers, they have to disclose the following: (1) significant changes in business strategy and scope; (2) major investment and transaction activities; (3) entry into major contracts that have significant financial impacts; (4) assumption and/or failure to honor significant debts; (5) whether they suffered significant losses; (6) significant changes in the external production and operation conditions; (7) changes in directors, or more than one-third of the supervisors or managers, or if the president or chief executive officials are unable to carry out their jobs; (8) changes in controlling rights of controllers or shareholders with more than 5% of shareholdings, and those in controllers or companies controlled by the controllers performing similar business; (9) significant decisions including dividends, capital increase, ownership structure, and those that reduce capital, conduct mergers or splits, file for dissolution or bankruptcy, or enter into bankruptcy proceedings; (10) major litigation or arbitration; and (11) criminal proceeding against the company senior directors, controllers, supervisors and/or senior management.

Bond issuers have to disclose the following events that might significantly influence their solvency: (1) significant changes in the ownership structure or the production and operation status; (2) changes in the credit rating; (3) the pledge, sale, transfer, or write-off of major assets; (4) failure to pay its due debts; 5) new debt or guarantees exceeding 20% of net assets; (6) giving up its creditor's rights or its property exceeding 10% of its net assets; (7) a major loss of more than 10% of its net assets; (8) significant decisions including dividends, capital increase, ownership structure, and those that reduce capital, conduct mergers or splits, file for dissolution or bankruptcy, or enter bankruptcy proceedings; (9) major litigation or arbitration; and (10) criminal proceeding against the companies, their controllers, directors, supervisors or senior management. In addition to those items identified by the Securities Law of 2019, the listing rules of the Shanghai Stock Exchange and Shenzhen Stock Exchange further provide quantitative thresholds for selective events, as summarized in Table 3.1. They are the quantitative thresholds for identifying material events in different categories of transactions.

Although the Securities Law of 2019 uses the term "misrepresentation" to describe the informational misconduct committed by obligors, it fails to provide a detailed definition of misrepresentation.[51] Article 17 of SPC's 2003 Provisions offers a definition of misrepresentation, which refers to those committed by the obligors to violate the informational duties established by securities law and/or making false or misleading statements, or omitting information disclosure of major events. Three specific types of misrepresentation are provided. The first is false records, which refer to the disclosure of nonexistent information. The second is misleading statements, which are information disclosures that materially impact investors and lead them to misjudge their investment decisions. The third is inappropriate disclosure, referring to failing to conduct information disclosures that in the appropriate time period or statutory way.

---

[51] Xu [25].

Table 3.1 Major events required to be disclosed by securities law

Percentage threshold		Absolute threshold		
Event	Threshold (%)	Event	Threshold (main board)	Threshold (GEM)
Total asset under transaction/Total asset	10	N.A	N.A	N.A
Transaction value/net asset	10	Transaction value	10 million	5 million
Net profit from transaction/total net profit	10	Net profit from transaction	1 million	1 million
Revenue from transaction/total revenue	10	Revenue from transaction	10 million	5 million
Related party transaction (individual)	N.A	Related party transaction	0.3 million	0.3 million
Related party transaction (legal entity)/net asset	0.5	Related party transaction	3 million	1 million
Disputed value in litigations or arbitrations/net asset	10	Disputed value in litigations or arbitrations	10 million	5 million
Expected net profit (percentage)	50	Expected net profit	N.A	N.A
Deviance of expected value from real value in financial report	10 (SHSE); 20 (SZSE)	Deviance of expected value from real value in financial report	N.A	N.A

Source Listing Rules of the Shenzhen Stock Exchange (2020) and Listing Rules of the Shanghai Stock Exchange (2020)

A critical element for the identification of misrepresentations is the materiality test.[52] Except for the lists of material information mandated by the securities law and regulation, both price-sensitive tests and investor decision tests are provided to test whether the relevant information is material. The Securities Law of 2005 has already required the obligor to disclose all price-sensitive information, and Article 19 of the Securities Law of 2019 explicitly adds the investor decision test for the first time. However, it is not clear how to apply both tests. Prior to the Securities Law of 2019, SPC's 2003 Provisions stipulated that civil litigation should meet administrative prerequisites, and Chinese courts used to treat administrative sanctions or

---

[52] Dai [26].

criminal judgements as proof of materiality. This informal judicial choice is recognized by the SPC, which issued the Minutes of Civil and Commercial Trials for All Courts Nationwide in 2019,[53] and Article 85 specifies that securities misconduct is regarded as satisfying materiality if it is sanctioned administratively. However, it left unanswered how to test the element of materiality in those cases filed without administrative sanctions.

Similarly, the assessment of materiality is also highly debated and fact-contingent in the U.S. The statutory rules fail to provide clear on-the-book guidance, and the case law is also ambiguous.[54] The U.S. Supreme Court holds that the information is material "if there is a substantial likelihood that a reasonable shareholder would consider it important",[55] or "that the disclosure of the omitted fact would have been viewed by the reasonable investor as having significantly altered the 'total mix' of information made available."[56] However, such standards are far from clear, and the ambiguity has caused significant inconsistency in lower-court judgements. The circuit-level judgements seem to adopt different interpretations of the "substantial likelihood" and fail to create clear expectations for securities market participants.[57] In addition, the content of "reasonable investors", which suffers from the influence of rational choice theory, is not clear by itself.[58] It has already been shown that different types of investors, such as retail investors and institutional investors, differ significantly in their expertise and preferences for risk, return and liquidity.[59]

The Securities Law of 2019 also significantly increases on-the-book liabilities for securities informational misconduct. Prior to the most recent revision, the legal liabilities stipulated in the Securities Law used to be trivial compared to the potential illegal profits.[60] The monetary fine for culpable individuals was between 0.03 million RMB and 0.3 million RMB, while that for legal entities was between 0.3 million RMB and 0.6 million RMB, which fails to effectively deter securities misconduct. Currently, Section 1 of Article 181 of the Securities Law of 2019 stipulates liabilities for IPO misrepresentation. If issuers omit or fabricate material information, they are subject to administrative fines between 2 and 20 million RMB if the issuance fails or administrative fines between 10 and 100% of the raised capital if the issuance is completed. Individuals directly responsible for misconduct are subject to administrative fines between 1 and 10 million. Section 2 further specifies the liabilities for the controlling shareholders and actual controllers of the issuers, who intentionally conduct or direct others to conduct the misrepresentation. They are subject to expulsion and administrative fines between 10 and 100% of the illegal gains; if there are

[53] See Quanguo Fayuan Minshangshi Shenpan Gongzuo Huiyi Jiyao, available at http://www.court.gov.cn/zixun-xiangqing-199691.html (Last accessed 31 October, 2021).

[54] Park [27].

[55] TSC Indus., Inc. v. Northway, Inc. 426 U.S. 438 (1976).

[56] Basic, Inc. v. Levinson, 485 U.S. 224 (1988).

[57] Madden [28].

[58] Schulzke and Berger-Walliser [29].

[59] Cremers and Sepe [30].

[60] Tomasic and Fu [31].

no illegal gains or the illegal gains are less than 20 million RMB, they are subject to administrative fines between 2 and 20 million RMB. Those individuals directly responsible for the misrepresentation are subject to administrative fines between 1 and 10 million RMB.

Article 197 further lays down the liabilities for informational obligors in the secondary market. Section 1 specifies that if they fail to file their reports as required by the securities law and regulation or fail to discharge their disclosure obligations, they should first correct their misconduct and are subject to a warning and administrative fines between 0.5 and 5 million RMB. Those directly responsible for the misconduct are subject to a warning and administrative fines between 0.2 and 2 million RMB. The controlling shareholders and controllers of the issuers intentionally conducting or concealing these misconducts are subject to administrative fines between 0.5 and 5 million RMB; for those individuals affiliated with these entities and assuming direct responsibility, they are subject to administrative fines between 0.2 and 2 million RMB.

Section 2 sets the liabilities for obligors who file reports or disclose information with false records, misleading statements, or significant omissions of information. They should first correct their misconduct and are subject to a warning and administrative fine between 1 and 10 million RMB; for those individuals affiliated with the obligors and directly responsible for the misconduct, they are subject to warning and administrative fines between 0.5 and 5 million RMB. The controlling shareholders and controllers of the issuers who intentionally commit or conceal the aforementioned misconduct are subject to administrative fines between 1 and 10 million RMB; for those individuals affiliated with these entities and assuming direct responsibility, they are subject to administrative fines between 0.5 and 5 million RMB.

The recent revision of the Criminal Law also significantly increases the criminal liabilities for misrepresentation and distinguishes the difference between misrepresentation in the primary and secondary markets.[61] The threshold for criminal liabilities is related to the seriousness of the misconduct. Article 160 of the Criminal Law of 2020 stipulates criminal liabilities for fraudulent securities issuance. For fraudulent securities issuances with significant size and serious negative impacts, the guilty parties are subject to imprisonment for up to five years and/or criminal fines between one and five times the illegal gains. For issuances with extremely large sizes and highly serious negative impacts, the guilty parties are subject to imprisonment between five years and ten years and criminal fines between one and five times the illegal gains. In addition, if the controlling shareholders and/or controllers intentionally organize and participate in the fraudulent issuances, they are subject to imprisonment for up to five years and/or the criminal fines between 20 and 100% of the illegally raised funds; for extremely large cases with serious negative impacts, they are subject to imprisonment of more than five years, and criminal fines between 20 and 100% of the illegally raised funds. Finally, if the guilty party is a legal entity, it is additionally subject to criminal fines between 20 and 100% of the illegally raised

---

[61] Ye [32].

funds. Article 181 further specifies criminal liabilities for secondary market misrepresentation. The guilty parties are subject to imprisonment of up to five years and/or criminal fines between 10,000 and 100,000 RMB.

Although the Criminal Law fails to provide detailed guidance on the threshold for criminal liabilities, the judiciary documents provide supplementary rules.[62] The Provisions for the Standards for Recording and Investigating Criminal Cases within the Jurisdiction of Public Security Bureau (II) issued by the Supreme People's Procuratorate and the Public Security Bureau[63] in 2010 specifies the thresholds for registering the cases by the Public Security Bureau. Article 5 stipulates that if one of the following conditions is satisfied, then the fraudulent IPO case should be recorded and investigated by the Public Security Bureau: (1) the size of the issuance is over 5 million RMB; (2) falsification of public documents; (3) the funds raised were used to carry out illegal activities; and (4) the funds raised were transferred or hidden. Article 4 further specifies the criteria for secondary market misrepresentation: (1) economic losses over 0.5 million RMB directly; (2) the falsely increased or decreased total asset is over 30%; (3) the falsely increased or decreased net profit is over 30%; (4) the total size of the unreported material events is over 50% of net assets in the last 12 months; (5) other legally issued securities were delisted or suspended multiple times; (6) unqualified issuers successfully conducted IPOs and listed on the stock exchange; (7) the issuers changed financial statements from profitable (loss) to loss (profitable); and (8) falsified financial statements were provided or the disclosure of material events omitted multiple times.

3.5.2   The Prohibition of Insider Trading and the Liability of Inside Traders

Chinese securities regulators are fully aware of the detrimental effects of insider trading on the healthy development of the securities market. As early as 1993, the Provisional Regulations on the Administration of Stock Issuance and Trading[64] contained articles prohibiting insider trading. However, these rules are too general to enforce, and both financial regulators and investors were not equipped with enough technical instruments to collect evidence of insider trading.[65] The Securities Law of 1998 already defined the core elements of insider trading, such as insiders and inside

---

[62] Ding [33].

[63] See Guanyu Gongan Jiguan Guanxia De Xingshi Anjian Li'an Zhuisu Biaozhun De Guiding (2), available at https://www.chinacourt.org/article/detail/2010/05/id/409249.shtml (Last accessed 31 October, 2021).

[64] See Gupiao Faxing yu Jiaoyi Guanli Zanxing Tiaoli (promulgated on 22 April 1993), available at http://www.gov.cn/zhengce/2020-12/25/content_5574619.htm (Last accessed 31 October, 2021).

[65] Huang [34].

information. However, it adopted a restrictive definition concerning insider trading, and several types of commonly seen strategies successfully escaped regulation.[66]

Chapter Three, titled "Prohibited Trading Behavior" of the Securities Law of 2019, listed the key elements in identifying insider trading. First, Article 50 of the Securities Law of 2019 categorizes inside traders into two groups, i.e., *de jure* insiders and those misappropriating inside information. The *de jure* insiders are further divided into corporate insiders and industrial insiders. The corporate insiders include eight groups, such as directors, supervisors and senior management, shareholders with more than 5% of stockholdings, business counterparts, acquirers, and employees of public agencies, and those defined by the State Council.[67] Industrial insiders are professionals and staff affiliated with stock exchanges, securities firms, securities registration and settlement institutions, self-regulatory organizations and regulatory authorities. They are prohibited from directly trading with or giving tips to others regarding material nonpublic information obtained due to their positions.[68] Second, insider information is defined as including the material nonpublic information concerning the operation, financial and other price-sensitive events, in addition to those events listed in Section 2 of Article 80 and Section 2 of Article 81 of the Securities Law of 2019. This is an improvement compared to prior versions of the Securities Law, which fail to explicitly provide such definitions.

In contrast, the case law in the U.S. has established three major doctrines concerning the identification of insider trading based on Section 10(b) of the Exchange Act and Rule 10b-5, which is also subjected to heated debate.[69] The first is the "fiduciary relationship theory",[70] which requires that inside traders have a fiduciary relationship with the source of the information so that they are subject to the obligation to disclose or abstain from trading based on the concerned material nonpublic information.[71] However, the "fiduciary relationship theory" significantly restricts the scope of enforcement actions, particularly in the case of mergers and acquisitions, where the employees of acquiring firms with no fiduciary duties to the target listed companies trade the securities of the latter firms.[72] The second is the "misappropriation theory", which revises the "fiduciary relationship theory" and only emphasizes that the trader should owe fiduciary duties to the source of information.[73] Another strand of cases addresses insider trading based on tipped inside information, which forms the "tipper-tippee theory".[74] The theory employs a two-stage perspective and requires that the tipper first maintain a special relationship with the information sources, which creates the duty to disclose or abstain; in addition,

---

[66] Qu [35].

[67] See Article 51 of the Securities Law of 2019.

[68] See Article 54 of the Securities Law of 2019.

[69] Bharara [36].

[70] Chiarella v. United States, 445 U.S. 222 (1980).

[71] Wang and Steinberg [37, p. 4].

[72] Ayres and Choi [38].

[73] United States v. O'Hagan, 521 U.S. 642 (1997).

[74] Dirks v. SEC, 463 U.S. 646 (1983).

the tipper should obtain personal benefits from the disclosure. The tippee could be liable if he or she knows or should know of the breach.[75]

The underlying theory concerning the identification of insider trading in China is manifested in the Guide for the Identification of Insider Trading Behavior in the Securities Markets (henceforth Insider Trading Guide),[76] which was issued by the CSRC in 2007 and circulated as an internal document. Although it has no *de jure* authority in either public or private enforcement, the CSRC and its affiliations follow its guidance in their enforcement actions. The Insider Trading Guide established that the possessors of material nonpublic information trading relevant securities during a preset information sensitive period are subject to insider trading liability unless good reasons are provided to justify the transactions.[77] The Insider Trading Guide was finally abolished by the CSRC in 2020, but its impacts are still present.[78] The Securities Law of 2019 adopts a rebuttable presumption about the subjective element of inside traders. For *de jure* insiders, if they know or should know about the information and then trade the relevant securities within the price-sensitive period, they are presumed to satisfy the subjective elements of insider trading liability. However, if the trading is based on a preset plan, it is not identified as insider trading.

In sum, the underlying theory concerning the identification of insider trading conducted by *de jure* corporate insiders is a combination of the fiduciary duty theory in *Chiarella v. United States*,[79] which restricts insider trading to insiders breaking the fiduciary or special relationship of trust and confidence with the trading counterparty, and the misappropriation theory established in the *United States v. O'Hagen*, which stipulates that any trader breaking a fiduciary or special relationship of trust and confidence with the source of material nonpublic information falls within the scope of insider trading. In addition, those concerning conduct by traders illegally misappropriating inside information are a combination of misappropriation theory and tipper-tippee theory established by *Dirks v. SEC*.

The administrative liabilities for insider trading were criticized as too light to deter the potential crime, and the Securities Law of 2019 revised the relevant rules and improved the administrative liabilities.[80] Article 191 stipulates that inside traders should first dispose of illegally held securities, return illegal gains and be subject to administrative fines between one and five times the illegal gains. If the illegal gains are less than 0.5 million RMB, the guilty parties are subject to administrative fines between 0.5 and 5 million RMB. If the trader is a legal entity, those staff directly

---

[75] Pritchard [39].

[76] See Zhengquan Shichang Neimu Jiaoyi Xingwei Rending Zhiyin (On trial), available at https://www.sohu.com/a/441290388_204085 (Last accessed 31 October, 2021).

[77] Howson [40].

[78] See The Decision on Revising and Abolishing Documents Relating to Securities and Futures Market, available at http://www.szse.cn/lawrules/csrcrules/notice/t20201118_583238.html (Last accessed 31 October, 2021).

[79] See Chiarella v. United States, 445 U.S. 222 (1980).

[80] Weng and Jia [41].

responsible for these transactions should be further sanctioned with warnings and administrative fines between 0.2 and 2 million RMB.

The revised Criminal Law also increases criminal liabilities for insider trading.[81] Article 180 of the Criminal Law of 2020 stipulates criminal liabilities for insider trading. For insider trading with serious negative impacts, the guilty parties are subject to imprisonment of up to five years and/or criminal fines between one and five times the illegal gains. For insider trading with highly serious negative impacts, the guilty parties are subject to imprisonment between five and ten years and criminal fines between one and five times the illegal gains.

Although the Securities Law and Criminal Law fails to provide criteria for the seriousness of insider trading, the Explanations on the Issues Concerning the Application of Insider Trading Law in Criminal Cases jointly issued by the SPC and Supreme People's Procuratorate[82] in 2012 offer detailed sentencing guidance. Article 6 indicates that if one of the following conditions is satisfied, then the inside trading has serious negative impacts: (1) trading volume is larger than 0.5 million RMB; (2) the deposit of the future trading margin is larger than 0.3 million RMB; (3) the profit or the avoidance of the loss is larger than 0.15 million RMB; (4) the frequency of the trading is more than 3 times; and (5) other conditions. Article 7 further stipulates that insider trading has highly serious negative impacts if one of the following conditions is met: (1) trading volume is larger than 2.5 million RMB; (2) the deposit of future trading margins is larger than 1.5 million RMB; (3) the profit or avoidance of the loss is larger than 0.75 million RMB; (4) the frequency of trading is more than 3 times; and (5) other conditions. An unfriendly arrangement for potential violators is that the aforementioned figures should be summed up if the same entity committed multiple acts of insider trading, and these misconducts are not sanctioned administratively or criminally.

3.5.3 The Prohibition of Market Manipulation and the Liability of Manipulators

Market manipulation has been a major regulatory concern since the 1990s. In 1996, the CSRC issued the Notice on the Prohibition of Securities Market Manipulation.[83] The Notice listed nine strategies to manipulate the market. Since then, the regulation of manipulation has followed a piecemeal fashion, and the theoretical foundation

---

[81] Ye et al. [32].

[82] See Guanyu Banli Neimu Jiaoyi and Xielu Neimu Xinxi Xingshi Anjian Juti Yingyong Falv Ruogan Wenti De Jieshi, available at https://www.chinacourt.org/law/detail/2012/03/id/145768.shtml (Last accessed 31 October, 2021).

[83] See Guanyu Yanjin Caozong Zhengquan Shichang Xingwei De Tongzhi, available at http://www.law-lib.com/law/law_view.asp?id=63567 (Last accessed 31 October, 2021).

for regulating market manipulation in China is not clear. In the international literature, manipulative behaviors can be grouped into three categories[84]: The first is action-based manipulation, which alters the real or expected value of the underlying assets with the aim of manipulating securities prices; the second is information-based manipulation, which is concerned with manipulation based on spreading false information; and the third is trade-based manipulation, which relies on transacting strategies to induce uninformed investors to trade.

Article 55 of the Securities Law of 2019 is concerned with the identification of securities market manipulation. Principally, any manipulative means that impacts or is utilized with an intention to impact the securities price and/or trading volume is regarded as market manipulation. Article 55 further defines the following seven specific manipulative behaviors: first, "Continuous Manipulation", which refers to those individually or jointly taking advantage of funding, shareholding or information and cooperatively or continuously transacting the target securities; second, "Matched Order", which refers to those in cooperation with others, transacting the securities at a preset time, price and manner; third, "Wash Sale", which refers to those transacting the securities among accounts controlled by the same entity; fourth, "Pinging", which refers to those repeatedly or voluminously bidding and cancelling orders without any intention of concluding the transaction; fifth, "Spoofing", which refers to those inducing investors to trade by way of false information or uncertain material information; sixth, "Scalping", which refers to those making comments, predictions, or investment suggestions about cross-securities and(or) issuers, and at the same time transacting in the opposite direction; and seven, "Cross-market manipulation", which refers to those making comments which refers to those manipulating activities.

The administrative liabilities for market manipulators are stipulated in Article 192 of the Securities Law of 2019. Manipulators should first dispose of illegally held securities, return illegal gains and be subject to administrative fines between one and ten times the amount of the illegal gains. If the illegal gains are less than 1 million RMB, the guilty parties are subject to administrative fines between 1 and 10 million RMB. If the manipulator is a legal entity, those staff directly responsible for the manipulative transactions should be further sanctioned with warnings and administrative fines between 0.5 and 5 million RMB.

Criminal liabilities are specified by Article 182 of the Criminal Law of 2020. The criteria for identifying misconduct are the same as those of the Securities Law of 2019. The difference lies in the seriousness of criminal misconduct. For manipulators with serious negative impacts, the guilty parties are subject to imprisonment of up to five years and/or criminal fines. For manipulators with highly serious negative impacts, the guilty parties are subject to imprisonment between five years and ten years and the criminal fine. In June 2019, the SPC and Supreme People's Procuratorate jointly released the Explanations on the Issues Concerning the Criminal Cases of Securities and Future Market Manipulation, which provides detailed sentencing guidance for

---

[84] Allen and Gale [42].

criminal cases.[85] Article 2 lists the manipulative actions with serious negative impacts on the securities market: first, controlling more than 10% of the floating shares and the cumulative turnover accounting for more than 20% of the total market turnover in ten consecutive trading days in the case of "Continuous Manipulation"; second, the cumulative turnover accounting for more than 20% of the total market turnover in ten consecutive trading days in the case of "Matched Order" and "Wash Sale"; third, the trading volume exceeding 10 million RMB for "Spoofing", "Scalping" and other informational manipulation; and fourth, illegal gains exceeding 1 million RMB.

In addition, according to Article 3, if the illegal gains are more than 0.5 million RMB and at the same time one of the following conditions is met, the market manipulation is regarded as having serious negative impacts: first, corporate insiders, including issuers, directors, supervisors, senior management and controllers committed the transactions; second, in merger and acquisition deals, the transacting counterparty and its directors, supervisors, senior management and controllers committed the transactions; third, the violator continued the manipulative transaction while knowing that they are being investigated; fourth, the violators have already received criminal sanctions due to market manipulation; fifth, the violators have already received criminal sanctions within the last two years due to market manipulation; and sixth, the market manipulation is performed when the market is experiencing abnormal and volatile fluctuations.

Finally, Article 4 specifies the conditions for manipulative actions with highly serious negative impacts: first, controlling more than 10% of the floating shares and cumulative turnover accounting for more than 50% of the total market turnover in ten consecutive trading days for "Continuous Manipulation"; second, cumulative turnover accounts for more than 50% of the total market turnover in ten consecutive trading days for "Matched Order" and "Wash Sale"; third, the trading volume exceeds 50 million RMB for "Spoofing", "Scalping" and other informational manipulation; fourth, illegal gains exceeding 10 million RMB; and finally, if the illegal gains are more than 5 million RMB and if, at the same time, one of the conditions mentioned in Article 3 is also met.

References

1. Huang, Y. (2002). *Selling China: Foreign direct investment during the reform era.* Cambridge University Press.
2. Walter, C., & Howie, F. (2003). *Privatizing China: The stock markets and their role in corporate reform.* Wiley.
3. Fang, L. (1994). China's corporatization experiment. *Duke Journal of Comparative & International Law, 5,* 149–269.
4. Pistor, K., & Xu, C. (2005). Governing stock markets in transition economies: Lessons from China. *American Law and Economics Review, 7*(1), 184–210.

---

[85] See Guanyu Banli Caozong Zhengquan, Qihuo Shichang Xingshi Anjian Shiyong Falv Ruogan Wenti De Jieshi, available at https://www.spp.gov.cn/spp/xwfbh/wsfbh/201906/t20190628_423 372.shtml (Last accessed 31 October, 2021).

5. Xu, C., & Zhuang, J. (1998). Why China grew: The role of decentralization. In P. Boone, S. Gomulka, & R. Layard (Eds.), *Emerging from communism: Lessons from Russia, China, and Eastern Europe* (pp. 183–212). MIT Press.

6. Du, J., & Xu, C. (2009). Which firms went public in China? A study of financial market regulation. *World Development, 37*(4), 812–824.

7. Chen, D. (2013). Developing a stock market without institutions: The China puzzle. *Journal of Corporate Law Studies, 13*(1), 151–184.

8. Xi, C. (2006). Private enforcement of securities law in China: Daqing Lianyi Co v Zhong Weida and others (2004) Heilongjiang High Court. *Journal of Comparative Law, 1*(2), 492–496.

9. Liu, G. S., & Sun, S. P. (2005). Identifying ultimate controlling shareholders in Chinese public corporations: An empirical survey. *Asia Program Working Paper No 2*. Available at http://www.chathamhouse.org.uk/files/3096_stateshareholding.pdf. Last accessed 31 Oct 2021.

10. Chen, Z. (2003). Capital markets and legal development: The China case. *China Economic Review, 14*(4), 451–472.

11. Clarke, D. C. (2010). Law without order in Chinese corporate governance institutions. *Northwestern Journal of International Law & Business, 30*(1), 131–200.

12. Guo, L., Ya, D., & Lien, D. (2016). The effects of China's split-share reform on firms' capital structure choice. *Applied Economics, 48*, 2530–2549.

13. Fan, J., Wong, T. J., & Zhang, T. (2007). Politically-connected CEOs, corporate governance, and post-IPO performance of China's partially privatized firms. *Journal of Financial Economics, 84*(2), 330–357.

14. Joyce, S. (2008). From non-tradable to tradable shares: Split share structure reform of China's listed companies. *Journal of Corporate Law Studies, 8*(1), 57–78.

15. Jiang, G., Lee, C. M. C., & Yue, H. (2010). Tunneling through intercorporate Loans: The China experience. *Journal of Financial Economics, 98*(1), 1–20.

16. Beltratti, A., Bortolotti, B., & Caccavaio, M. (2016). Stock Market efficiency in China: Evidence from the split-share reform. *The Quarterly Review of Economics and Finance, 60*, 125–137.

17. Liao, L., Liu, B., & Wang, H. (2014). China's secondary privatization: Perspectives from the split-share structure reform. *Journal of Financial Economics, 113*(3), 500–518.

18. China Securities Regulatory Commission. (2010). *Twenty years of China's capital markets* (p. 346). China CITIC Press.

19. Hachem, K. (2018). Shadow banking in China. *Annual Review of Financial Economics, 10*, 287–308.

20. Liang, Y. (2016). Shadow banking in China: Implications for financial stability and macroeconomic rebalancing. *The Chinese Economy, 49*, 148–160.

21. Allen, F., & Gu, X. (2020). Shadow banking in China compared to other countries. *The Manchester School*, forthcoming.

22. Gompers, P., & Lerner, J. (2001). The venture capital revolution. *Journal of Economic Perspectives, 15*(2), 145–168.

23. Black, B. S., & Gilson, R. J. (1998). Venture capital and the structure of capital markets: Banks versus stock markets. *Journal of Financial Economics, 47*(3), 243–277.

24. Wu, X., & Fang, H. (2021). 30 years of China's Capital markets: Exploration and transformation. *Finance and Trade Economics, 42*(4), 20–36. (In Chinese)

25. Xu, W. (2017). Private securities litigation and investor compensation: An empirical analysis of the securities misrepresentation cases. *Journal of Shandong University (Philosophy and Social Sciences), 2017*(3), 67–75. (In Chinese).

26. Dai, L. (2006). The judicial application of the causation test of the false statement doctrine in securities litigation in China. *Pacific Rim Law & Policy Journal, 15*, 733–764.

27. Park, J. J. (2009). Assessing the materiality of financial misstatements. *Journal of Corporation Law, 34*, 513–565.

28. Madden, T. M. (2015). Significance and the materiality tautology. *Journal of Business & Technology Law, 10*, 217–244.

29. Schulzke, K. S., & Berger-Walliser, G. (2017). Toward a unified theory of materiality in securities law. *Columbia Journal of Transnational Law, 56*, 6–70.

30. Cremers, M., & Sepe, S. M. (2016). Shareholder value of empowered boards. *Stanford Law Review*, 67–148.
31. Tomasic, R., & Fu, F. (1999). The securities law of the People's Republic of China: An overview. *Australian Journal of Corporate Law, 10*, 268–289.
32. Ye, Z., Lin, W., Safari, N., & Singh, C. (2020). Controlling insider dealing through criminal enforcement in China. *Journal of Financial Crime, 27*(4), 1061–1073.
33. Ding, H. (2011). An analysis of the criminal liability of misrepresentation in securities market. *Journal of Lanzhou University (Social Sciences), 39*(04), 131–135.
34. Huang, H. (2005). The regulation of insider trading in China: A critical review and proposals for reform. *Australian Journal of Corporate Law, 17*, 1–42.
35. Qu, C. Z. (2001). An outsider's view of China's insider trading law. *Pacific Rim Law & Policy Journal, 10*, 327–352.
36. Bharara, P. (2020). Report of the Bharara task force on insider trading. Available at https://www.bhararataskforce.com. Last accessed 31 Oct 2021
37. Wang, W., & Steinberg, M. I. (2010). *Insider trading*. Oxford University Press.
38. Ayres, I., & Choi, S. (2002). Internalizing outsider trading. *Michigan Law Review, 101*, 313–408.
39. Pritchard, A. C. (2015). Dirks and the genesis of personal benefit. *SMU Law Review, 68*, 857–875.
40. Howson, N. C. (2012). Enforcement without foundation? Insider trading and China's administrative law crisis. *The American Journal of Comparative Law, 60*, 955–1002.
41. Weng, C. X., & Jia, J. (2016). Assessing the administrative sanctions regime for insider trading in China: An empirical approach. *Asian Journal of Comparative Law, 10*, 343–358.
42. Allen, F., & Gale, D. (1992). Stock-price manipulation. *The Review of Financial Studies, 5*(3), 503–529.

Chapter 4
Public Enforcement Initiated by the CSRC and Its Regional Offices

China has a centralized securities enforcement model in which public regulators play a dominant role.[1] Public agencies that are responsible for enforcing securities law include the China Securities Regulatory Commission (CSRC) and its 38 regional offices (ROs), the Shanghai Stock Exchange (SHSE) and the Shenzhen Stock Exchange (SZSE), and securities self-regulatory organizations. Whereas public enforcement in China is performed in part by imposing a variety of sanctions on fraudulent firms; it is often claimed in the literature that they do not deter securities fraud and fail to sustain a healthy stock market.[2] This chapter systemically analyzes the enforcement efforts of the CSRC and its regional offices, which are placed at the center of the enforcement regime in China.

4.1 CSRC and Its Enforcement Proceedings

According to Article 7 of the Securities Law of 2019, the CSRC is given authority to regulate the securities market in China and sets up ROs to facilitate its regulatory duties. The CSRC has established ROs in every provincial region and in two special regulatory offices in Shanghai and Shenzhen, where the two stock exchanges are located. ROs are responsible for regulating listed companies, financial services companies and intermediaries in accordance with the authorization of the CSRC.

---

[1] Before 2016, courts could accept private securities litigation subject to the condition that an administrative penalty (or a criminal sanction) had previously been imposed for the alleged fraud. In other words, private enforcement was dependent on public enforcement. However, after the SPC issued the Reply to the Questions in Commercial Cases on December 24, 2015, the administrative prerequisites were removed. For details of this Reply, see http://www.pkulaw.cn/fulltext_form.aspx?Db=chl&Gid=9f64e621836ab2c1bdfb. (Last accessed 31 October, 2021).

[2] Mark Humphery-Jenner, 2013. Strong Financial Laws without Strong Enforcement: Is Good Law Always Better Than No Law? *Journal of Empirical Legal Studies* 10(2): 288–324.

© The Author(s), under exclusive license to Springer Nature Singapore Pte Ltd. 2022
W. Xu, *The Enforcement of Securities Law in China*,
https://doi.org/10.1007/978-981-19-0904-7_4

Previously, they exercised incomplete enforcement authority, could only impose nonadministrative sanctions and were not active enforcers of securities law. This situation changed in 2011, when the CSRC started to systemically reform the enforcement regime and encouraged ROs to enforce securities law through a pilot project that delegated the authority to impose administrative sanctions to ROs in Shanghai, Guangdong and Shenzhen.[3] In October 2013, the CSRC further expanded the scope of the delegation, and all ROs obtained the authority to impose sanctions.[4] The CSRC issued the Opinions on Further Strengthening Securities Law Inspection and Enforcement[5] to streamline the enforcement proceeding, and law enforcement was among the top policy priorities. According to the Provisions of the ROs to Impose Administrative Sanction,[6] the commission-level enforcement department is only responsible for investigating and sanctioning major cases, while ROs are responsible for cases within their jurisdictions. The enforcement proceedings initiated by ROs are relatively independent and the ROs are only required to file records with the CSRC.

Article 170 of the Securities Law of 2019 lists a broad range of enforcement tactics that could be employed by the CSRC. The first group is administrative sanctions, which include warnings, administrative fines, disgorgement, correction, disqualification and being closed down. As stipulated in the Administrative Penalties Law of 2021, the substantive and procedural requirements for the categories and institutions of administrative sanctions are strictly restricted, and the CSRC could only impose the aforementioned instruments. Administrative sanctions could result in derivative costs to those sanctioned, particularly the listed companies. First, according to the SPC's 2003 Provisions, only civil cases that meet administrative prerequisites are admitted by Chinese courts. Hence, those sanctioned administratively will be exposed to the risk of private litigations. Second, those companies and their affiliated sanctions will lose the qualification for special regulatory treatment and be subject to restrictions in certain transactions. For example, individuals sanctioned administratively will not be eligible for senior management positions of listed companies for three years.[7] Listed companies sanctioned administratively will not be eligible for seasonal offerings for three years.[8]

The second group is nonadministrative sanctions, which, according to Article 2 of the Measures for Implementing the Nonadministrative Sanctions in the Securities and

---

[3] See CSRC Delegated the Authority to Issue Administrative Sanction to Shanghai, Guangdong and Shenzhen in Pilot Project, available at http://news.hexun.com/2010-11-02/125372590.html. (Last accessed 31 October, 2021).

[4] See CSRC Delegated the Authority to Issue Administrative Sanction Comprehensively, available at http://finance.people.com.cn/stock/n/2013/0930/c67815-23082442.html. (Last accessed 31 October, 2021).

[5] See Guanyu Jinyibu Jiaqiang Jicha Zhifa Gongzuo De Yijian, available at http://www.csrc.gov.cn/pub/newsite/zjhxwfb/xwdd/201308/t20130819_232829.html. (Last accessed 31 October, 2021).

[6] See Paichu Jigou Xingzheng Chufa Gongzuo Guiding, available at http://www.csrc.gov.cn/pub/newsite/zjhxwfb/xwdd/201309/t20130927_235486.html. (Last accessed 31 October, 2021).

[7] See Article 44 of Listing Rules of Shanghai Stock Exchange of 2019.

[8] See Article 39 of the Administrative Measures for the Securities Offering by Companies.

Futures Market (Draft for Soliciting Comments),[9] explicitly includes sixteen types of sanctions, i.e., (1) correction order; (2) conversation with regulator; (3) warning letter; (4) public explanation; (5) periodic reports; (6) temporarily refusing to accept documents related to administrative license; (7) restricting securities subscription; (8) suspension or termination of merger, acquisition and restructuring; (9) disqualifying candidates; (10) increasing the number of internal compliance inspections; (11) public criticism; (12) punishment against relevant personnel; (13) replacing directors, supervisors and senior managers or restricting their authorization; (14) stopping the approval of new business; (15) restricting the business activities of securities and futures institutions; and (16) restricting the rights of shareholders or ordering them to transfer shares. The costs to those with sanctions against them, particularly the listed companies, increased after the SPC issued the Provisions on the Issues Concerning Securities Representative Litigation (Henceforth SPC's 2020 Provisions)[10] in July 2020, and its Article 5 increased the scope of cases admitted by Chinese courts, only requiring that plaintiffs submit preliminary proofs, which include the statement of charges, the evidence of administrative sanctions decisions, criminal judgments, disciplinary or self-regulatory sanctions issued by the stock exchanges and securities trading venues approved by the State Council against the defendants, or confession material of the defendants, for potential misconducts in the case adjudicated with representative litigation. Consequently, entities sanctioned by the CSRC and its ROs nonadministratively are also exposed to the risks of private litigation.

In terms of procedural norms, the CSRC issued its first Principles for Investigating and Sanctioning Securities and Futures Cases[11] and Principles for Evidential Matters of Investigating and Sanctioning Securities and Futures Cases[12] in 1999. The enforcement proceeding can be further divided into the stages of informal investigation, filing and registering the case, formal investigation and case closing, which are shown in Fig. 4.1. In the informal investigation stage, the enforcement department receiving case tips evaluates its merits based on informal communications and information collection. The case tips are primarily from other departments of the CSRC, self-regulatory organizations, whistleblowing sources and the media. The CSRC established the hotline "12386" in 2013 for whistleblowing. According to

---

[9] The current version of the Measures for Implementing the Nonadministrative Sanctions in the Securities and Futures Market was issued in 2018. However, the Administrative Penalties Law was significantly revised in 2021, and some of the articles of the Measures are inconsistent with the revised Administrative Penalties Law. Consequently, the draft for soliciting comments is used here to reflect the most recent view of the CSRC, see Zhengquan Qihuo Shichang Jiandu Guanli Cuoshi Shishi Banfa (Zhengqiu Yijian Gao), available at http://www.csrc.gov.cn/zjhpublic/zjh/202003/P02 0200327611784619869.pdf. (Last accessed 31 October, 2021).

[10] See Guanyu Zhengquan Jiufen Daibiaoren Susong Ruogan Wenti De Guiding, available at http://www.court.gov.cn/zixun-xiangqing-245501.html. (Last accessed 31 October, 2021).

[11] See Diaocha Chuli Zhengquan Qihuo Weifa Weigui Anjian Jiben Zhunze, available at http://www.ine.cn/regulation/exchangelaw/911319420.html. (Last accessed 31 October, 2021).

[12] See Diaocha Chuli Zhengquan Qihuo Weifa Weigui Anjian Zhengju Zhunze, available at https://www.chinacourt.org/law/detail/1999/12/id/36140.shtml. (Last accessed 31 October, 2021).

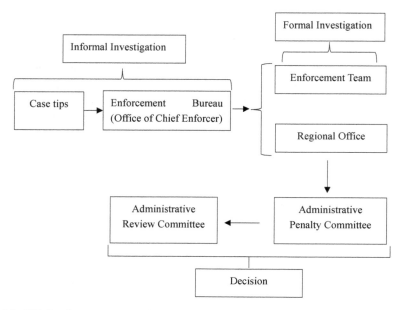

Fig. 4.1 CSRC enforcement proceeding

one recent media release, approximately 400 tips are reported every day, and the CSRC has dealt with more than 480,000 tips up until 2021.[13]

However, the whistleblowing program seems to play a negligible role, as it fails to mitigate the information disadvantage of public enforcers. The CSRC receives a large number of case tips every year, which are of little help to investigations. Article 167 of the Securities Law of 2019 established the whistleblowing program, which only accepts real-name reporting and requires that securities regulators award those tippers who provide critical information for case investigation. In 2020, the CSRC also revised the Interim Provisions on Reporting Legal Violations of Securities and Futures Market, which was first issued in 2014.[14] Article 13 of the Interim Provisions outlines the monetary awards to whistleblowers. Section 4.1 stipulates that the whistleblowers are entitled to 1% of the fine and disgorgement if the violators are sanctioned administratively and the monetary penalties are above 100,000 RMB or to 100,000 RMB if the violators are sanctioned criminally. Section 4.2 further specifies that whistleblowers are entitled to no more than 300,000 RMB if the information provided is of significant importance in major nationwide cases. For corporate insiders, the maximum award could be 600,000 RMB. Obviously, such monetary awards are insufficient to attract valuable tips, and whistleblowers are mainly driven

---

[13] See 12,386 Hotline Has Recovered 132 Million RMB for Investors, available at https://www.sohu.com/a/365937407_115433. (Last accessed 31 October, 2021).

[14] See Zhengquan Qihuo Weifa Weigui Xingwei Jubao Gongzuo Zanxing Guiding, available at http://www.csrc.gov.cn/pub/zjhpublic/zjh/202001/P020200121556622909959.pdf. (Last accessed 31 October, 2021).

by ethical concerns.[15] The CSRC receives a large number of tips, but they only make a marginal contribution to public enforcement proceedings.

In contrast, the SEC has long valued the importance of the whistleblower program for public enforcement and is committed to providing high-powered monetary incentives for tippers.[16] The Dodd-Frank Act enacted a landmark reform by adding a section on "Securities Whistleblower Incentives and Protection".[17] A specialized unit, the Office of the Whistleblower (OWB), as mandated by Sect. 924(d) of the Dodd-Frank Act, was established in the Enforcement Division of the SEC to administer the whistleblower program. To qualify for the monetary award, the tippers should voluntarily provide the information that is original and that leads the SEC to successful enforcement actions. In addition, the monetary sanctions due to the case tips should be over 1 million dollars. The award is set between 10 and 30% of the monetary sanctions collected,[18] and in the majority of cases, the whistleblowers receive 30% of the monetary sanctions. Another important improvement advanced by the Dodd-Frank Act is the confidentiality protection of tippers. They are allowed to anonymously file a report with the help of an attorney, and employers are forbidden from striking back against whistleblowers. The SEC could bring enforcement actions against employers retaliating against whistleblowers, should the latter report such cases to the OWB. The SEC has awarded a total of 562 million dollars to 106 individuals through the whistleblower program between 2010 and 2020. The year 2020 has witnessed the largest annual award to whistleblowers. SEC granted approximately 175 million dollars to 39 tippers, with the largest individual award amounting to over 114 million dollars.[19] The aforementioned rewards also bring about significant benefits. The SEC estimates that the monetary sanctions due to whistleblowing have been more than 2.7 billion dollars, which significantly deters potential misconduct.[20]

If the enforcement departments of the CSRC decide to pursue the case and launch a formal investigation, it has to submit the case material to the Enforcement Bureau, which is responsible for the coordination of the enforcement proceedings, for registration. The CSRC has promulgated undisclosed internal guidance for evaluating if the case should be registered.[21] The Enforcement Team of the CSRC mainly investigates major cases of misrepresentation, insider trading, or market manipulation,

---

[15] For example, CSRC has released the information for rewarding whistleblower related to three administrative enforcement proceedings, available at http://www.gov.cn/xinwen/2019-08/03/content_5418387.htm. (Last accessed 31 October, 2021).

[16] Joseph L. Zales [1].

[17] Pub. L. No. 111–203, § 922(a), 124 Stat. 1841 (2010).

[18] 15 U.S.C. § 78u-6(b)(1).

[19] Securities and Exchange Commission. 2020 Annual Report to Congress: Whistleblower Program, available at https://www.sec.gov/files/2020%20Annual%20Report_0.pdf. (Last accessed 31 October, 2021).

[20] Securities and Exchange Commission. 2020 Annual Report to Congress: Whistleblower Program, available at https://www.sec.gov/files/2020%20Annual%20Report_0.pdf. (Last accessed 31 October, 2021).

[21] CSRC [2].

whereas the ROs investigate minor cases within their jurisdictions. Cases are further divided into three categories based on the severity of the misconduct according to Article 5 of the Opinions on Further Strengthening Securities Law Inspection and Enforcement.[22] The cases are categorized as A-level, B-level and C-level, with the A-level case of the highest significance.

Once the CSRC decides to register the case, the Notice Letter of Investigation is sent to the investigated parties. Then, it enters the stage of the formal investigation. Article 179 of the Securities Law of 2019 grants the CSRC broad investigative authority, including information and evidence collection, seizing the accounts of potential violators, and restricting travel aboard. However, the CSRC lacks the authority to search and issue subpoenas, which limits its investigative ability and requires the CSRC to cooperate with the Public Security Bureau.[23] To protect the legitimate interests of those investigated, the onsite investigation should be carried out by at least two staff members, according to the CSRC Measures for the Implementation of Freezing and Sealing Up Procedure.[24] The final investigative step is the preparation for the investigative report. Article 22 of the Principles for Investigating and Sanctioning Securities and Futures Cases provides a framework for the report, which summarizes the basis of the case registration, the identified violations, the evidence and the recommended sanctions.

The Enforcement Bureau will review the report and submit it to the Administrative Penalty Committee, which is governed by the Organizational Rules of the Administrative Penalty Committee.[25] Regular cases will be chaired by one committee member, and two additional members will join the hearing proceedings. Simple cases can be heard by only one member through a simplified procedure. Before the Administrative Penalty Committee finalizes the sanction, the sanctioned will receive the preliminary decision and be granted the right to conduct a hearing conference.[26] The conference will be heard by three to five members of the SEC and is mainly for violators to explain and defend themselves. Unfortunately, the hearing conference is an internal procedure of the CSRC and seldom reverts the preliminary decision. After the hearing, the final report will be submitted to the vise commissioner supervising the enforcement division for approval.

---

[22] See Guanyu Jinyibu Jiaqiang Jicha Zhifa Gongzuo De Yijian, available at http://www.csrc.gov. cn/pub/newsite/jcj/gzdt/201311/t20131105_237463.html. (Last accessed 31 October, 2021).

[23] See Yiwei Liu [3].

[24] See Dongjie Chafeng Shishi Banfa, available at http://www.csrc.gov.cn/pub/newsite/flb/flfg/ bmgz/zhl/201310/t20131016_236269.html. (Last accessed 31 October, 2021).

[25] see Xingzheng Chufa Weiyuanhui Zuzhi Guize of 2021, available at http://www.csrc.gov.cn/pub/ zjhpublic/zjh/202103/P020210312577179068544.pdf. (Last accessed 31 October, 2021).

[26] See CSRC Provisions for Hearing of the Administrative Sanction (Xingzheng Chufa Tingzheng Guize), available at http://www.csrc.gov.cn/pub/zjhpublic/G00306201/201511/P02015110647410 7818224.pdf. (Last accessed 31 October, 2021).

After receiving the final sanction, those sanctioned could resort to the administrative review procedure of the CSRC.[27] The department responsible for this procedure is the Legal Bureau. The administrative review procedure has been criticized for being unlikely to bring about any meaningful change regarding the defendants because one department of the CSRC, instead of an independent third party, will conduct the whole review process. A recent empirical study finds that only one case out of 24 sanction decisions made by the CSRC was repealed due to insufficient evidence.[28]

4.2 Enforcement Inputs of the CSRC

Public enforcement outputs are, to a large extent, determined by the inputs of regulatory agencies. It is difficult or impossible to deter securities fraud effectively without sufficient resources.[29] Jackson and Roe proposed measuring the regulatory input of securities regulators using the annual budget and staffing numbers.[30] This subsection follows their approach and presents a time-series distribution of the CSRCs' regulatory inputs. Based on the statistics released by the annual reports of the CSRC, Table 4.1 shows the annual budget and standardized annual budget of the CSRC and its ROs between 2011 and 2019.

The first column of Table 4.1 shows that the annual budget of the CSRC was approximately 772 million RMB in 2011 and has since increased significantly. In 2019, the budget reached 1.34 billion RMB, with an average growth rate of 6.6%. The third column presents the standardized annual budget, which is calculated by dividing the annual budget by the market capitalization at the end of the same year. The standardized annual budget decreased significantly between 2014 and 2015, which is attributed to the fact that it was a bull market. On average, regulatory costs are approximately 2768 RMB per 100 million RMB of market capitalization. Further analysis of the components of the CSRC's annual budget shows that a small proportion of the budget was devoted to enforcement proceedings. Taking the annual budget of 2015 as an example, the column "Financial spending" is 920 million RMB, and its sub column "Financial regulation spending" is approximately 300 million RMB, which accounts for only 30% of its total budget.[31]

Table 4.2 shows the time-series changes in the number of staff of the CSRC and its ROs. The average staffing number is approximately 3,100 and has a growth rate of 3.75%. Human resources are mostly devoted to ROs, which employ approximately

---

[27] See CSRC Measures for Administrative Review (Xingzheng Fuyi Banfa), available at http://www.gov.cn/gongbao/content/2003/content_62245.htm. (Last accessed 31 October, 2021).

[28] See Yiwei Liu [3], p. 25.

[29] Sunstein and Stewart [4].

[30] Jackson and Roe [5].

[31] See The 2015 CSRC Annual Budget Report, available at http://www.gov.cn/xinwen/2015-04/17/content_2848812.htm. (Last accessed 31 October, 2021).

Table 4.1 The annual budget of the CSRC between 2011 and 2019

Year	Annual budget (100 million RMB)	Annual growth rate (%)	Standardized annual budget(/100 million market capitalization)	Annual growth rate (%)
2019	13.40	11.39	2259.95	−18.30%
2018	12.03	2.04	2766.00	33.04
2017	11.79	12.18	2079.05	0.43
2016	10.51	5.84	2070.18	10.76
2015	9.93	4.64	1868.99	−26.63
2014	9.49	−1.96	2547.33	−37.09
2013	9.68	14.15	4048.90	9.99
2012	8.48	9.84	3681.23	2.41
2011	7.72	1.31	3594.74	25.21
Average	10.07	6.60	2768.49	−0.02

Note (1) The annual budget is obtained from the CSRC's annual report
(2) The "Standardized Annual Budget" is calculated with market capitalization as the denominator

Table 4.2 The number of staff of the CSRC between 2011 and 2019

Year	Number of staff	Annual growth rate (%)	Standardized number of staff	Annual growth rate (%)
2019	3256	3.07	0.86	−2.20
2018	3159	2.33	0.88	−0.49
2017	3087	0.85	0.89	−11.68
2016	3061	−1.16	1.00	−8.45
2015	3097	−2.21	1.10	−9.61
2014	3167	−0.50	1.21	−5.22
2013	3183	10.10	1.28	10.32
2012	2891	5.32	1.16	−1.10
2011	2745	6.03	1.17	−6.61
Average	3072	2.65	1.06	−3.89

Note (1) The annual number of staff is obtained from the CSRC's annual report
(2) The "Standardized Staffing Number" is calculated with the number of listed companies as the denominator

75% of the total staff.[32] Resource allocations reflect the informational advantage of local regulators and can facilitate the responsiveness of regulatory interventions. The third column standardized the staffing number with the number of listed companies. The standardized staffing number has recently decreased, which reflects the fact that

[32] See The 2015 CSRC Annual Report, p.11, available at http://www.gov.cn/xinwen/site1/201 50417/88221429274164491.pdf. (Last accessed 31 October, 2021).

the number of listed companies has grown at a higher rate than that of CSRC staffing. The fast growth in the number of listed companies is partly due to deregulation in entry to the securities market. Another human resource dimension is the training of the staff. Until the end of 2012, approximately 97.5% of the staff held a bachelor's degree, while at the commission level, approximately 76.1% of the staff had received a master's degree and 16.4% held a doctoral degree.[33] A challenge faced by the CSRC is that experienced staff are moving to market institutions, which significantly undermines the efficiency of public enforcement.

CSRC appears to be short of disposable resources. To make things most comparable, the annual budget of 2012 is taken as an example. According to disclosed data, the annual budget of the CSRC was 134.84 million dollars in 2012,[34] whereas its American counterpart, the SEC, spent 1.29 billion dollars that same year.[35] After adjusting to stock market capitalization, the normalized budget of the SEC is approximately 69.09 dollars per million market capitalizations, whereas for the CSRC, the normalized budget is 36.47 dollars per million market capitalizations.[36] Compared to the cross-country data reported by Jackson and Roe, the CSRC's annual budget of 16,319.98 dollars per billion dollars of GDP ranks relatively low in their sample. Therefore, it may be reasonable to argue that China's enforcement regime is similar to the regimes of civil law countries, such as Japan and Germany, which invest limited resources in enforcing their securities laws. This argument contradicts, at least partially, the legal origin theory that claims that civil law countries regulate their markets more intensively.[37] However, the negative effects due to the shortage in the CSRC budget are partly mitigated by the following three factors. First, it should be noted that China has adopted a stringent *ex ante* screening process to ensure the quality of listed companies. For example, the quota system established when the two stock exchanges were just established has been proven to provide incentives for regional governments to compete with each other and select high-quality firms to list on the market.[38] Second, the costs for human capital are relatively low in China, and a smaller budget could support a relatively large number of personnel. Third, the CSRC has multiple affiliated institutions, such as stock exchanges and industrial associations, which could share part of the daily regulatory duties.

---

[33] See The 2012 CSRC Annual Report, p.7, available at http://www.csrc.gov.cn/pub/newsite/zjhjs/zjhnb/201307/P020130722555052657179.pdf. (Last accessed 31 October, 2021).

[34] See The 2012 CSRC Annual Budget Report, and the budget is adjusted to dollars utilizing the exchange rate 6.2855 of December 31, 2012, available at http://www.gov.cn/gzdt/2012-04/23/content_2120877.htm. (Last accessed 31 October, 2021).

[35] The number is drawn from the SEC website under the account actual obligation; see http://www.sec.gov/foia/docs/budgetact.htm, last access 2014/10/10. (Last accessed 31 October, 2021).

[36] The data for annual stock market capitalization are drawn from the website of the World Bank. The market capitalization in 2012 for the U.S. was 18,668,333 million dollars, whereas for China, the amount was 3,697,376 million dollars. see http://data.worldbank.org/indicator/CM.MKT.LCAP.CD?order=wbapi_data_value_2012+wbapi_data_value+wbapi_data_value-last&sort=desc. (Last accessed 31 October, 2021).

[37] Rafael La Porta et al. [6], p. 286.

[38] Katharina Pistor and Chenggang Xu [7].

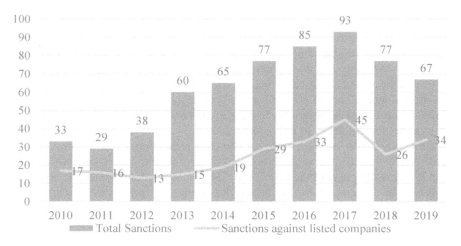

Fig. 4.2 CSRC enforcement outputs between 2011 and 2019. *Source* China stock market and accounting research database (CSMAR database)[39]

4.3   Enforcement Outputs of the CSRC

4.3.1   *Enforcement Outputs at Commission Level*

After decentralizing the enforcement authority, the number of enforcement actions of the CSRC exhibits an upward trend, but at a relatively low rate. As shown in Fig. 4.2, the CSRC imposed a total of 624 administrative sanctions between 2010 and 2019. From 2010 to 2012, the annual enforcement outputs were less than 40, but they quickly increased to nearly 100 in 2017. Enforcement proceedings against listed companies account for between 30 and 50% of the yearly total; the remainder are against individuals and other legal entities. It is worth mentioning that the administrative sanctions of the CSRC and its ROs have significant third-party effects on the protection of minority shareholders because these sanctions are prerequisites for private securities litigation. Before 2002, injured investors enjoyed no *de facto* rights to bring lawsuits for compensation due to the SPC's 2001 Notice. The situation changed after the SPC issued the SPC's 2002 Notice, which, for the first time, explicitly allowed lower courts to accept civil cases for compensation brought by private parties. However, the SPC's 2002 Notice sets an administrative prerequisite for private actions, i.e., it requires that private litigations be based on sanction decisions made by public agencies, particularly the CSRC and the MOF, or on the courts'

---

[39] CSMAR Database is one of the largest financial data suppliers in China, available at http://www.gtarsc.com. (Last accessed 31 October, 2021).

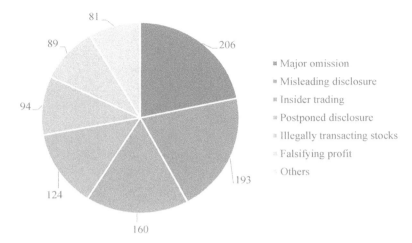

Fig. 4.3 The distribution of misconducts sanctioned by CSRC. *Source* CSMAR database

criminal judgments.[40] Consequently, the enforcement proceedings initiated by the CSRC and its ROs also matter for harmed investors because they partly determine the availability of potential judiciary compensation.

Figure 4.3 presents the distribution of the enforcement actions among different types of misconduct. Informational infractions are the primary type of misconduct committed by market participants. "Major omission", "Misleading disclosure", "Postponed disclosure" and "Falsifying profit" were sanctioned 206 times, 193 times, 124 times and 89 times, respectively. Second, insider trading was sanctioned 160 times. The sanctioned entities are mainly corporate insiders, for example, the chairman of the board, the CEO, and other senior management. The third type is "illegally transacting stocks", which was sanctioned 94 times. This mostly concerns entities prohibited by law and regulations from trading stocks. Finally, other misconducts, including "Falsifying asset", "Manipulating stock price", "False disclosure" and "Misappropriating asset", were sanctioned 16 times, 16 times, 15 times and 11 times, respectively. However, the figures presented should be interpreted with caution because the data are obtained from the announcements made by listed companies, which are mandated to disclose information that might influence themselves.

Another factor that deters securities misconduct is the liabilities for violators. Rational market participants expect that they can profit from illegal activities, and consequently, monetary penalties are an important strategy to reduce their expected profits. Figure 4.4 presents the fines and disgorgements collected by the CSRC between 2011 and 2019, which have grown exponentially since 2013. In 2018, the

---

[40] Although Article 5 of the Provisions Concerning Securities Representative Litigation reduces the administrative prerequisites of private securities litigations, it still stipulates that the ordinary representative action should meet the preliminary prerequisites that defendants are sanctioned administratively, criminally, nonadministratively or by stock exchanges.

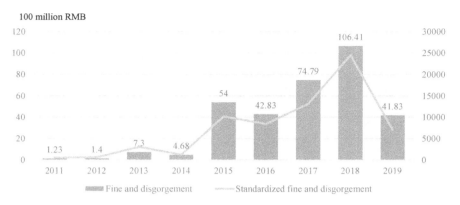

Fig. 4.4 The fine and disgorgement collected by the CSRC between 2011 and 2019

monetary penalty reached 10.64 billion RMB, which is nearly 100 times the amount in 2010. The curve line is the distribution of the standardized monetary penalty with the denominator of market capitalization. In 2011, the monetary penalty per 100 million market capitalizations was only 420, and it quickly increased to 24,466 per 100 million market capitalizations. Increased monetary penalties improve enforcement intensity and, hence, deter potential securities misconduct. However, it also has the side effect of drawing capital out of the securities market. Unlike the rules in other jurisdictions, the monetary penalties collected by the CSRC cannot be distributed to harmed investors but rather are handed over to the National Treasury. Functionally speaking, monetary penalties are likely to reduce the funding available to compensate harmed investors and represent a capital outflow from the market.

The way that Chinese financial regulators deal with monetary penalties is in sharp contrast to the globally popular mixed enforcement model, which tends to combine both functions of deterrence and compensation. For example, the monetary penalties collected by the SEC will be used to form fair funds, which are dedicated to compensating harmed investors. Between 2002 and 2013, the SEC established 243 fair funds and paid harmed investors 14.5 billion dollars, which surpassed its total budget of 12.1 billion dollars during the same period.[41] Section 308 of the Sarbanes–Oxley Act grants the SEC the authority to establish fair funds, which allows public enforcement to achieve both functions of deterrence and compensation.[42] The SEC serves as a public class counsel and represents a harmed investor to seek compensation.[43] Prior to authorization, monetary penalties should be paid to the Treasury's General Fund. Section 929B of the Dodd-Frank Act further lifts constraints on the source of the funds that can be used to establish fair funds. Previously, the SEC had to obtain disgorgement if it wanted to inject fines into the fair fund. Empirical studies show that public enforcement tends to complement private enforcement and

---

[41] Urska Velikonja [8].

[42] Barbara Black [9].

[43] Verity Winship [10].

intervenes in cases where class actions fail to function well.[44] For example, the SEC often sanctions securities firms, which are not the primary entities to compensate harmed investors, and administrative fines cannot be covered by directors' and officers' liability insurance. However, fair funds might suffer from potential caveats; they could overlap with class actions and lead to a waste of resources.[45]

The CSRC also imposes limits on market entry for individuals who are directly responsible for securities misconduct. Those sanctioned could be restricted from assuming the position of directors, supervisors and senior management and from performing securities business, such as working at securities companies, which will significantly reduce the future revenue that could be obtained by violators. The CSRC issued 69 sanctions against 126 individuals between 2011 and 2015. Finally, the enforcement proceedings of the CSRC also impose indirect costs on violators. First, sanctioned entities experience reputational damage, and their stocks suffer from significant negative abnormal returns after the information is released to the market.[46] Second, in the case of legal entities, public enforcement will increase the turnover rate of their senior management.[47] Third, sanctioned financial intermediaries are likely to lose market share, and their bargaining power is reduced. For example, in securities misrepresentation cases, the CSRC will sanction not only the issuers but also securities firms, accounting firms and law firms that fail to fulfill their gatekeeper functions. Those sanctioned accounting firms are found to lose their high-quality clients, and their ability to acquire new clients is undermined.[48]

4.3.2 Enforcement Outputs at the Regional Office Level

After the reform decentralized the enforcement authority, the enforcement outputs of the CSRC increased significantly. According to the announcements made by listed companies between 2011 and 2019, ROs issued 1472 sanctions, accounting for more than three-fifths of the total public enforcement outputs. The current governance structure of China's public enforcement of securities law mimics its authoritarian political regime, which has been called an RDA model.[49] The RDA model combines the attributes of centralization and decentralization. On the one hand, the Chinese political and personnel governance structure is highly centralized. Subnational government officials are appointed and promoted from above, which serves as a powerful incentive to induce regional officials to follow the central government's policies.[50] More specifically, this personnel control system is a nested network in

---

[44] Urska Velikonja [8].

[45] See Adam Zimmerman [11].

[46] Gongmeng Chen et al. [12].

[47] Gongmeng Chen et al. [12].

[48] Li et al. [13].

[49] Chenggang Xu [14].

[50] Pranab Bardhan [15].

which the center directly controls key positions at the provincial level and grants each tier of subnational government the power to appoint key officials at the next level below. Each subnational government level oversees the appointment, evaluation, promotion and dismissal of its subordinate-level regional leaders.[51]

On the other hand, substantial powers are also delegated to subnational governments. They have a general responsibility for initiating and coordinating reforms, providing public services, and making and enforcing laws within their jurisdictions. This regime is argued to have decisively contributed to China's miraculous economic growth by encouraging interregional competition around certain performance indicators, such as GDP (total or per capita), GDP growth rate, and foreign direct investment (FDI), and by using regional experiments to initiate and test new reform policies that weaken political resistance and reduce uncertainties.[52]

The relationship between the CSRC and its local agencies replicates the relationship between China's central and local governments. On the one hand, local agencies are subject to the CSRC's orders (particularly its personnel power), which means that authority is highly centralized. On the other hand, local agencies are granted considerable power to regulate listed companies, leading to a certain degree of decentralization. With a properly designed incentive mechanism, such as the performance target system prevalent in China's governance system, officials in local agencies can be motivated to focus on the particular objectives preferred by their principals, such as an aggressive enforcement strategy.[53] Officials in local agencies may also be incentivized to compete with each other on certain indicators established by the CSRC, such as sanctions issued or fines collected each year, and may, therefore, become even more aggressive than what is intended by the target system. Moreover, an RDA-like governance structure may help improve the performance of China's public enforcement in securities law by taking advantage of the territorial proximity (and hence information accessibility) between local agencies and targeted listed companies. Local agencies have an informational advantage over the CSRC with regard to listed companies and may, therefore, implement securities law more efficiently and more effectively. Finally, an RDA-like structure may help the CSRC distance itself from blame-generating situations in which local agencies fail to enforce securities law effectively. In other words, local agencies act as 'buffer zones' that protect the CSRC from social dissatisfaction and cushion the CSRC from potential crises.

Table 4.3 summarizes the distribution of the annual sanctions issued by ROs. In Panel A, the number of sanctions issued for each year is reported. The enforcement actions of the ROs were relatively small in 2010. In 2012, the number increased to 152, which is nearly 10 times that in 2010, and remained stable between 2013 and 2016. It further increased after 2017, reaching the highest point of 276 sanctions in 2019. Panel B presents the distribution of the number of sanctions by different types of misconduct. Because one decision could sanction multiple infractions, the 1,472 sanctions presented in Panel A record 2,107 infractions in total. The primary

---

[51] Xin Wan et al. [16].

[52] Hehui Jin et al. [17].

[53] Xiaodong Zhu [18].

Table 4.3 The distribution of RO sanctions by year and type of misconduct

Panel A distribution by year

Year	2010	2011	2012	2013	2014	2015	2016	2017	2018	2019
Frequency	17	62	152	154	105	147	145	198	216	276
Percentage (%)	1.15	4.21	10.33	10.46	7.13	9.99	9.85	13.45	14.67	18.75

Panel B distribution by type of misconduct

Year	Major omission	Postponed disclosure	Misleading disclosure	Accounting irregularities	Illegally transacting stocks	Falsifying disclosure	Misappropriating assets	Illegal guarantees	Falsifying profits	Changing the use of capital raised	Others
Frequency	553	454	340	267	116	100	89	73	55	44	16
Percentage (%)	26.25	21.55	16.14	12.67	5.51	4.75	4.22	3.46	2.61	2.09	0.76

Table 4.4 Distribution of the sanctions by RO and year

	2010	2011	2012	2013	2014	2015	2016	2017	2018	2019	Total
Guangdong RO	1	3	32	19	3	11	14	28	12	17	140
Shanghai RO	1	2	10	21	11	17	12	14	22	28	138
Shenzhen RO	3	7	17	12	8	9	8	9	10	22	105
Zhejiang RO	0	2	5	7	6	5	7	22	19	30	103
Jiangsu RO	1	1	16	15	4	6	3	10	11	14	81
Sichuan RO	0	2	13	10	8	7	8	7	13	9	77
Shanxi RO	0	3	4	7	8	16	9	8	9	8	72
Henan RO	1	5	15	14	8	13	5	1	3	0	65
Hubei RO	0	0	2	5	5	7	9	14	10	12	64
Shandong RO	3	5	6	4	3	2	9	7	9	15	63
Fujian RO	1	7	3	3	6	2	5	9	10	11	57
Others	6	25	29	37	35	52	56	69	88	110	507

misconducts are informational infractions, including "Major omission" and "Postponed disclosure". "Misleading disclosure", "Accounting irregularities", "Falsifying disclosure" and "Falsifying profits", which are sanctioned 553 times, 454 times, 340 times, 267 times, 100 times and 55 times, respectively. In addition, ROs sanctioned "illegally transacting stocks" 116 times. Finally, "Misappropriating assets", "Illegal guarantees" and "Changing the use of capital raised" are sanctioned occasionally. One interesting phenomenon is that the two most serious misconducts, i.e., "IPO fraud" and "Market manipulation" are not sanctioned by ROs, and "Insider trading" is not sanctioned frequently. This likely reflects the division of labor between the CSRC and ROs, where the former is responsible for these high-profile cases.

Table 4.4 further presents the distribution of the annual enforcement outputs by ROs between 2010 and 2019. The most active enforcers are the ROs in Guangdong, Shanghai, Shenzhen and Zhejiang, which imposed 140, 138, 105 and 103 sanctions, respectively. These provincial regions are those with the largest number of listed companies, which partly leads to their relatively high enforcement outputs. In total, 11 out of 36 ROs imposed more than 50 sanctions, and their total enforcement actions accounted for 66% of the total outputs. The pilot reform project decentralizing the authority to impose administrative sanctions on ROs in Guangdong, Shanghai and Shenzhen, which has created a competitive environment, seems to have generated significant positive effects. The outputs for these three ROs increased most significantly in 2012, those for the RO in Guangdong increased 867%, from 3 sanctions in 2011 to 32 sanctions in 2012, those for the RO in Shanghai increased 400%, from 2 to 11 sanctions, and those for the RO in Shenzhen increased 43%, from 7 to 17 sanctions.

The sanctioned include both listed companies and nonlisted companies as well as individuals. Figure 4.5 shows the distribution of the sanctions against these two groups of entities between 2011 and 2019. Sanctions against listed companies account

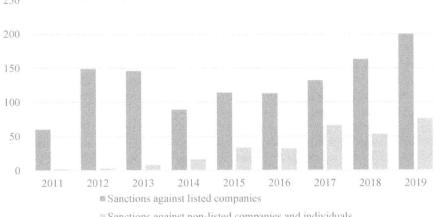

Fig. 4.5 Distribution of sanctions against listed companies and nonlisted companies and individuals between 2011 and 2019

for approximately two-thirds of the total enforcement outputs. Because the data are obtained from the announcements made by listed companies, the figure might under-estimate the enforcement outputs of ROs against nonlisted companies and individ-uals. Sanctions against nonlisted companies and individuals not affiliated with listed companies are not taken into account. For sanctioned listed companies, approxi-mately 90% of them received the nonadministrative sanction "Correction", and other frequently used penalties include "Explain publicly", "Censure letter" and "Credit records of the securities market". Administrative sanctions, including "Warning" and(or) "Fine" are only employed in approximately 7% of the cases. For sanctioned nonlisted companies and individuals, the majority receive "Censure letters", and approximately 10% receive the administrative sanctions of "Warning" and/or "Fine".

4.4 Is CSRC's Enforcement Action Biased?

4.4.1 Hypotheses and Sample

One major concern raised by Landes and Posner about a monopolistic public enforcer is the risk of discretionary nonenforcement.[54] Selective enforcement is a salient threat to the development of the securities market in China, given that the CSRC enjoys *de facto* exclusive authority in public enforcement and that a high percentage of listed companies are owned or controlled by various levels of the government. It may be

---

[54] Landes and Posner [19].

argued that the strategy of focusing on law enforcement could, in certain circumstances, generate positive net social gains given the limited resources at the disposal of the CSRC.[55] A prior study using the enforcement data disclosed by the CSRC's annual reports found that it maintains a relatively "level playing field" for listed companies, except for the fact that central government-controlled firms (CGCFs) receive favorable treatment.[56] Consequently, the hypothesis tested in this subsection is whether the CSRC and its ROs have been selectively exercising enforcement against private firms and SOEs.

The sample used to test this hypothesis is obtained from the CSMAR Database, a leading financial data provider in China. In contrast to previous studies, which obtained their data on regulatory outputs from regulators' websites, this study adopts a different approach by collecting information on enforcement outcomes from regulated firms, which are required to disclose these sanctions to the public.[57] Hence, a sanction-based measure of regulatory output, rather than individual- or firm-based measures, is used in this subsection.[58] The sample consists of sanctions disclosed by listed companies between 2003 and 2015. In our sample, there are 1,083 listed companies that have received certain types of sanctions, of which 36.57% (396) and 63.43% (687) are listed on the SHSE and SZSE, respectively. Based on the type of ownership, i.e., the identities of their controllers, these listed companies are classified into five groups: private firm (PF), foreign firm (FF), municipal-government-controlled firm (MGCF), provincial-government-controlled firm (PGCF) and CGCF.[59]

4.4.2 Empirical Findings

In this subsection, we examine the enforcement preferences of regulators against listed companies.[60] An enforcement intensity index (EII), which is calculated with

---

[55] Lando and Shavell [20].

[56] Tianshu Zhou [21].

[57] Listed companies are required to disclose major events that may influence the price of their securities and derivatives. The definition of a major event is given by Article 30 of the *Administrative Measures for the Disclosure of Information of Listed Companies* (promulgated by CSRC in Jan. 30th, 2007). More specifically, Article 30 (11) requires that listed companies make public announcements when they are under public investigation or receive criminal or major administrative sanctions, or when their directors, supervisors and senior managers are subject to public investigation or coercive measures.

[58] A sanction-based measure means that the regulatory output is the number of sanction decisions made by various regulators, rather than the number of individuals or firms punished in each decision. It is highly likely that one sanction decision involves multiple individuals or firms.

[59] For listed companies that were sanctioned in 2015, information on the identities of their controllers is not available. Hence, we use the data reported at the end of 2014 as a substitute.

[60] The dataset used in this subsection excludes those sanctions issued by MOF and those against FFs because these numbers are too small to conduct meaningful in-depth analysis. Hence, the sample size is reduced to 2108 sanctions against listed companies.

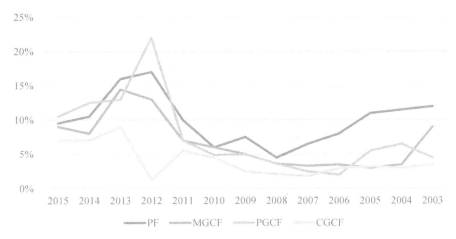

Fig. 4.6 The enforcement intensity index for listed companies with different types of ownership

Eq. (4.1) by dividing the annual number of sanctions received by listed companies with certain ownership by the total number of listed companies with the same ownership in that year, is used to measure the probability of receiving public sanctions.

$$\text{EII} = \text{(The annual number of sanctions received by PF/MGCF/PGCF/CGCF)}$$
$$/\text{(The annual number of PF/MGCF/PGCF/CGCF listed on the market)} (4.1)$$

Figure 4.6 presents the EII for each group of firms. Clearly, PFs suffered from an enforcement bias and had the highest EII; MGCFs and PGCFs were in the middle; and CGCFs had the lowest EII. In 2003, the probability of a PF being sanctioned was approximately 11.56%, while for CGCFs it was only approximately 3.26%. However, the gap started to shrink after 2005 because the number of PFs increased quickly during this time, even though the absolute number of sanctions received by each group of firms remained stable. EIIs for all groups of firms increased significantly and showed a similar trend after 2010, partially due to the increase in the ROs' outputs. According to the EII measure, the problem of selective enforcement against PFs was a prominent concern in the early years of the twenty-first century. This bias, however, has been mitigated in recent years, with only CGCFs still enjoying an obvious preferential treatment from public regulators.[61]

We further examine the enforcement preferences of different regulators and construct an enforcement preference index (EPI), which is calculated using Eq. (4.2). The EPI compares the probability of being sanctioned for firms with different types of ownership with the probability of all firms being sanctioned. The logic behind

---

[61] It must be recognized that we cannot rule out the possibility that CGCFs have established a better corporate governance structure that leads to fewer infringements.

the ratio is simple: if a regulator has no bias in enforcing the securities law against a given type of firm, the value of the EPI should be close to 1. If a regulator over- or underenforces the securities law, the value of the EPI should be larger or smaller than 1. Table 4.5 reports the EPIs for each regulator from 2003 to 2015.

$$
\begin{aligned}
\text{EPI} = {} & \text{(Probability of being sanctioned for PF/MGCF/PGCF/CGCF)} \\
& /\text{(Probability of being sanctioned for all firms)} \\
= {} & \text{(Number of sanctions against PF/MGCF/PGCF/CGCF} \\
& /\text{Number of listed PF/MGCF/PGCF/CGCF)} \\
& /\text{(Number of Total sanctions/Number of listed companies)} \quad (4.2)
\end{aligned}
$$

The last row of Table 4.5 reports the average EPI of firms with different types of ownership for each regulator over our sample period. The EPI against PFs is significantly higher than 1, indicating that PFs receive a disproportionately higher percentage of sanctions. In contrast, CGCFs are sanctioned less often than other groups of firms. If looking into the enforcement outputs of each regulator from a time-series perspective, we can find different enforcement patterns among these regulators. Panel A reports the CSRC's EPI against different groups of firms. Before 2012, MGCFs and PGCFs also enjoyed obvious preferential treatment when compared to PFs, but the situation changed thereafter when they were sanctioned more frequently by the CSRC.

Panel B presents the ROs' EPI. Before 2009, the ROs sanctioned listed companies sporadically (accounting for approximately 3% of the total output), and their outputs significantly increased after 2010, when RO (SZ), RO (GD) and RO (SH) were granted the authority to issue administrative sanctions. The EPIs of the ROs against PFs, MGCFs and PGCFs are similar after 2011 and those against CGCFs are significantly lower. Panel C and Panel D report the EPIs of the two stock exchanges, SHSE and SZSE, which also differ from each other in enforcement patterns. Starting in 2011, SHSE went easy on PFs and enforced regulations more intensively against CGCFs. In contrast, SZSE has a higher EPI compared to PFs. It is worth noting that one reason that PFs have fared relatively well in recent years (i.e., they are sanctioned less intensively) is in part because the number of listed PFs increased by approximately 20%, while the number of other groups of firms remained stable, which dilutes the EPIs against PFs.

We may also gauge enforcement intensity using the severity of issued sanctions. In our sample, regulators mainly used nonadministrative sanctions and four types of administrative sanctions: criticism, warning, censure and fines, which are arranged in ascending order of severity.[62] We construct an enforcement severity ratio (ESR) to measure the magnitude of discrimination against firms with different types of ownership, which is calculated according to Eq. (4.3) by dividing the number of each type of penalty received by each group of firms by the number of sanctions received

---

[62] The other two possible administrative sanctions are disgorgement of illegal gains and disqualifications.

Table 4.5 The enforcement preference index of different regulators against listed companies with different types of ownership

Year	Panel A. CSRC				Panel B. RO				Panel C. SHSE				Panel D. SZSE			
	PF	MGCF	PGCF	CGCF	PF	MGCF	PGCF	CGCF	PF	MGCF	PGCF	CGCF	PF	MGCF	PGCF	CGCF
2015	0.94	0.97	2.00	0.58	1.06	0.99	1.06	0.71	0.79	1.52	1.11	1.21	1.23	0.50	1.02	0.59
2014	1.12	0.67	1.67	0.40	0.96	1.13	1.39	0.73	0.88	0.91	1.75	1.09	1.39	0.28	0.61	0.44
2013	1.02	1.38	1.06	0.41	1.04	1.19	0.96	0.64	1.20	0.45	0.69	1.07	1.29	0.61	0.74	0.50
2012	1.06	1.13	1.22	0.46	1.06	0.75	1.22	0.91	0.84	1.23	0.80	1.49	1.09	0.81	1.52	0.51
2011	1.21	0.91	0.99	0.36	1.19	0.90	1.00	0.45	0.45	1.37	0.00	3.28	1.27	0.51	0.49	0.97
2010	1.37	1.19	0.00	0.38	0.97	1.30	1.45	0.36	1.42	0.00	2.35	0.00	1.17	0.76	0.37	1.24
2009	1.07	0.94	1.11	0.83	1.25	1.09	0.97	0.31	1.86	0.81	0.00	0.00	1.52	0.56	0.99	0.37
2008	1.19	0.97	1.37	0.36	1.28	1.09	0.69	0.53	0.85	1.21	1.14	0.89	1.39	0.91	0.86	0.44
2007	1.69	0.62	0.31	0.76	2.21	0.00	1.12	0.00	1.59	1.02	0.00	0.55	1.53	1.05	0.78	0.00
2006	1.65	0.93	0.30	0.51	0.00	0.00	0.00	0.00	1.70	0.77	0.37	0.63	1.93	0.65	0.42	0.36
2005	2.33	0.38	0.42	0.37	0.00	0.00	0.00	0.00	2.30	0.32	0.35	0.62	1.62	0.61	1.34	0.36
2004	1.49	0.64	1.69	0.23	2.15	0.46	1.04	0.00	2.50	0.15	0.70	0.33	1.70	0.70	0.87	0.49
2003	1.35	1.36	0.56	0.00	2.97	0.50	0.00	0.00	1.16	1.25	0.38	0.75	1.42	1.04	0.71	0.50
Avg	1.34	0.93	0.98	0.43	1.24	0.72	0.84	0.36	1.35	0.85	0.74	0.92	1.43	0.69	0.82	0.52

Table 4.6 The enforcement severity ratio for listed companies with different types of ownership

	Nonadministrative sanctions (%)	Criticism (%)	Warning (%)	Censure (%)	Fine (%)
PF	61.79	16.43	8.18	10.93	11.24
MGCF	54.01	18.09	6.72	13.95	13.70
PGCF	64.92	12.90	5.24	11.29	11.29
CGCF	72.22	13.64	4.55	6.57	7.07

by each group of firms. If firms with certain ownership are treated favorably, on average, there may be a greater probability that they receive less severe punishments and less probability that they receive more severe punishments.

$$\text{ESR} = \text{(The number of each type of penalty against PF/MGCF/PGCF/CGCF)}$$
$$/\text{(The number of total sanctions received byPF/MGCF/PGCF/CGCF)}$$
$$(4.3)$$

Table 4.6 presents the ESRs of listed companies with different types of ownership. Generally, CGCFs have the highest probability of receiving the lightest penalties, such as nonadministrative sanctions, and the lowest probability of receiving more serious penalties, including criticism, warning, censure and fines. In contrast, PFs and MGCFs have a higher probability of being sanctioned most severely. Their ESRs for nonadministrative sanctions are the lowest, while they have a much higher chance of receiving more severe administrative sanctions.

It is not difficult to explain the enforcement discrimination faced by private companies in China. This is just a microcosm of the larger picture of China's economy, particularly its financial system. It is claimed that China's financial system conforms to the stereotype of financial repression theory. For example, Huang and Wang argue that "despite more than 30 years' of economic reform, the Chinese economy still possesses the typical characteristics of financial repression: heavily regulated interest rates, state-influenced credit allocation, frequently adjusted reserve requirements and tightly controlled capital accounts".[63] Johansson also claims that "repressive financial policies constitute a central problem in the Chinese economic system".[64]

Under such a repressed financial environment, scarce financial resources, particularly credit, have been systematically and continually allocated to less profitable but more politically preferable ventures, particularly SOEs, whereas private firms, which have become the driving force behind China's economic growth, are forced to rely on informal and even underground credit channels to finance their survival. The narrow private sector (i.e., domestically privately owned and individual businesses)

---

[63] Huang and Wang [22].

[64] Johansson [23], pp. 45–64.

accounted for only 7.4–13.5% of total bank loans issued from 2002 to 2008.[65] In contrast, SOEs, particularly those under the control of the central government, are the main beneficiaries of the financial rents generated by distorted financial policies.[66] Brandt and Zhu find that over the 1998–2003 period, the state sector, which includes companies in which governments have significant ownership shares, continued to absorb between one-half and two-thirds of new bank lending.[67]

This phenomenon could be attributed to the governmental preference for the state-owned sector. Haggard and Huang report that "despite the well-documented process of economic reform in China, the domestic private sector remains relatively small and subject to a variety of policy and economic constraints".[68] It is also understandable that, in terms of enforcement, SOEs controlled by the central government are more favored by regulators than are SOEs controlled by local governments. After several rounds of reform and reorganization, a number of powerful central SOEs have emerged as "national champions" in sectors of strategic importance, with unprecedentedly high levels of remuneration and managerial independence from governmental agencies. A certain number of leaders from these SOEs are represented in important Party fora, such as the Central Committee, and therefore can exert significant influence over China's economic policies. As Brødsgaard reports, "once a CEO has been elected member of the Central Committee he or she will try to influence policy-making within his or her field of expertise", and "leaders with a background in business have an opportunity to advance the interests of the business groups and industrial sectors in which they have worked".[69] These SOEs have become powerful interest groups, and enforcement against them may be a politically unwise decision.

4.5 Is CSRC's Enforcement Action "Toothless"?

4.5.1 Hypothesis Development

Law and finance scholarship has shown that public enforcement is positively associated with securities market development. Hence, Hypothesis 4.1 concerning the "enforcement-finance nexus" is tested in this subsection using the external shock brought about by enforcement reform in China. The pilot project launched by the CSRC to decentralize and delegate its enforcement authority to ROs in Guangdong, Shanghai and Shenzhen was announced on October 26, 2010. According to RDA theory, the reform should be expected to exogenously increase enforcement intensity

---

[65] See All-China Federation of Industry and Commerce, 2009. Report on the Development of Private Economy in China 2008–2009, available at http://www.scio.gov.cn/zggk/gqbg/2009/Document/380620/380620.htm. (Last accessed 31 October, 2021).

[66] See Xu and Gui [24], pp. 139–163.

[67] Brandt and Zhu [25].

[68] Haggard and Huang [26].

[69] Brødsgaard [27].

against listed companies in these regions compared to those in other regions. Hence, it is hypothesized that the value of the shares affected by such reform is likely to increase due to improved investor protections.

H4.1 (Enforcement-Finance Nexus): The portfolio of stocks issued by companies in the jurisdictions of Shenzhen, Guangdong and Shanghai experienced significant and positive abnormal returns on the date when the pilot project was announced.

Although both administrative and nonadministrative sanctions are public enforcement actions, the costs brought about by these two types of sanctions differ significantly. First, they represent the differing attitudes of public regulators toward the seriousness of the misconduct, which should lead to different reputational costs. Second, harmed investors could file private actions against sanctioned firms for civil compensation with administrative sanctions. Hence, the market should react more significantly to the announcement of administrative sanctions. Furthermore, according to the efficient market hypothesis,[70] the stock price will fully reflect new information once it is released. Hence, Hypothesis 4.2a predicts different market reactions to different announcements.

H4.2a (Effects of Administrative Sanction): The stock price will react to the announcement of administrative enforcement proceedings and most significantly to the *Investigation Announcement*, when the information concerning the enforcement action is first officially disclosed to the market.
H4.2b (Effects of Nonadministrative Sanction): Announcements of nonadministrative sanctions are unlikely to negatively affect the stock prices of sanctioned firms.

4.5.2 Sample Description

Our data are obtained from the CSMAR Database and WIND Corporation (WIND), both of which are leading financial data providers in China. The CSMAR Database collects information on the enforcement outputs of the CSRC and its ROs, which indicates the exact dates when sanctions against listed companies are made public and allows us to examine stock market reactions accordingly. We further cross-check the CSMAR data by accessing the website of the CNINF,[71] a website designated by the CSRC as the official platform for listed companies to disclose information. We then complement the CSMAR data with information from the CNINF. When there are mismatches between the two data sources, we use the CNINF data.

We managed to retrieve 691 distinct sanctions against listed companies that were published between January 1, 2014 and December 31, 2018, the composition of which

---

[70] Eugene Fama [28].

[71] See the website of the CNINF, available at http://www.cninfo.com.cn/new/index. (Last accessed 31 October, 2021).

Table 4.7 Distribution of sampled sanctions

		CSRC	RO
Informational Misconducts	Administrative sanction	75	78
	Nonadministrative sanction	2	422
Noninformational Misconducts	Administrative sanction	13	0
	Nonadministrative sanction	10	91

Source CSMAR database

is shown in Table 4.7.[72] Our main sample consists of 577 sanctions for informational misconduct of listed companies. The CSRC and its ROs issued a similar number of administrative sanctions for informational misconduct of listed companies during our sample period. However, ROs issued 422 nonadministrative sanctions, which accounted for approximately 73% of our main sample.

4.5.3 Stock Market Reactions to Enforcement Actions

The event studies methodology, which has been widely applied in analyzing the effects of securities enforcement, is used to estimate the AR of stock prices of selected firms during the event window. The event date is the first trading day when a listed company makes an announcement that it has received a sanction (or sanctions) from certain agencies. The daily AR is calculated with Eq. (4.4).

$$AR_{it} = R_{it} - \hat{R}_{it} \tag{4.4}$$

where R_{it} and $\hat{R}_{it}$ are the daily returns and expected returns of stock i on day t, respectively.

The expected return $\hat{R}_{it}$ is estimated using the standard market model, as shown in Eq. (4.5).

$$\hat{R}_{it} = \hat{\alpha}_i + \hat{\beta}_i * R_{mt} + \hat{\varepsilon}_{it} \tag{4.5}$$

---

[72] We exclude 190 sanctions issued by the CSRC and 198 sanctions issued by ROs against individuals and nonlisted companies during our sample period. For example, a large percentage of sanctions excluded are those against insider trading, where the guilty parties are senior management or block holders of the listed companies.

Table 4.8 Event studies on market reactions to pilot project with the one-sided SQ test

	Panel A Shanghai		Panel B Shenzhen		Panel C Guangdong	
Trading Day	AR (%)	p value	AR (%)	p value	AR (%)	p value
2010–10-25	−0.16	0.59	−0.12	0.59	−0.23	0.78
2010–10-26	−0.20	0.64	0.22	0.21	−0.12	0.64
2010–10-27	−0.22	0.69	0.43*	0.07	0.45**	0.047

Note (1) *, **, *** represent 10%, 5% and 1% significance levels

where R_{mt} is the proxy for market return on day t, and $\hat{\alpha}_i$ and $\hat{\beta}_i$ are estimated over a period of 150 trading days prior to the event window. We obtain the data on daily returns of individual stocks and proxies for market returns from the CSMAR Database.

4.5.3.1   Enforcement-Finance Nexus

To test Hypothesis 4.1 that the market should respond positively to the reform that decentralized the CSRC's enforcement authority and delegated some of its authority to its ROs, we perform event studies using the sample of all A-shares listed before October 26, 2010. To correct for potential correlation among individual stocks, three equally weighted portfolios of A-shares issued by listed companies in the jurisdictions of the Guangdong RO (128 A-shares), the Shenzhen RO (140 A-shares) and the Shanghai RO (166 A-shares) are formed. The average daily returns of these three portfolios are regarded as R_{it} in Eq. (4.4). In addition, an equally weighted portfolio of 1,490 A-shares issued by listed companies in the jurisdictions of other regions is used as the proxy for market return, i.e., R_{mt}. Finally, $\hat{\alpha}_i$ and $\hat{\beta}_i$ are estimated over a period of 150 trading days prior to the event window.

Because portfolio returns are used, the event studies are similar to the single-firm-single-event setup, which renders the standard parametric significance test prone to potential biases. Following the suggestions made by a prior study,[73] we report the p value of the one-sided "SQ Test", which is based on the same pre-event window of 150 trading days that we employ to estimate Eq. (4.2) following the estimated AR. Table 4.8 reports the event studies' outcomes. The portfolios of shares issued by listed companies in Shenzhen and Guangdong enjoyed positive and significant ARs on the next trading day following the announcement of the pilot project. However, this is not the case for those shares in Shanghai.

Although we find some positive and significant evidence supporting Hypothesis 4.1 concerning the "enforcement-finance nexus", the magnitude of this effect is relatively small and therefore of little economic significance. However, our results are potentially subject to the caveat that the market expects the enforcement intensity

---

[73] Gelbach et al. [29].

in the regions not included in the pilot project to eventually increase; hence, the stock prices have already accounted for such changes.

4.5.3.2   Effects of Administrative Sanctions

This subsection focuses on market reactions to the announcements that listed companies are being investigated or have been sanctioned administratively by public regulators. The direct monetary costs brought about by such sanctions are very small. As mandated by the Securities Law of 2014, a majority of sanctioned firms suffered monetary penalties less than 600,000 RMB due to statutory limits. It is therefore indeterminant whether market participants will care about these enforcement actions. On the other hand, these sanctions could result in indirect costs to the reputational capital of sanctioned firms, which would cause significant drops in their share prices.

Our empirical study has two advantages. First, it collects an updated sample and contains the entire sample of administrative and nonadministrative enforcement proceedings initiated by the CSRC and its ROs. Second, it takes the institutional features of Chinese public enforcement into consideration. There is a procedural difference between administrative and nonadministrative proceedings. Administrative proceedings can be divided into three stages, and hence, there are three separate disclosure events. The first event is when the CSRC or its ROs issue a brief notice to a listed firm, indicating that a case against the firm has been built and the investigation against the firm has commenced (Investigation Announcement). This is the first time that information regarding the risk of a potential sanction faced by the company is made public. The second date is when the CSRC or its ROs issue a preliminary decision on the sanctions (Preliminary Announcement). The firm is informed of its rights, particularly the right to explain to and negotiate with regulators. The last date is when the firm receives the final and formal sanction from the CSRC or its ROs (Sanction Announcement). The whole administrative proceeding may take years to fully reflect the impact of information disclosure on stock price. We estimate the stock price reactions to the three material announcements concerning the progress of the administrative enforcement proceedings, i.e., Investigation Announcement, Preliminary Announcement, and Sanction Announcement. Information concerning public enforcement is first disclosed in the Investigation Announcement. Consequently, if the market is efficient, the stock price should not react to the Preliminary Announcement and Sanction Announcement, or should at least react to a lesser extent.

Table 4.9 reports the event studies testing Hypothesis 4.2a and Hypothesis 4.2b. For Panel A, Panel B and Panel C, our sample starts with all 153 administrative enforcement proceedings and further excludes those shares that suspended trading over the $(-7, 7)$ event window around the announcement dates. For Panel D, the sample starts with all 424 nonadministrative sanctions and further excludes those shares that suspended trading on the event date. The expected return is estimated

Table 4.9 Stock price reactions to enforcement actions

Trading day	Panel A investigation announcement				Panel B preliminary announcement				Panel C sanction announcement				Panel D Nonadministrative Sanction			
	Sample size	Mean AR (%)	Median AR (%)	"z value", Wilcoxon sign-rank test	Sample size	Mean AR (%)	Median AR (%)	"z value", Wilcoxon sign-rank test	Sample size	Mean AR (%)	Median AR (%)	"z value", Wilcoxon sign-rank test	Sample size	Mean AR (%)	Median AR (%)	"z value", Wilcoxon Sign-rank Test
7	107	-0.18	-0.43	-0.77	97	0.22	0.10	1.33	110	-0.21	-0.34	-1.37	367	-0.02	-0.04	-0.63
6	107	-0.1	-0.04	-0.38	97	-0.01	0.29	0.30	110	-0.12	-0.07	-0.33	367	0.03	-0.01	-0.25
5	107	-0.76	-0.4	-2.64***	97	-0.54	-0.51	-2.23**	110	0.10	0.02	0.09	367	-0.15	-0.21	-1.53
4	107	-0.91	-0.37	-3.00***	97	-0.29	-0.19	-1.20	110	0.36	0.07	0.56	367	-0.14	-0.01	-1.29
3	107	-0.72	-0.45	-1.92*	97	-0.55	-0.42	-1.60	110	0.20	-0.10	0.10	367	-0.04	-0.08	-1.07
2	107	-0.90	-0.51	-2.54**	97	-0.31	-0.39	-1.37	110	-0.24	-0.47	-1.81*	367	0.08	-0.06	-0.34
1	107	-2.39	-1.32	-6.41***	97	0.49	0.07	0.51	110	-0.32	-0.16	-1.38	367	-0.11	-0.13	-1.23
0	107	-5.54	-5.74	-8.38***	97	1.55	1.16	3.46***	110	0.99	0.85	3.22***	367	-0.67	-0.56	-4.90***
-1	107	-0.81	-0.61	-2.86***	97	0.67	0.27	1.77*	110	-0.07	-0.15	-1.08	367	-0.07	-0.12	-0.88
-2	107	-0.45	-0.34	-1.38	97	0.75	0.33	2.16**	110	0.18	0.03	0.30	367	-0.13	-0.18	-1.32
-3	107	-0.08	-0.13	-0.47	97	-0.07	0.03	-0.06	110	0.27	0.15	010	367	-0.09	-0.14	-1.15
-4	107	-0.004	0.04	0.34	97	-0.32	-0.29	-1.25	110	0.39	0.27	0.92	367	-0.03	-0.13	-0.82
-5	107	-0.18	-0.31	-0.81	97	-0.29	0.17	-0.06	110	-0.10	-0.04	-0.68	367	-0.13	-0.11	-1.52
-6	107	-0.10	-0.11	-0.92	97	-0.52	-0.55	-1.87*	110	0.26	-0.03	0.36	367	0.08	0.02	0.49
-7	107	-0.02	-0.44	-0.83	97	0.21	-0.004	0.26	110	0.73	0.41	2.38**	367	0.12	0.004	0.17

Note (1) *, **, *** represent 10, 5 and 1% significance levels

(2) The sample size differs among Panels A, B and C because some firms seem to fail to make the disclosure when they receive investigation or preliminary sanctions, and some are suspended from trading when they disclose that they are in an enforcement proceeding.

with the daily return of each share and the SHSZ300[74] proxy for market return. $\hat{\alpha}_i$ and $\hat{\beta}_i$ are estimated over a period of 150 trading days prior to the event window. We report the "z value" of the Wilcoxon sign-rank test with the null hypothesis that the median is zero, along with the mean and median values of the daily AR of our sample stocks over the $(-7, 7)$ event window.

Panel A shows the results of the *Investigation Announcement*. These stocks experience a significant and negative daily AR over the $(-1, 5)$ event window, and the cumulative average abnormal return is -12.03%, which is much higher than that estimated by previous studies. The average daily AR on the event date (Day 0) and the first trading day after the event date (Day 1) are of the largest magnitude, approximately -5.52% and -2.22%, respectively. The magnitude of the market reaction is in sharp contrast to those reported in prior studies, which suggests that it is better to take a dynamic view of enforcement actions.[75]

Panel B reports the mean and median values of the daily AR of our sample stocks over the $(-7, 7)$ event window of the *Preliminary Announcement*. It is interesting to note that our sample stocks experience a significant and positive (rather than a negative) AR of 1.549% on the event date, and a cumulative AR of 2.97% over the $(-2, 0)$ event window. This may be due to the fact that the *Preliminary Announcement* for the first time discloses the details concerning the misconduct and proposed sanctions, which reduces the uncertainty by moving forward in the regulatory process[76] or corrects the overreaction by the market toward the sanctioned firms at the first stage of the enforcement process.

Panel C reports the mean and median values of the daily AR of our sample stocks over the $(-7, 7)$ event window of the *Sanction Announcement*. There is a significant but very slightly positive stock price reaction of approximately 0.985% on the event date. The results of Table 4.9 generally confirm the predictions made by Hypothesis 2a that the market reacts to public enforcement proceedings and reacts most significantly when the information is disclosed to the market for the first time.

Panel D reports the event studies result of the nonadministrative sanctions issued by the CSRC and its ROs and tests Hypothesis 2b that the stock market will not significantly react to such sanctions. Because there is only one (rather than three) stage for nonadministrative enforcement proceedings (the announcement of a final decision), the table only reports the mean and median values of the daily AR of our sample stocks over the $(-7, 7)$ event window of *Sanction Announcement*. The sample stocks experience a significant and negative AR of approximately -0.562%

---

[74] SHSZ300 is a capitalization-weighted market index constructed by the China Securities Index Co., Ltd, which selects sample stocks based on market capitalization and liquidity. For more details on SHSZ300, see http://www.csindex.com.cn/sseportal/csiportal/zs/jbxx/report.do?code= 000300&&subdir=1. (Last accessed 31 October, 2021).

[75] The prior study has also documented the time-varying market reactions to the enforcement of insider trading, see Diane Del Guercio et al. [30].

[76] More details of the investigation and its outcomes are disclosed in this stage. It may be argued that the market reacts positively to more information, regardless of whether the information is good news or bad news, as even bad news is better than no news.

on the event date.[77] All ARs on the rest of the trading days in the event window are not significant.

The event studies' results for enforcement actions are generally consistent with our previous intuitive discussions. First, unlike prior research, we find that the costs of administrative enforcement proceedings for sanctioned firms are very high, as measured by firm value reduction. Second, once the information concerning the enforcement actions is officially disclosed to the public, the stock prices of sanctioned firms tend not to react significantly to additional announcements, which adds very little new information. Finally, the costs ascribed to the nonadministrative sanctions are statistically significant but economically insignificant. Although the existing literature has already shown that public enforcement in China imposes high costs on sanctioned firms, such as share price decline and forced turnover of senior management, the enforcement intensity is still regarded as insufficient to efficiently deter securities misconduct. This perception should be updated, given that the outputs of public enforcement have increased significantly in recent years. More specifically, the total outputs of public enforcers quadrupled in 2012 compared to 2008.

In addition, the perception could be due to a caveat with the current literature, i.e., the public enforcement regime is investigated in a piecemeal manner and the enforcement efforts of the 38 ROs, which account for more than 70% of the CSRC's staff and nearly 50% of its enforcement actions, are overlooked. This is probably due to the difficulty of obtaining relevant information about the operation of the CSRC's ROs, which is hard to acquire from public channels such as the websites or public announcements of these agencies. In addition, the institutional details concerning the administrative enforcement proceedings are overlooked. Sanctioned firms will disclose multiple announcements, including Investigation Announcements, Preliminary Announcements and Sanction Announcements. If these announcements are distinguished and event studies are applied separately to different groups of events, the sanctioned listed companies would experience a significant decline in their market capitalization around the time of the Investigation Announcement.

References

1. Zales, J. L. (2016). $22 trillion lost, zero wall street executives jailed: Prosecutors should utilize whistleblowers to establish criminal intent. *Notre Dame Journal of International and Comparative Law, 6*, 167–188.
2. CSRC. (2013). *Report on the development of legal governance in China's capital market*. Law Press China.
3. Liu, Y. (2018). The investigation, sanction and review proceedings of securities regulators against misconducts. In B. Peng (Ed.), *Disciplining capital market* (pp. 3–32). Law Press China.

---

[77] We further perform event studies on the two nonadministrative sanctions issued by the CSRC separately, and find that the ARs of the sanctioned shares on the event date are −6.735% with a one-Sided SQ test "p value" of 3.26 and −3.12% with a one-Sided SQ test "p value" of 12.7%.

4. Sunstein, C. R., & Stewart, R. B. (1982). Public programs and private rights. *Harvard Law Review, 95*(6), 1193–1322.
5. Jackson, H. E., & Roe, M. J. (2009). Public and private enforcement of securities laws: Resource-based evidence. *Journal of Financial Economics, 93*, 207–238.
6. La Porta, R., Lopez-de-Silanes, F., & Shleifer, A. (2008). The economic consequences of legal origins. *Journal of Economic Literature 46*(2), 285–332.
7. Pistor, K., & Xu, C. (2005). Governing stock markets in transition economies: Lessons from China. *American Law and Economics Review, 7*(1), 184–210.
8. Velikonja, U. (2015). Public compensation for private harm: Evidence from the SEC's fair fund distributions. *Stanford Law Review, 67*, 331–395.
9. Black, B. (2008). Should the SEC Be a collection agency for defrauded investors? *Business Lawyer, 63*, 317–346.
10. Winship, V. (2008). Fair funds and the SEC's compensation of injured investors. *Florida Law Review, 60*, 1103–1144.
11. Zimmerman, A. (2011). Distributing justice. *New York University Law Review, 86*, 500–572.
12. Chen, G., Firth, M., Gao, D. N., & Rui, O. M. (2005). Is China's securities regulatory agency a toothless tiger? Evidence from enforcement actions. *Journal of Accounting and Public Policy, 24*, 451–488.
13. Li, X., Cao, Q., & Sun, L. (2016). Audit reputation damage and client portfolio changes: Based on empirical evidence of CSRC administrative punishment from 1999 to 2014. *Accounting Research, 2016*(4), 85–91. (In Chinese).
14. Xu, C. (2011). The fundamental institutions of China's reforms and development. *Journal of Economic Literature, 49*(4), 1076–1151.
15. Bardhan, P. (2020). The Chinese governance system: Its strengths and weaknesses in a comparative development perspective. *China Economic Review, 61*, 101430.
16. Wan, X., Ma, Y., & Zhang, K. (2015). Political determinants of intergovernmental transfers in a regionally decentralized authoritarian regime: Evidence from China. *Applied Economics, 47*(27), 2803–2820.
17. Jin, H., Qian, Y., & Weingast, B. R. (2005). Regional decentralization and fiscal incentives: Federalism, Chinese style. *Journal of Public Economics, 89*, 1719–1742.
18. Zhu, X. (2012). Understanding China's growth: Past, present, and future. *Journal of Economic Perspectives, 26*(4), 103–124.
19. Landes, W. M., & Posner, R. A. (1975). The private enforcement of law. *The Journal of Legal Studies, 4*(1), 1–46.
20. Lando, H., & Shavell, S. (2004). The advantage of focusing law enforcement effort. *International Review of Law and Economics, 24*(2), 209–218.
21. Zhou, T. (2015). Is the CSRC protecting a 'level playing field' in China's capital markets: Public enforcement, fragmented authoritarianism and corporatism. *Journal of Corporate Law Studies, 15*(2), 377–406.
22. Huang, Y., & Wang, X. (2011). Does financial repression inhibit or facilitate economic growth? A case study of Chinese reform experience. *Oxford Bulletin of Economics and Statistics, 73*(6), 833–855.
23. Johansson, A. C. (2012). Financial repression and china's economic imbalances. In H. McKay & L. Song (Eds.), *Rebalancing and sustaining growth in China* (pp. 45–64). ANUE-Press.
24. Xu, G., & Gui, B. (2015). Why are China's state-owned enterprises so profitable? A financial repression perspective. In N. Philipsen, S. Weishaar, & G. Xu (Eds.), *Market integration: The EU experience and implications for regulatory reform in China* (pp. 139–163). Springer.
25. Brandt, L., & Zhu, X. (2007). China's banking sector and economic growth. In C. Calomiris (Ed.), *China's financial transition at a crossroads* (pp. 86–136). Columbia University Press.
26. Haggard, S., & Huang, Y. (2008). The political economy of private-sector development in China. In L. Brandt & T. G. Rawski (Eds.), *China's great economic transformation* (pp. 337–374). Cambridge University Press.
27. Brødsgaard, K. E. (2012). Politics and business group formation in China: The party in control? *The China Quarterly, 211*, 624–648.

28. Fama, E. (1970). Efficient capital markets: A review of theory and empirical work. *Journal of Finance, 25*, 383–417.
29. Gelbach, J. B., Helland, E., & Klick, J. (2013). Valid inference in single-firm, single-event studies. *American Law and Economics Review, 15*, 495–541.
30. Guercio, D.D., Odders-White, E.R., & Ready, M.J. (2017). The deterrent effect of the securities and exchange commission's enforcement intensity on illegal insider trading: Evidence from run-up before news events. *Journal of Law and Economics 60*, 269–307

Chapter 5
Complementary Public Enforcement Proceedings

Except for the formal enforcement proceedings initiated by the CSRC and its ROs, the public enforcement regime in China also comprised alternative enforcement proceedings administered by the CSRC and those initiated by self-regulatory organizations. This chapter discusses these public enforcement efforts.

5.1 Alternative Enforcement Proceedings Administered by the CSRC

Realizing the importance of compensating harmed investors, the CSRC also experimented with two alternative enforcement proceedings, i.e., a prioritized compensation scheme and an administrative settlement, which placed investor compensation at the center of the enforcement regime. However, the two institutions are still in the pilot project stage and are not widely applied in practice.

5.1.1 Prioritized Compensation Scheme

Article 93 of the Securities Law of 2019 stipulates the prioritized compensation scheme, which could be applied in all types of securities fraud cases. As its name suggests, the scheme values investor compensation. In situations where violators have caused substantial damage to investors through securities fraud, the controlling shareholders, controllers and/or securities firms of concern could authorize the investor protection agency to negotiate a compensation arrangement before any administrative or judiciary proceedings. The prioritized compensation scheme is mainly about efficiently compensating harmed investors and encourages a variety of entities to contribute to the fund. Those entities assuming the joint and several obligations could first compensate investors and then collect proportional damages from other

© The Author(s), under exclusive license to Springer Nature Singapore Pte Ltd. 2022   81
W. Xu, *The Enforcement of Securities Law in China*,
https://doi.org/10.1007/978-981-19-0904-7_5

Table 5.1 Case information of prioritized compensation fund

Issuer	Compensator	Established date	Sanction date	Size of the fund	Compensation paid	Percentage to lawful damages (%)
Wanfu Shengke[1]	Pingan Securities	10 May, 2013	24 September, 2013	300 million	179 million	99.56
Hailianxun[2]	Controllers	18 July, 2014	14 November, 2014	200 million	89 million	98.81
Xintai Dianqi[3]	Xingye Securities	July 9, 2016	25 July, 2016	550 million	242 million	99.46

obligators. The CSRC mainly serves as the mediator, which facilitates the concerned parties to conclude a compensatory contract.

The primary incentive for violators to compensate investors before any enforcement proceedings are completed using a prioritized compensation regime is to obtain regulatory leniency from the CSRC, which regards the harm caused to investors as a major element for evaluating the seriousness of committed misconduct. A generous investor compensation plan could significantly reduce the magnitude of the administrative sanctions. Consequently, although the CSRC is not directly involved as the signing party of the compensatory contract, it has played a leading role in the proceeding. There have been three cases of prioritized compensation, i.e., the "Wanfu Shengke case", "Hailianxun case" and "Xintai Dianqi case". These cases are all concerned with fraudulent IPOs, the main features of which are summarized in Table 5.1.

The first element of the compensatory fund is the identity of the establisher, which contributes capital. Interestingly, as shown in the first column of Table 5.1, only in one case do the controllers of the issuers pay for compensation, whereas in the other two cases, the securities firms pay harmed investors. This could be due to the following three reasons. First, the guilty parties differ in their expected proportionate liability; hence, those assuming a small percentage of the joint and several obligations are unlikely to establish such compensatory funds. Second, the size of the compensation is relatively large, and only entities with deep pockets will have the ability to establish the fund. The issuers and their controllers are sometimes close to insolvency and are not able to assume compensatory liabilities. Finally, the expected profits from the

[1] See The Case of Wanfu Shengke and the Pilot Project of Compensating Investors, available at http://www.csrc.gov.cn/pub/newsite/tzzbh1/tbtzzjy/tbfxff/201508/t20150803_282336.html. (Last accessed 31 October, 2021).

[2] See The Controllers Should Compensate Harmed Investors: The Case of Hailianxun, available at https://www.investor.org.cn/learning_center/investor_education_base/gallery/xinsanban_2579/202007/t20200701_440832.shtml. (Last accessed 31 October, 2021).

[3] See The Termination of the Compensatory Fund of Xintai Dianqi, available at http://www.sipf.com.cn/investor/notice63.html. (Last accessed 31 October, 2021).

scheme vary among the guilty parties. Securities firms, which are under the direct regulation of the CSRC, are more likely to cooperate with the CSRC and help it mitigate the expected embarrassment and political pressure due to a massive number of harmed investors. Securities firms could also obtain larger expected benefits by compensating harmed investors, for example, in exchange for a lenient administrative sanction and avoiding more severe administrative sanctions, such as the suspension of their regular business.

The second element is the establishment date of the fund. It is clear from the second and third columns that the establishment date is prior to the sanction date, which suggests that it is highly likely that violators would exchange compensating harmed investors for a lenient administrative sanction. The third element is the size of the fund and the fund distributed. Although the sizes of the funds are quite large, only approximately half of the fund is paid to investors. The fund distribution is much larger than the total damages paid by violators in previous civil ligations.

The last element is compensatory efficiency. According to Article 18 of the SPC's 2003 Provisions, the causal relationship between misrepresentation and damages is only satisfied if the investors buy the stock between the implementation date and the revelation date of the misrepresentation and sell or hold stock after the revelation date of the misrepresentation. Those investors suffering from losses due to the afore-mentioned transactions are qualified participants of the prioritized compensation proceeding. Similar to securities civil litigation, the prioritized compensation regime adopts the opt-in design, in which harmed investors will have to actively select into the compensatory agreement. Based on previous cases, the opt-in design does not work well for investors, and the percentage of harmed investors receiving compensation is very small. The three analyzed cases concern fraudulent IPOs, which have the advantage that causality is obvious and that investors subscribing new shares and suffering from investment losses are qualified payees. To increase the compensatory rate, these funds have actively reached out to qualified investors, reminding them to accept the compensation. The last column shows that approximately 99% of the qualified investors are compensated by the fund, which suggests that the arrangement is relatively efficient in compensating harmed investors.

5.1.2   Administrative Settlement Regime

The administrative settlement regime is an application of institutional design in administrative law to the securities market. It represents a tradeoff between compensation efficiency and the availability of justice and transforms the confrontation relationship between the regulatory agency and the violators in administrative sanction proceedings to a cooperative relationship. The involved parties are trying to develop a solution to achieve the policy goals, which include investor compensation, continuous and normal operation of the violators, and deterrence of securities misconduct.

The CSRC promulgated the Measures for the Pilot Project of the Implementation of Administrative Settlement in Securities Market[4] in 2015. However, administrative settlement is not frequently used, and there have only been two cases thereafter. Article 171 of the Securities Law of 2019 formalizes the regime and provides that in the investigative process of the CSRC, in the situation where the investigated parties propose to correct misconduct, compensate investors and eliminate adverse effects within a reasonable period, the CSRC could suspend the investigation. If the investigated entities met its promises, the CSRC could terminate the investigation; otherwise, it could restart the process.

Based on the revised Securities Law, the CSRC released the Measures for the Implementation of Administrative Settlement in Securities and Future Market (For Consultation) (Henceforth Administrative Settlement Measures (For Consultation)) in 2020. Article 4 of the Administrative Settlement Measures (For Consultation) stipulates four scenarios in which the CSRC could accept the proposal from the investigated entity to reach an administrative settlement: first, the facts and applicable legal rules are ambiguous and unclear; second, the investigated entities promise to take effective measures to correct misconduct, compensate investors and eliminate adverse effects; and fourth, it is beneficial to investor protection, enforcement efficiency and recovery of market stability. The CSRC repeatedly emphasizes that administrative settlement is not a procedure for violators to escape administrative and criminal penalties.

Article 5 further specifies six scenarios in which securities administrative settlement is not applicable: first, the investigated are concerned with criminal cases; second, the investigated have been sanctioned criminally within three years, or administratively within one year; third, the proposal has already been rejected and the investigated have resubmitted it without any new evidence; four, the application for the administrative settlement is accepted but fails to conclude the agreement, and the applicants make a resubmission without any further evidence; five, the investigated entity, that has already concluded the agreement with the CSRC but failed to fulfill the obligations, resubmits the proposal; and sixth, CSRC regards that the case is not suitable for administrative agreement from the perspective of prudent regulation principles.

Similarly, the most important incentive for applicants to arrive at a settlement with the CSRC is to reduce the magnitude of the potential administrative sanctions. Article 9 of the Administrative Settlement Measures (For Consultation) specifies the time window for violators to propose an administrative settlement, which covers the date of the investigation notice and that of the final decision. On the other hand, the most important driver for the CSRC to promote administrative settlement is to save administrative resources. Consequently, as investigations progress, the CSRC becomes more reluctant to accept a settlement proposal.

---

[4] See Xingzheng Hejie Shidian Shishi Banfa, available at http://www.csrc.gov.cn/xizang/xxfw/gfxwj/201508/t20150802_282275.htm. (Last accessed 31 October, 2021).

It should be noted that administrative settlement in China is significantly different from that in the U.S., in which the SEC seeks to save valuable enforcement resources.[5] It is also extremely popular among securities market participants and shows that nearly 90% of the SEC's enforcement proceedings end with a settlement.[6] In most enforcement actions, staff members will draft a settlement agreement and submit it to the Office of Chief Counsel, and the final version of the settlement agreement will be approved by the Director of the Division of Enforcement.[7] The agreement normally includes deferred prosecution or nonprosecution agreements and requires that violators pay monetary fines and disgorgement and adopt new internal procedures.

In a typical enforcement action, such as the administrative disciplinary proceeding, courts will also play an important role and review SEC actions. The Enforcement Division of SEC will serve as the plaintiff and have to prepare for evidential proof to establish that defendants have committed securities misconduct.[8] In addition to proving the existence of statutory violations, the Enforcement Division also has to demonstrate that misconduct is committed "willfully".[9] The proposed settlement decree of the SEC needs to be approved by the courts. In the case of SEC v. Citigroup Global Markets, Inc.,[10] the Second Circuit reviewed the consent decree and clarified the standards for judiciary review, which focused on procedural appropriateness instead of examining substantive content.

The difference between public enforcement in China and the U.S. is highly likely to be ascribed to the following factors. First, the investigation and sanctions are internal proceedings of the CSRC, although they are subject to an external review if the sanctioned bring about administrative litigation; in contrast, the enforcement actions of the SEC are under judiciary review and are heard by federal judges or its own internal administrative law judges. The SEC faces significantly higher uncertainty than the CSRC in the outcomes of public enforcement. Second, violators could obtain significantly higher benefits from the settlement deal with the SEC. In China, the administrative and civil liabilities for potential violators remain relatively low, and the administrative settlement only brings limited additional benefits from the perspective of administrative counterparts. In the U.S., the settlement normally will include the "no-admit/no-deny" clause, which renders the question of whether it has committed any securities misconduct unsettled.[11] The settlement deal will significantly reduce damages to the reputational capital of the administrative counterpart, and because of the lack of judiciary hearing, it is not found guilty, which makes it possible for the insurance company to pay the settlement.[12]

---

[5] Arthur [1].

[6] See Cox et al. [2].

[7] SEC Enforcement Manual, at §2.5.1.

[8] Cox and Thomas [3].

[9] Arthur F. [4].

[10] 752 F.3d 285 (2d Cir. 2014).

[11] See Winship and Robbennolt [5].

[12] See Baker and Griffith [6].

5.2 Enforcement Efforts of the Stock Exchanges

Article 96 of the Securities Law of 2019 specifies that the two national stock exchanges, i.e., the Shanghai Stock Exchange and Shenzhen Stock Exchanges,[13] are self-regulatory organizations of the securities market and assume the responsibilities of direct market supervision and self-regulation. Unlike stock exchanges in the U.S., which operate as a public company and relatively independently from the SEC, the two stock exchanges in China are membership-based and under the *de facto* control of the CSRC, which has received the authority to appoint senior management of both exchanges.[14]

The CSRC and the two stock exchanges have divided their labor, with the latter complementing the functions of the former. The two stock exchanges are mainly responsible for real-time monitoring and front-line supervision and enforcement. Stock exchanges have not received the authority to impose administrative sanctions but could impose self-regulatory penalties, which are nonadministrative sanctions. Based on the listing rules of the two stock exchanges, self-regulatory penalties mainly include self-regulatory management measures against minor infractions and self-regulatory disciplinary measures against more severe infractions. The former category includes "Explanation", "Warning letter", "Regulatory conversation", "Mandatory training", and "Disqualification"; while the latter includes "Criticism", "Censure", "Limiting or abolishing transacting right" and "Membership cancellation". One significant advantage of the sanctions issued by the stock exchanges is timeliness; they normally react to potential misconduct within a very short time and can discipline misconduct at its early stage. It normally takes only a few months between the discovery of misconduct and the issuance of self-regulatory penalties; in contrast, the CSRC normally takes years to complete its administrative enforcement proceedings.

Figure 5.1 shows the enforcement outputs of the two stock exchanges against listed companies and their related parties between 2010 and 2019. A total of 1,932 sanctions were made in this period, of which 978 sanctions were made by the Shenzhen Stock Exchange, and 953 sanctions were made by the Shanghai Stock Exchange. In the time-series dimension, both stock exchanges maintained relatively low enforcement outputs before 2013, particularly the Shanghai Stock Exchange, which had fewer than 20 sanctions. The situation changed in 2014, and both stock exchanges started to increase their outputs, which could be ascribed to the competition between the two exchanges.

---

[13] In September 2021, the Beijing Stock Exchange was established as the third national exchange, but it has a very short history and hence is not analyzed here. In addition, the Article 96 of the Securities Law of 2019 also recognizes the legal status of the stock trading venues, which is the National Equities Exchange and Quotations, an over-the-counter market and not covered by this book. For a recent discussion on the junior stock exchanges in China, see Wenming Xu, Shaogang Zhu & Zhicheng Wu [7].

[14] Liebman and Milhaupt [8].

Fig. 5.1 Enforcement outputs of the shanghai and shenzhen stock exchange

Because a sanction decision could be imposed against multiple infractions, Table 5.2 reports the distributions of the types of misconduct for 2,682 infractions. Panel A shows the misconduct sanctioned by the Shanghai Stock Exchange. "Postponed disclosure", "Major omission" and "Falsifying records" are among the most frequently sanctioned misconducts, which were punished 496 times, 198 times and 197 times, respectively. In total, the aforementioned misconducts account for approximately 67% of the total outputs. In addition, "Illegally transacting stocks" are sanctioned 219 times, accounting for 16.37% of the total outputs. Panel B presents the misconduct sanctioned by the Shenzhen Stock Exchange. "Postponed disclosure", "Falsifying records" and "Major omission" are among the most often sanctioned misconducts, which are punished 430 times, 257 times and 191 times, respectively. In total, the aforementioned misconducts account for approximately 65% of the total outputs. Similarly, "Illegally transacting stocks" are sanctioned 221 times, accounting for 17.19% of the total outputs. The data provided in Table 5.2 suggest that the primary function of the stock exchange is to maintain the integrity and quality of information disclosure and stock trading. Particularly, both exchanges target the misconduct of the "Postponed disclosure", which, according to Article 115 of the Securities Law of 2019, is one of its major front-line responsibilities.

The mechanism by which the enforcement actions of stock exchanges influence the firms they regulate is mainly shaming, with significant impacts on the reputational capital of sanctioned entities. An empirical study shows that the listed shares receiving "criticism" from the Shanghai Stock Exchange and Shenzhen Stock Exchange suffer from −2.1% and −1% cumulative abnormal returns on average over the 3-day window, respectively.[15] In addition, stock exchanges take a preventive measure by issuing a "Letter of concern", which is not punitive in nature, in events in which securities misconduct is highly likely to emerge. It is found that

---

[15] Liebman and Milhaupt [8].

Table 5.2 Distribution of the infractions sanctioned between 2010 and 2019

Panel A Shanghai stock exchange

Infractions	Postponed disclosure	Illegally transacting stocks	Major omission	Falsifying records	False disclosure	Misappropriating assets	Illegal guarantee	Others
Number	496	219	198	197	87	47	35	59
Percentage (%)	37.07	16.37	14.80	14.72	6.50	3.51	2.62	4.41

Panel B Shenzhen stock exchange

Infractions	Postponed disclosure	Falsifying records	Illegally transacting stocks	Major omission	Misappropriating assets	Illegal guarantees	Accounting irregularities	Others
Number	430	257	231	191	72	50	40	73
Percentage (%)	31.99	19.12	17.19	14.21	5.36	3.72	2.98	5.43%

share price experience a significant negative abnormal return if the listed companies revise their corporate charter and adopt takeover defenses after receiving the "Letter of concern".[16] The findings suggest that the "Letter of concern" successfully increases the propensity of issuers to adopt value-decreasing articles in their corporate charters.

5.3 Enforcement Efforts of the Securities Association of China

The Securities Association of China, founded in August 1991, is an industrial self-regulatory organization for the securities industry. Chapter 11 of the Securities Law of 2019 is titled "Securities Association of China" and lays down its basic organizational structure and regulatory responsibilities. As required by Sect. 5.2 of the Article of the Securities Law of 2019, all securities firms should join the Securities Association of China. It has two types of enforcement authority. The first is to enforce the securities self-regulatory rules and monitor, investigate and sanction the misconduct committed by member entities and their affiliates. The Securities Association of China can only impose nonadministrative sanctions, which include self-disciplinary measures and self-management measures. The second authority is to act as the mediator for disputes between members and between members and investors.

At the end of 2016, there were 1,123 members of the Securities Association of China, between firms and other organizational entities. According to Article 9 and Article 10 of the Measures for Implementing Self-regulatory Management and Disciplinary Sanctions,[17] the Securities Association of China can impose both self-regulatory management sanctions and self-regulatory disciplinary sanctions against registered members and their affiliates. The former mainly includes "Regulatory conversation", "Warning", "Mandatory training" and "Correction", whereas the latter includes "Criticism", "Condemnation", "Suspension" and "Disqualification". In 2015 and 2016, the Securities Association of China imposed 599 and 1,188 self-regulatory sanctions, respectively. The most frequent misconducts sanctioned are "Misconducts in IPO", "Illegal securities consulting companies" and "Illegal securities companies". The Securities Association of China also employed a "black list" measure to combat these misconducts; sanctioned entities are included in this list, which is disclosed to the general public.

---

[16] Zeng [9].

[17] See Zilv Cuoshi Shishi Banfa, available at https://www.sac.net.cn/flgz/zlgz/202007/t20200715_143281.html. (Last accessed 31 October, 2021).

Table 5.3 Distribution of the enforcement outputs of the ministry of finance by type of infraction

	Accounting irregularities	Misleading disclosure	False records	Postponed disclosure	Major omission
Frequency	14	3	3	1	3
Percentage	58%	12.5%	12.5%	4.2%	12.5%

5.4 Enforcement Efforts of the Ministry of Finance

The Ministry of Finance is responsible for administering and enforcing the Accounting Law of China and maintaining the integrity of the accounting system of the listed companies. According to the Measures for Supervising and Administrating Financial Departments,[18] its regulatory boundary mainly focuses on ensuring high-quality compliance with accounting rules. In addition, it also promulgates the Working Rules for Random Spot Check,[19] which defines the procedures for reviewing the quality of the accounting system. Between 2010 and 2019, the Ministry of Finance imposed a total of 19 sanctions against listed companies. Table 5.3 shows the distribution by type of infraction.

In accordance with its regulatory responsibilities, the most frequently sanctioned misconduct is "Accounting irregularities", which account for approximately 58% of the total enforcement outputs. The sanctions imposed by the Ministry of Finance mainly include the "Revocation of the subsidiary qualification", "Revocation of business permit" and "Monetary fine". However, the monetary penalties are small in magnitude, ranging from 30,000 RMB to 334,000 RMB. The enforcement instruments of the Ministry of Finance against misconduct in the securities market are limited, and its role in securities law enforcement is relatively marginal.

5.5 Criminal Enforcement Proceedings

The outputs of criminal enforcement actions are relatively small, which is partly because criminal sanctions rely heavily on case inference from the CSRC. Table 5.4 surveys the criminal cases against informational misconduct on the internet and presents a summary of 19 criminal judgments. These cases are mainly referred to the local Public Security Bureau by the CSRC. There is an upward trend in the number of criminal judgments in recent years based on the limited sample. It can also be observed that the primary entities with criminal sanctions against them are listed companies and their president, CEO, CFO, and accountants from the accounting

---

[18] See Measures for Supervision and Administration of Financial Departments (Caizheng Bumen Jiandu Guanli Banfa), available at http://www.gov.cn/flfg/2012-03/19/content_2094400.htm. (Last accessed 31 October, 2021).

[19] See Suiji Choucha Gongzuo Xize, available at http://www.gov.cn/xinwen/2016-10/14/content_5 119089.htm. (Last accessed 31 October, 2021).

Table 5.4 Information concerning criminal proceedings against informational misconducts

No	Date	Listed companies	Entities sanctioned	Provincial regions
1	2011	Gaoxin Zhangtong	President of the board; CFO; CEO, and vice CEO	Jiangsu Province
2	2013	Yunan Lvdadi	Listed companies; President of the board; CEO; CFO; Financial Consultant	Yunnan Province
3	2014	Wanfu shengke	Listed companies; President of the board; CEO; CFO; Accountants of the Licheng accounting firms	Hunan Province
4	2017	Boyuan touzi	President of the board; CEO; CFO; Staff in the accounting department	Guangdong Province
5	2017	Huarui Fengdian	President of the board; CFO	Beijing City
6	2018	Zhonghengtong	Listed companies; President of the board; CFO; staff of the securities firms; staff of the accounting firms	Shanghai City
7	2018	Haixin shiping	President of the board; Board secretary	Shanghai City
8	2018	Huaze gunie	CEO and others	Sichuan Province
9	2019	Yabaite	N.A	Jiangsu Province
10	2018	Jinya keji	N.A	Sichuan Province
11	2019	Xintai dianqi	Listed companies; President of the board; CEO	Liaoning Province
12	2019	Duolun Group	President of the board	Shanghai City
13	2020	Zhongyida	President of the board; CEO; vice President of the board; CFO and vice CEO of subsidiary company	Shanghai City
14	2020	Shanghai putian	President of the board; CEO; CFO; Chief Accountant	Shanghai City
15	2021	Jiuhao Group	President of the board; Director; vice CFO	Zhejiang Province
16	2020	Zhangzidao	N.A	Liaoning Province
17	2020	Kangdexin	N.A	Jiangsu Province
18	2021	Tianxiang huanjing	N.A	Sichuang Province
19	2021	Kangmei yaoye	N.A	Guangdong Province

firms. Occasionally, the vice president, the staff in the accounting department of the listed companies, and the financial consultants are sanctioned. Finally, geographically, the cases are widely distributed in different provincial regions, although the absolute frequency is larger in the southeastern region, where the economy is more active and developed, and a higher percentage of listed companies are located.

In criminal sanctions against insider trading, those sanctioned most frequently have close relationships with corporate insiders or frequently contact corporate insiders in the information-sensitive period. For example, as is revealed by one case, the defendant is a close friend of the board secretary, who is aware of the information concerning an undisclosed acquisition of the listed company. The board secretary is also on the list of corporate insiders.[20] Both individuals frequently contacted each other by telephone, internet apps, and in-person meetings, and the defendant brought nearly two million shares between 14 April 2016 and 25 April 2016. The shares were sold in approximately half a year, and the defendant made a profit of 1.1 million RMB. In another judgment selected by SPC as the national reference case, it is clarified that the concerning information is not required to actually change the stock price. Instead, it is sufficient to be qualified as inside information if it has the potential to impact the stock price from the perspective of a regular person.

Finally, for market manipulation, recent criminal enforcement proceedings have focused on these new manipulative schemes. For example, as revealed in one judgment issued by the First Intermediate People's Court in Shanghai City, the defendants employed a trading strategy that repeatedly filed bids and ask orders for two stocks and then canceled these transacting orders before they were concluded. The manipulative strategy intended to use the order flow to impact market expectations about the equilibrium price. The total bid and ask volume submitted by the defendants surpassed 50% of the total market bid and ask volume for the two stocks, and the defendants' profit was more than 25 million RMB.[21]

5.6   Is Public Enforcement of the CSRC and Stock Exchanges Responsive?

The theory of responsive enforcement argues that public enforcement should respond to the reactions of counterparties and adopt a "tit-for-tat strategy" based on a dynamic relationship of "deterrence-cooperation". This subsection tries to analyze the enforcement outputs of the CSRC and the stock exchanges against listed companies in China from the perspective of responsive regulation.

---

[20] See (2019) Yue 03 Xingchu No. 473.

[21] See Market Manipulation by Danghanbo et al., available at https://www.chinacourt.org/article/detail/2020/09/id/5471335.shtml. (Last accessed 31 October, 2021).

Table 5.5 Categorization of punitive administrative measures

Reputational sanctions	Warning
Monetary sanctions	Fine, Disgorgement, Confiscation of business revenue
Behavioral sanctions	N.A
Disqualification sanction	Suspension of business, Revocation of license, Exclusion of market entry
Administrative detention	N.A

5.6.1   The Categorical Analysis of the Enforcement Outputs

The enforcement outputs analyzed include those initiated by the CSRC and the two stock exchanges, which can be divided into the categories of administrative sanctions and nonadministrative sanctions. The former can only be imposed by the CSRC and its ROs, and the latter can be imposed by all regulators. According to Article 9 of the Administrative Penalties Law of 2021, administrative sanctions are divided into five groups, i.e., reputational sanctions, monetary sanctions, behavioral sanctions, disqualification and administrative detention.[22] By searching the securities law and regulation, the specific punitive measures are identified and classified into five groups, as shown in Table 5.5. The reputational sanction, that is, "warning", is the most lenient administrative sanction and mainly impacts the reputational capital of those sanctioned. It is seldom used alone but rather together with other administrative sanctions. The second group is monetary sanctions, which include "Fine", "Disgorgement" and "Confiscation of business revenue". The disqualification sanctions exclude violators from the securities market and deprive them of future potential profits, which are among the most serious sanctions. The securities administrative sanctions do not include any "Behavioral sanctions" or "Administrative detention".

Similarly, the nonadministrative sanctions could also be grouped into the aforementioned categories. Using the terms of the "Supervision and Management" and/or "Legal Responsibilities" to survey sections in the securities law and regulation, it is shown that there are 49 specific measures in the enforcement toolbox of the CSRC and its ROs. In addition, SHSE Measures for Implementing Disciplinary and Supervisory Sanctions of 2019[23] and SZSE Measures for Implementing Disciplinary and Supervisory Sanctions of 2020[24] explicitly list 38 self-regulatory measures. However, not all these nonadministrative sanctions target listed companies. Table 5.6 presents the classification of these measures according to the aforementioned categories.

---

[22] Ma [10].

[23] See Shanghai Zhengquan Jiaoyisuo Jilv Chufen He Jianguan Cuoshi Shishi Banfa (2019 Nian Xiuding), available at http://www.sse.com.cn/lawandrules/sserules/organization/c/c_20191011_4 925638.shtml. (Last accessed 31 October, 2021).

[24] See Shenzhen Zhengquan Jiaoyisuo Zilv Jianguan Cuoshi he Jilv Chufen Shishi Banfa (2020 Nian Xiuding), available at http://www.szse.cn/disclosure/notice/general/t20201231_584056.html. (Last accessed 31 October, 2021).

Table 5.6 Categorization of nonadministrative disciplinary measures

Restorable measure	Correction, rectification, loss recovery
Reputational measure	Censure, Credit records, Criticism, Regulatory concern, Regulatory conversation, Warning, Regulatory letter
Monetary measure	N.A
Behavioral measure	Sanctioning concerned employees, Explanation, Public apology, Replacement of directors, supervisors and senior management, Hiring securities firms and other financial intermediaries to review and issue opinions, Suspension or termination of mergers and acquisitions, Increasing compliance checking, Restricting the business activities of securities companies, and Restricting the dividend or payment to directors, supervisors and senior management
Disqualification measures[25]	Unsuitable for certain positions, Suspending acceptance of application for administrative permits, and Suspending the fast information disclosure channel
Regulatory detention	N.A

In contrast to administrative sanctions, some of the nonadministrative sanctions are not punitive but restorable measures in nature, which mainly include "Correction", "Rectification" and "Loss recovery". They try to correct the misconduct and/or restore the current situation to the original state prior to the misconduct. In addition, punitive nonadministrative sanctions include "Reputational measures", "Behavioral measures" and "Disqualification". "Reputational measures" are most lenient and include "Censure", "Credit records", "Criticism", "Regulatory concern", "Regulatory conversation", "Warning" and "Regulatory letter". "Behavioral measures" are the main requirements imposed by regulators for regulated entities to perform certain actions. The final category is "Disqualification", which includes "Unsuitable for certain positions", "Suspending acceptance of application for administrative permits" and "Suspending the fast information disclosure channel".

5.6.2   The Tested Hypotheses

Responsive enforcement distinguishes punitive enforcement actions and cooperative enforcement actions and emphasizes that regulatory agencies should encourage a culture of cooperation. The aforementioned enforcement actions can be divided into three groups based on the degree of punitiveness. The first is cooperative enforcement instruments, which mainly include restorable measures. Second, weak-punitive enforcement instruments, which are mainly sanctions with relatively bearable costs,

---

[25] Only the two stock exchanges impose the nonadministrative sanction of "Suspending the fast information disclosure channel".

include "Reputational measures", "Behavior measures" and "Reputational sanctions". These measures are mainly informational or mandate the involved parties to perform certain tasks to deter securities misconduct. Finally, the strong-punitive enforcement instruments, which impose the highest costs on the sanctioned, include "Disqualification measures", "Disqualification sanctions" and "Fines". This group of methods is the most confrontational and likely to cause conflicts with counterparties.

Two predictions could be derived from the theory of responsive enforcement. First, the enforcement outputs should follow a pyramidal distribution. Strong punitive enforcement actions should be the least likely to be imposed and are mainly employed to deter potential misconduct. In contrast, weak-punitive enforcement actions should be the most frequently used instruments.

Hypothesis 5.1. The enforcement outputs of the CSRC and stock exchanges should follow a pyramidal distribution.

In addition, responsive enforcement does not claim to rely only on cooperative enforcement instruments; instead, it emphasizes that regulators begin with cooperative enforcement instruments to encourage cooperation from regulatory counterparties. However, if the latter fail to correct the misconduct, compensate relevant damage, or perform other requirements imposed by the regulatory agencies, the regulatory agencies should escalate and increase the punitiveness of the sanctions.

Hypothesis 5.2. If violators repeatedly commit securities misconduct, enforcement sanctions should be escalated, and more punitive sanctions should be adopted.

5.6.3 Empirical Findings

In this subsection, the sample comprises the 3,688 sanctions issued by the CSRC and the two stock exchanges against the listed companies between 2009 and 2020.

5.6.3.1 The Pyramidal Distribution Hypothesis

Responsive enforcement proposes establishing a "deterrence-cooperation" dynamic model and predicts that the enforcement outputs follow a pyramidal distribution by the punitive degree of the sanctions imposed. Based on the analysis in the hypothesis development section, the sampled sanctions are grouped into five categories: "Strong-punitive administrative sanction", "Weak-punitive administrative sanction", "Strong-punitive nonadministrative sanction", "Weak-punitive nonadministrative sanction" and "Cooperative nonadministrative sanction". Figure 5.2 presents the annual enforcement outputs divided into the five groups. It is clear from the figure that the enforcement outputs are relatively small before 2012; their increase thereafter

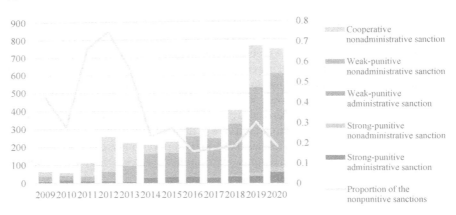

Fig. 5.2 The distribution of the enforcement actions by their punitiveness magnitude

is mainly due to the number of less punitive sanctions. The CSRC prefers "Strong-punitive administrative sanction" and imposes "Fines" and "Warnings" 342 times and 339 times, respectively. ROs mainly use "Cooperative nonadministrative sanctions", including the issuance of "Corrections" and "Rectifications" 464 times and 561 times, respectively, and "Weak-punitive nonadministrative sanctions", including the issuance of "Warnings" and "Credit records" 618 times and 136 times, respectively.

The Shanghai Stock Exchange favors the "Weak-punitive nonadministrative sanction" and actively imposed "Criticism", "Censure" and "Regulatory concern" 290 times, 132 times and 321 times, respectively. Similarly, the Shenzhen Stock Exchange prefers "Cooperative nonadministrative sanctions" and "Weak-punitive nonadministrative sanctions". The former includes the issuance of "Correction" 467 times, and the latter includes the issuance of "Criticism", "Censure" and "Regulatory letter" 550 times, 198 times and 150 times, respectively.

The enforcement pattern goes through a change from the state where "Cooperative nonadministrative sanctions" account for the highest percentage to a new situation in which "weak-punitive nonadministrative sanctions" account for the highest percentage. The curved line represents the change in the "proportion of nonpunitive sanctions", which clearly shows that "Cooperative nonadministrative sanctions" declined from its highest point of 75.2% in 2012 to approximately 20% in recent years. In addition, "Weak-punitive nonadministrative sanctions" increased proportionally and now account for more than 60% of the total enforcement outputs. In general, the enforcement outputs of the CSRC and the two stock exchanges conform to a pyramidal distribution, consistent with the predictions of responsive enforcement theory.

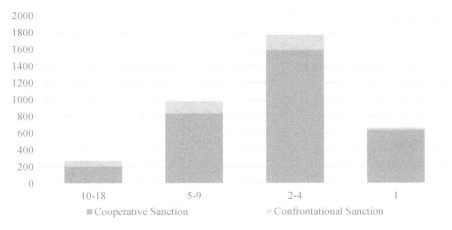

Fig. 5.3 The distribution of the sanction frequency

5.6.3.2   The Escalation Hypothesis

The second prediction made by responsive enforcement theory concerns the escalation of enforcement sanctions. For repeated violators, the punitiveness of the sanctions issued should increase. Figure 5.3 shows the distribution of the frequency of firms sanctioned over 2009 and 2019. The sample is divided into four groups based on the frequency of the sanctions received. The first group includes firms sanctioned between 10 and 18 times and are the most frequent violators. A total of 23 firms received 271 sanctions between 2009 and 2019, of which 66 sanctions were punitive and accounted for 24% of the total sanctions received. The second group includes those sanctioned between 5 and 9 times and includes 161 firms that received 981 sanctions, of which 146 sanctions were punitive and accounted for 15% of the total sanctions received. The third group includes those sanctioned between 2 and 4 times. This group included 667 firms that received 1,774 sanctions, of which 181 sanctions were punitive and accounted for 10% of the total sanctions received. The final group includes those sanctioned one time. This group includes 662 firms that received 24 punitive sanctions, which accounted for 4% of the total sanctions received. The descriptive analysis shows that as the frequency of sanctions of listed companies increases, the likelihood of receiving punitive sanctions also increases.

Table 5.7 presents a simple regressional analysis to test the escalation hypothesis, and the sample comprises 2967 sanctions issued between 2014 and 2020.[26] The dependent variable is the dummy variable "PUNITIVE", which indicates whether the sanctions received are punitive. The two key explanatory variables are chosen to proxy for the willingness to cooperate with sanctioned listed companies. The first is the dummy variable "SANCTIONONE", which indicates whether the sanctioned

---

[26] The sanctions issued between 2009 and 2013 are excluded because the historical sanction frequency of the listed firms is used as explanatory variable.

Table 5.7 Tests of the escalation hypothesis

	(1)	(2)	(3)	(4)
SANCTIONFIVE	0.28** (0.12)		0.30** (0.16)	
NUMFIVE			-0.021 (0.039)	
SANCTIONONE		0.33*** (0.11)		0.44** (0.17)
NUMONE				−0.086 (0.073)
SOE	NO	NO	-0.48*** (0.17)	−0.47*** (0.17)
Industrial Dummies	NO	NO	YES	YES
Year Dummies	NO	NO	YES	YES
Constant	−2.21*** (0.1)	−2.19*** (0.09)	−1.49*** (0.38)	−1.47*** (0.38)
Sample	2.967	29.67	2.939	2.939
Pseudo R-squared	0.0025	0.0038	0.031	0.033

firms have received any sanctions in one year prior to the sanction year. The second is the dummy variable "SANCTIONFIVE", which indicates whether the sanctioned firms have received any sanctions in five years prior to the sanction year. The other controlling variables include "NUMFIVE" representing the number of sanctions received in five years, "NUMONE" representing the number of sanctions received in one year, "SOE", which is a dummy variable indicating whether the listed company is an SOE, industrial dummies and year dummies. The regression is estimated with the logit model, and the standard errors are clustered by listed companies.

The empirical analysis reported in Table 5.7 generally supports the Escalation Hypothesis: firms sanctioned before are more likely to be sanctioned with punitive sanctions. In Column (1), a univariate regression is performed, and the coefficient of the variable "SANCTIONFIVE" is positive and significant at the 5% level. In Column (2), a similar univariate regression is performed, and the coefficient of the variable "SANCTIONONE" is 0.33 and significant at the 5% level. The results suggest that the odds of a firm receiving punitive sanctions increase if it has been sanctioned within five years or one year. Columns (3) and (4) report the results of multivariate regressions with additional controls. The results are similar to those reported in the previous two columns. The number of sanctions received by a given firm in the previous year or five years has no predictive power for the odds of receiving punitive sanctions. In addition, SOEs are less likely to be sanctioned punitively.

References

1. Mathews, A. (1975). Effective defense of SEC investigations: Laying the foundation for successful disposition of subsequent civil administrative and criminal proceedings. *Emory Law Journal, 24*, 567–638.
2. Cox, J.D., Hillman, R.W., Langevoort, D.C., Lipton, A.M., Sjostrom, W.K. (2020). *Securities regulation: Cases and materials* (9th ed.), Wolters Kluwer, 910.
3. Cox, J. D., & Thomas, R. S. (2019). Revolving elites: The unexplored risk of capturing the SEC. *Georgetown Law Journal, 107*(4), 845–922.
4. Mathews, A. F. (1980). Litigation and settlement of SEC administrative enforcement proceedings. *Catholic University Law Review, 29*(2), 215–312.
5. Winship, V., & Robbennolt, J. K. (2018). An empirical study of admissions in SEC settlements. *Arizona Law Review, 60*, 1–66.
6. Baker, T., & Griffith, S. J. (2007). The missing monitor in corporate governance: The directors' and officers' liability insurer. *Georgetown Law Journal, 95*, 1795–1822.
7. Wenming, X., Zhu, S., & Zhicheng, W. (2020). Building a junior stock exchange: Lessons from China. *European Business Organization Law Review, 21*, 139–170.
8. Liebman, B. L., & Milhaupt, C. J. (2008). Reputational sanctions in China's securities market. *Columbia Law Review, 108*, 929–983.
9. Zeng, S. (2019). Regulating draconian takeover defenses with soft law: Empirical evidence from event studies in China. *European Business Organization Law Review, 20*(4), 823–854.
10. Ma, H. (2020). Several controversial issues in the revision of administrative penalty law. *East China University of Political Science and Law Journal, 2020*(4), 6–16. (In Chinese).

Chapter 6
SPC's 2003 Provisions and the Collective Action Problem of Securities Litigation

The most important governing rules of securities private enforcement have undergone significant changes since the revised Securities Law of 2019.[1] Prior to the revision, SPC's 2003 Provisions were the primary guidelines for private enforcement and regarded as investor unfriendly. Although the Securities Law of 2019 established a multidimensional securities litigation system, SPC's 2003 provisions are still the basis for several key elements of securities litigation. This chapter first discusses the SPC's 2003 Provisions and relevant rules concerning securities litigation promulgated prior to the Securities Law of 2019 and empirically examines the enforcement outputs and potential collective action problems due to the "opt-in" design of private securities litigation.

6.1 Institutional Background

Private enforcement of securities law was absent in China in the 1990s, although the securities law on the books granted harmed investors the right to pursue tortious compensation in civil litigation. Entering the twenty-first century, harmed investors started to bring civil litigations against those listed companies that committed securities misrepresentation and were sanctioned administratively by the CSRC. Due to concerns about the disorder that might be caused by the surging number of civil litigations, the SPC promulgated the SPC's 2001 Notice on 21 September 2001, and lower courts were instructed to reject hearing those securities fraud cases.[2] Considering that most listed companies were SOEs, the implied political preference was to protect the

---

[1] The institutional innovation concerning securities litigation is also regarded as the most important reform by the Chinese legislature, see The Revised Securities Law Is Released, available at http://www.npc.gov.cn/npc/c30834/202001/748d4354d334497595ecdd1591f122a4.shtml. (Last accessed 31 October, 2021).

[2] CSRC criticized SPC's 2001 Notice when it was promulgated, see Pistor and Xu [1].

state sector from paying compensation to harmed investors, which would deteriorate its balance sheet and is *de facto* a transfer of state assets to private parties. Such judiciary attitudes have attracted overwhelming criticism from regulatory agencies, academics and market practitioners.

In less than four months, the SPC changed its prior position and issued SPC's 2002 Notice, allowing lower courts to accept suits brought on the grounds of misrepresentation,[3] given that the defendants have been administratively sanctioned by the CSRC or received criminal judgements. It is noted that victims of concealed positive information are likely to fall out of legal protection because the causality between false disclosure and investors' losses is found only when they buy securities after the false disclosure is made and sell securities after the misrepresentation is publicly revealed.[4] In January 2003, the SPC's 2003 Provisions was issued and specified the detailed substantive and procedural rules for securities misrepresentation cases. The securities litigation system designed by SPC's 2003 Provisions is investor unfriendly and at best compensation-oriented and significantly differs from the American model, which mixes deterrence and compensation functions.[5] Highly intensive American private enforcement even leads to unbearable costs of frivolous suits, and PSLRA was enacted to curb the widespread frivolous suits and agency problems of plaintiff attorneys.[6]

Private suits initiated by harmed Chinese investors were repressed and suffered from significant procedural hurdles. First, the provisions restricted the scope of qualified plaintiffs to investors suffering from losses due to misrepresentation, and those due to insider trading and market manipulation were excluded.[7] Though almost a decade later, the SPC changed its position and admitted the civil compensation cases based upon insider trading and market manipulation,[8] but the court system was cautious about adjudicating such cases due to the lack of relevant judiciary rules.

The scope of defendants is broadly defined. Although issuers and listed companies are primary defendants of civil litigation, several other entities also assume joint and several obligations if they cannot prove that they have no fault in misconduct. The first group includes the directors, supervisors and senior management of the issuers and listed companies.[9] The second group comprises securities underwriters and sponsors and their directors, supervisors and senior management, who assume joint and several

---

[3] Hutchens [2].

[4] Article 5 of SPC's 2003 Provisions expands the ground for private litigation and includes those administrative sanctions made by other agencies that are empowered to impose administrative sanctions and criminal judgements determined by courts.

[5] Cox [3].

[6] Choi [4].

[7] Article 1 of SPC's 2003 Provisions.

[8] See Article 20 of Some Opinions on Further Strengthening Trial Concerning Financial Disputes (Guanyu Jinyibu Jiaqiang Jinrong Shenpan Gongzuo De Ruogan Yijian), available at http://www.csrc.gov.cn/newsite/flb/flfg/sfjs_8249/201805/t20180518_338327.html. (Last accessed 31 October, 2021).

[9] Article 21 of SPC's 2003 Provisions.

obligations to their liabilities, should they fail to prove that they have no fault.[10] The third group contains other financial service firms, including securities firms, accounting firms, law firms, and asset evaluation firms, which assume proportional joints and several obligations. They should compensate investors to the extent that they are responsible, should they fail to prove that they have no fault.[11] However, those individuals rarely pay compensation out of their own pockets, leading to the problem of circularity.

Furthermore, the intermediate-level courts at the place where the defendant firms are located have territorial jurisdiction, which significantly increases plaintiffs' burdens to pursue such suits.[12] Listed companies are major economic players in regional areas and maintain relatively strong political ties, which might compromise judicial independence and disadvantage investor plaintiffs.

Third, an administrative prerequisite requires that private suits be based on sanctions of public agencies or courts' criminal judgements. This rule has caused drastic disputes. The administrative prerequisite that restricts the freedom of investors to bring civil litigations and deprives them of judiciary protection has been criticized.[13] However, a recent empirical study on the actual cases brought about by harmed investors shows that the number of cases brought to the courts is significantly smaller than that of cases sanctioned by the CSRC.[14] Consequently, the author argues that administrative hurdles are not the primary obstacles for investors to obtain judiciary relief and proposes that an inefficient court system is the major impediment.[15] It is argued that administrative prerequisites should bring value to listed companies, considering the capability of the judiciary system and the long history of public-oriented regulation.[16]

Finally, SPC's 2003 Provisions aggravate the collective action problem in shareholder litigations and requires that they be brought as individual or joint actions instead of U.S.-style class actions.[17] Hence, aggrieved investors need to actively "opt into" the enforcement proceedings and assume participation costs. It is highly likely that the expected costs from pursuing civil litigation outweigh the expected benefits, and harmed investors are apathetic toward the right of bringing civil litigation.

Substantially, Sect. 6 of the SPC's 2003 Provisions explicitly specifies that such cases fall in the category of tort disputes instead of contractual disputes. Based on the basic principle of tort law in China, investors seeking tortious compensation should

---

[10] Article 23 of SPC's 2003 Provisions.

[11] Article 24 of SPC's 2003 Provisions.

[12] Lu [5].

[13] Guo and Ong [6].

[14] Huang [7].

[15] The most recent judiciary reform concerning the adjudication of the financial disputes is the establishment of Shanghai Financial Court, Financial Division of Shenzhen Financial Court, and Beijing Financial Court.

[16] Layton [8].

[17] Article 12 of SPC's 2003 Provisions.

prove the following elements. First, the defendant has committed securities misconduct, such as misrepresentation. It is emphasized that misrepresentation refers to false records, misleading statements of material events, or omitting or improperly disclosing major events.[18] The derivative benefits of the administrative prerequisite lie in the fact that Chinese courts implicitly regard the administrative sanction as compelling proof of the misconduct and materiality of the information concerned.[19] A recent judiciary rule enacted by the SPC explicitly confirms such a position and requires that the lower courts treat the cases with administrative sanctions as satisfying materiality tests.

Second, the defendant should intentionally commit misconduct, which is equalized to the "scienter" in American securities cases.[20] Those organizations and individuals sanctioned by the CSRC administratively are regarded as intentionally committing misrepresentation. The plaintiffs have saved the trouble of proving the subject intent of the defendants, which makes it difficult to collect relevant evidence.

Third, misconduct should cause damage suffered by the plaintiff, which requires that investors' losses are due to misrepresentation. SPC's 2003 Provisions narrowly defines the causation and the underlying rationale for proving causal relationships by adopting a strictive form of fraud-on-the-market theory. Only those investors buying securities between the misrepresentation date and the revealing date of misrepresentation and selling these securities post the revealing date could regard the losses due to these transactions as caused by the misrepresentation.[21] Specifically, the losses due to the following five types of transactions are regarded as uncorrelated with the misrepresentation.[22] First, investors sell securities prior to the revealing date, which means that misrepresented information is always in the market information mix during their buying and selling decisions and hence causes any difference. Second, the investors transact after the revealing date. The losses due to such transactions are not caused by misrepresentation because the market has already adjusted for the corrected information. Third, the investors are aware of the misrepresentation. Fourth, the losses are due to systematic risk. However, no judiciary rules define the boundary of systematic risk, which causes significant inconsistency in the judgements delivered by lower courts. Finally, investors transact securities with malicious intent or to manipulate the market.

The side benefits of the administrative prerequisite are a relatively high success rate for proving the three required elements for tort cases, i.e., existence of misconduct, subjective intent and causation. The most significant disputes revolve around the estimation of tortious damages. The calculation of civil compensation in general comprises the difference in investment and the relevant interests and stamp duty. However, the volume is calculated in two ways. First, if the investors sell the securities prior to the reference date, then the damage is calculated by multiplying the

---

[18] Article 17 of SPC's 2003 Provisions.

[19] The element of materiality is a highly debated concept, see Jonathan Macey et al. [9].

[20] Ernst and Ernst v. Hochfelder, 425 U.S. 185 (1976).

[21] Article 18 of SPC's 2003 Provisions.

[22] Article 19 of SPC's 2003 Provisions.

difference in securities price by the holding volume. Second, if the investors still hold the securities post the reference date, then the damages are calculated by multiplying the difference between the buying price and the average price between the revealing date and the reference date and the holding volume.

The calculation of civil compensation is based on the following three dates, which are defined in Article 20 of SPC's 2003 Provisions. First, the implementation date is the date when the misrepresentation was performed. Generally, this date is subject to little dispute when defendants are sanctioned administratively. The CSRC or its ROs will explicitly identify misconduct and its relevant implementation dates in sanction decisions, which will be quoted by courts adjudicating civil cases.

Second, the revealing date is the time when the market learns about misconduct for the first time, which is a heatedly debated element. The revealing date comprises two different times.[23] On the one hand, if the misrepresentation is passively revealed, for example, by media or public agencies, the revealing date is the time when such misconduct is first published by national media (disclosure time). On the other hand, if the misrepresentation is corrected by the informational obligor, then the revealing date is the time when such correction is disclosed by the media accredited by the CSRC, and the announcement is made to the general public by listed companies (correction time). In judiciary practice, the court system seems to adopt a conservative attitude only when the details of the misconduct are learned by the market through authoritative channels so that the revealing date is recognized. However, it is normally too late because the market price might have already adjusted to the expected disclosure when the news or announcement suggests the expected investigation or sanctions. From the perspective of an efficient capital market, market participants have already expected the reveal of the misrepresentation, and the market price has adjusted to such information.

6.2 The Enforcement Outputs of Securities Litigation

To empirically analyze the outputs of private securities litigation, Table 6.1 presents the distribution of the 1747 judgements made between November 2013 and December 2016 and disclosed by China Judgements Online. These judgements concerned 40 defendants and 2746 investors, and 47 law firms provided legal service to harmed investors. In the time-series dimension, the numbers of judgements made in 2016, 2015, 2014 and 2013 were 894, 506, 279 and 68, respectively. To save space, only defendants sued by more than 30 plaintiffs and the top 10 law firms are reported, and the rest of the defendants and law firms are grouped into "Others". It is worth mentioning that the sample used in this section is not the complete sample of judgements delivered in these years because some of the judgements are not disclosed by law or at the discretion of the adjudicated courts.[24]

---

[23] Article 20 of SPC's 2003 Provisions.

[24] The estimated percentage of cases disclosed is approximately 50%, see Zhuang Liu et al. [10].

Table 6.1 The outputs of securities litigation between 2013 and 2017

Law firm Defendant	Huarong	Saijie	Dongfang Jianqiao	Yingke	Huiye	Yufeng	Minglun	Jialanda	Benben	Huanyu Jinmao	Others	Total	Sanction date	Sanction entity	Court	Compensation (RMB)	Pct. of investor (%)
Ningbo Fubang (宁波富邦)	47	0	7	0	0	21	0	0	0	0	4	79	2012/06	CSRC	Ningbo Inter. Ct	1,465,782	0.35
Foshan Zhaoming (佛山照明)	98	357	174	73	2	21	0	98	68	9	79	979	2012/11	CSRC	Guangzhou Inter. Ct	63,676,892.16	0.63
Weifang Yaxing (潍坊亚星)	1	6	18	0	0	0	0	0	0	0	0	25	2013/01	CSRC	Jinan Inter. Ct	2227	0.11
Yunnan Yutou (云南云投)	34	1	0	35	6	0	0	0	0	0	17	93	2013/05	CSRC	Kunming Inter. Ct	587,122.30	0.63
Shanghai Yidian (上海仪电)	7	62	36	1	0	5	0	0	0	3	10	124	2013/08	CSRC	Shanghai 1st Inter. Ct	1,723,672.23	0.19
Wuchang Yu (武昌鱼)	13	0	11	0	0	0	0	0	0	0	7	31	2013/10	Hubei RO	Wuhan Inter. Ct	84,373.85	0.09
Hengtian Hailong (恒天海龙)	12	0	1	8	19	0	14	0	0	0	14	68	2013/11	CSRC	Jinan Inter. Ct	1,634,507.93	0.08
Nanjing Fangzhi (南京纺织)	14	11	22	24	13	1	38	0	0	2	8	133	2014/04	CSRC	Nanjing Inter. Ct	285,233.91	1.25

(continued)

Table 6.1 (continued)

Law firm Defendant	Huarong	Saijie	Dongfang Jianqiao	Yingke	Huiye	Yufeng	Minglun	Jialanda	Benben	Huanyu Jinmao	Others	Total	Sanction date	Sanction entity	Court	Compensation (RMB)	Pct. of investor (%)
Qinshang Guangdian (勤上光电)	16	0	7	0	0	0	0	0	0	3	4	30	2014/05	Guangdong RO	Guangzhou Inter. Ct	9,671,628.87	0.09
Hubei Shanxia (湖北三峡)	2	0	36	0	0	0	1	0	0	1	0	40	2014/12	Hubei RO	Wuhan Inter. Ct	3,213,982.72	0.10
Shanghai Shenkai (上海神开)	13	8	5	3	0	1	0	0	0	1	0	30	2015/02	Shanghai RO	Shanghai 1st Inter. Ct	112,605.32	0.14
Xiexin Jicheng (协鑫集成)	114	5	27	21	0	0	0	0	0	2	1	170	2015/06	CSRC	Shanghai 1st Inter. Ct	3,893,388.50	0.07
Hairun Guangfu (海润光伏)	28	6	32	26	1	14	23	0	0	16	26	172	2015/10	Jiangsu RO	Nanjing Inter. Ct	16,250,445.43	0.08
Others	207	102	108	59	100	69	28	0	12	35	52	772	N.A	N.A	N.A	N.A	N.A
Total	606	558	484	250	141	132	104	98	80	71	222	2746	N.A	N.A	N.A	102,601,862.22	N.A

Note (1) Those defendants against which fewer than five suits are brought are classified into the group titled "Miscellaneous"

(2) The number of plaintiffs represented is counted according to law firms instead of lawyers. To avoid double counting, the information on the first instance and the second instance is recorded once

(3) To calculate the "Percentage of total shareholders", the number of shareholders disclosed in the annual report of the listed companies at the time when the CSRC made the sanctions is used. It is worth noting that occasionally, the shareholders of the listed companies controlled by the defendants could bring cases instead of those of the defendant firms

The securities fraud litigation market is very small and inactive. The demand for legal services is limited: in more than three years, only 2746 shareholders have actively sought judicial relief. Nearly all plaintiffs are individuals, and no institutional investors in A/B-share markets are involved in these suits. To measure the participatory rate of the harmed investors of sanctioned firms in securities litigation, an indicator of the "Pct. of Investor", which equals the number of shareholders actually bringing the suits divided by the number of shareholders reported by the listed companies in the prior annual report. For listed companies sued by more than 30 shareholders, the percentage of shareholders actually seeking compensation ranged between 1.25 and 0.07%, and the average is approximately 0.22%. This is a relatively low participatory rate of the shareholders. A large number of potentially harmed investors are "rationally apathetic" to the right granted by SPC's 2002 Notice, which leads to a shortage of demand for legal services. Caution needs to be exercised in interpreting our data because the sample is small and the results of private bargaining outside the courtroom are not available.

From the supply side, the law firms specializing in this field are mostly regional firms, and national elite law firms, for example, those in the "Red Circle",[25] fail to provide legal service to plaintiffs. This could be ascribed to the fact that national elite law firms have strong ties with established listed companies and would prefer not to irritate their potential or existing clients by serving plaintiff parties. The top three law firms are "Shanghai Huarong", "Shanghai Saijie" and "Dongfang Jianqiao", which represent 606, 558 and 484 plaintiffs, respectively. The plaintiffs mainly bring litigations based on the administrative sanctions issued by the CSRC or its ROs, and firms sanctioned by the CSRC do not seem to pay much for harmed investors. The "opt-in" feature imposes significant economic obstacles to gathering small claims together and limits the expected number of plaintiffs that could be represented by a given law firm.

Consequently, informational obligators face extremely limited litigation risks. In approximately three years, only 40 informational violators were named defendants. For these defendants, only 13 were sued by more than 30 plaintiffs. The occurrence of securities litigation is rare, and even if they are actually sued, the expected costs are trivial for defendants. The 40 sanctioned firms in total paid 102 million RMB, and the largest sum of civil compensation was approximately 64 million RMB paid by "Foshan Zhaoming". Only seven listed companies paid more than 1 million RMB in the sampled three years, and the minimum compensation paid was just 2227 RMB.

The agency problem of plaintiffs' attorneys further compromises their role as representatives. Most minority investors do not have knowledge of the expected damages allowed, which leads to asymmetric information between shareholders and their attorneys. The claimed damages are consequently inflated both to encourage aggrieved investors to file suits and to generate larger contingent fees. However, the costs of inflated claimed damages are assumed by plaintiffs. The losing parties are liable for the prevailing parties' court costs, which are calculated according to

---

[25] The Chinese national elite law firms are tagged with the "Red Circle" (Hongquan Suo) by Asian Legal Business, see https://china.legalbusinessonline.com/. (Last accessed 31 October, 2021).

the claimed damage instead of the allowed damage. If investors lose the case, they have to pay the court costs calculated with claimed damages, which are often not negligible. If they win the case, they also have to pay for the proportion of the court costs calculated according to the difference between claimed and allowed damages. The significant court costs further reduce the compensation and the incentives of injured investors to opt into civil proceedings.

The number of private enforcement outputs is small compared to that in the American markets, where 144 and 161 federal securities class actions against misrepresentations in financial documents were filed in 2012 and 2013, respectively.[26] The number of securities class actions further increased to more than 400 cases in 2017 and has maintained a stable level ever since.[27] The Federal Rules of Civil Procedure established the class action procedure in 1966, and Rule 23 specifies the conditions for the certification of the class action. Class members must face similar legal or factual problems, and the class is formed according to the "opt-out" principle, which by default regards investors as opting into litigation unless they explicitly opt out of the class action. The institutional design maximizes the number of harmed investors participating in civil litigation and hence minimizes the average costs of obtaining judiciary relief. However, private enforcement in the U.S. is subject to significant risks of frivolous suits because entrepreneur lawyers control litigation and try to maximize their own interests instead of the interests of the plaintiff class.[28] Entrepreneur lawyers tend to bring securities class actions against those firms whose share prices decline significantly and take advantage of the discovery procedure to exert pressure on defendants to arrive at a settlement, regardless of the merits of the case.[29] Although investors seem to be successfully compensated,[30] listed companies, particularly high-tech companies, are harassed by such meritless suits and pay huge costs to cope with them.

In sum, although SPC's 2002 Notice granted aggrieved investors the right to seek compensation from companies undertaking misrepresentation, retail investors seem to be apathetic to these rights. Entrepreneur lawyers fail to solve the collective action problem satisfactorily. On the one hand, unlike U.S.-style class actions, in which injured investors are automatically opted into the class and bounded by any agreements reached by the class and defendants unless they expressly opt out, aggrieved investors need to actively opt into securities litigations in China. On the other hand, the agency costs of plaintiff attorneys further reduce the expected compensation from civil litigations. Hence, retail investors are unlikely to pay premiums for the right to seek compensation.

---

[26] See Cornerstone Research: Securities Class Action Filings: 2013 Year in Review (2013), available at http://securities.stanford.edu/research-reports/1996-2013/Cornerstone-Research-Securities-Class-Action-Filings-2013-YIR.pdf. (Last accessed 31 October, 2021).

[27] The American market is exceptional in private enforcement even compared to those in more developed jurisdictions, see John Armour et al. [11].

[28] Choi [12].

[29] Bebchuk [13].

[30] According to the theory of circularity, harmed investors holding a portfolio of stocks are compensated with their own money, see Fisch [14].

6.3   The Calculation of the Tortious Compensation

The lower courts seem to adopt an inconsistent and to some extent arbitrary way to calculate the damages to harmed investors, which increases the uncertainty about investor compensation. Table 6.2 shows the elements in damage estimation as revealed by the judgements concerning the 13 defendants listed in Table 6.1. First and foremost, the lower courts have unanimously adopted the following estimation formula in accordance with the SPC's 2003 Provisions, which equals the difference between the buying and selling price multiplied by the qualified trading volume, excluding the losses due to systematic risk. Consequently, the "implementation date", "revealing date" and "calculation of systematic risk" are the three core elements in estimating civil compensation.

First, the "implementation date" is decided based on the information disclosed by the administrative sanctions. The CSRC and its ROs will explicitly identify the misconduct committed by defendants and the exact dates of the misconduct. The court will decide the implementation date with reference to these sanctions. Sometimes, disputes arise when defendants commit multiple misconducts, and both parties have different preferences about the "implementation date". Plaintiffs normally prefer the implementation date, after which the largest buying volume is undertaken, whereas defendants tend to prefer the date after which the smallest buying volume is undertaken.

The second element is the revealing date. Theoretically, misconduct could be revealed by multiple resources. Occasionally, informational obligators might self-disclose misconduct. In addition, the media will uncover certain misconduct before any financial regulators intervene and be the first source through which the market learns about the misrepresentation. Another two leading disclosure sources of the misrepresentation are the announcements for non-administrative sanctions issued by the CSRC or its ROs and the investigation announcement for administrative sanctions. The non-administrative sanction is a relatively soft penalty, and hence, its decision process is comparatively less time-consuming. It is not uncommon that informational obligators are first sanctioned nonadministratively, and then the investigation process for administrative sanctions begins.

As discussed previously, because of the significant potential costs to violators, administrative sanctions have to go through a lengthy process, which could be broadly defined as the stage for investigation, preliminary sanction and final sanction. Required by Chinese securities law, listed companies will have to disclose relevant information when they first receive the notice for the aforementioned stages. The "Investigation Notice" is special in the sense that it is very simple because, at this time, the exact details of the misconduct are unknown to the regulators, so the announcements made by the listed companies will include only listed companies that are under administrative investigation. The listed companies will make two further announcements concerning administrative sanctions: one about preliminary sanction, and the other about final sanctions. Normally, the content of the announcement

Table 6.2 The elements concerning calculating the tortious compensation

Defendant	Implementation date	Revealing date	Calculation of systematic risk
Ningbo Fubang (宁波富邦)	Date mandated by the securities law for disclosing major litigation	Self-disclosure date	The percentage changes in the average of industrial index and SZSE index
Foshan Zhaoming (佛山照明)	Announcement day of transaction	Announcement day of non-administrative sanction	The percentage changes in the SZSE index
Weifang Yaxing (潍坊亚星)	Date mandated by the securities law for major event	Investigation announcement	Not admitted by the adjudicating court
Yunnan Yutou (云南云投)	Date for disclosing prospectus	Investigation announcement	Not discussed
Shanghai Yidian (上海仪电)	Date mandated by the securities law for disclosing shareholding	Self-disclosed date	Not discussed
Wuchang Yu (武昌鱼)	Date mandated by the securities law for disclosing major litigation	Investigation announcement	The percentage changes in the market index
Hengtian Hailong (恒天海龙)	Date for Annual report	Investigation announcement	The percentage changes in the average of industrial index and SZSE index
Nanjing Fangzhi (南京纺织)	Date for Annual report	Investigation announcement	Not discussed
Qinshang Guangdian (勤上光电)	Date mandated by the securities law for major asset acquisition	Investigation announcement	Not admitted by the adjudicating court
Hubei Shanxia (湖北三峡)	Date for Annual report	Investigation announcement	Not admitted by the adjudicating court
Shanghai Shenkai (上海神开)	Date for Annual report	Investigation announcement	Not discussed
Xiexin Jicheng (协鑫集成)	Date mandated by the securities law for major event	Investigation announcement	Not admitted by the adjudicating court
Hairun Guangfu (海润光伏)	Announcement day of dividend	Investigation announcement	Not admitted by the adjudicating court

for preliminary sanction will be quite close to that for final sanction and documents the details about the misconduct committed by the listed companies.

As shown by the judiciary decisions, the above dates were all identified as the revealing date by different lower courts. The most commonly recognized date is when listed companies announce that they have received the Investigation Notice. This choice is most likely to be the first time that the market is aware of misconduct if there was no prior media coverage or announcement for non-administrative sanctions, which in accordance with the efficient market hypothesis, the market price will incorporate historical information in the weak-form efficient market. In addition, in our sampled cases, the Ningbo Intermediate Court recognized the date when the listed company "Ningbo Fubang" disclosed and corrected the misconduct as the revealing date. Finally, in several other unreported cases, Chinese courts sometimes recognize the date when national media reports misconduct as the revealing date.[31] In other unreported cases, the date for the announcement of preliminary sanctions is regarded as the revealing date. The reasons provided by the adjudicating courts for such decision is that the Investigation Notice is too ambiguous and fails to provide any detailed information about the misconducts, which fails the criteria for "revelation of the misconducts".

The last element for calculating the civil compensation is the determination of the losses due to systematic risk. SPC's idea is straightforward; civil compensation is tortious rather than a save clause for investor investment. Hence, losses unrelated to misrepresentation should be carved out. Unfortunately, the securities law fails to provide any guidance on the sources and calculation of such risks. Based on the disclosed judgements, lower courts have followed three strategies. First, the topic is completely overlooked in the decision, which could be ascribed to the fact that the defendants fail to bring about such defense. Second, the decisions mention that the defendants have raised the defense but fail to provide the exact sources of such risks. The adjudicating courts hence overturn their claims that the losses of the plaintiffs are caused by systematic risk.

Finally, the defendants raise the defense of systematic risk, and the adjudicating courts accept such arguments. However, the exact way to determine the impacts of systematic risk could vary. On the one hand, the market index could be selected as a proxy for systematic risk, and its percentage changes during the holding period are excluded from the losses of the plaintiffs. For example, the Guangzhou Intermediate Court decided that the losses caused by the misrepresentation of "Foshan Zhaoming" should exclude the percentage changes in the SZSE index during the same period. On the other hand, the industrial index is selected, and its percentage changes are excluded from investor losses. For example, the Jinan Intermediate Court used the average of the market index and chemical fiber segment index to adjust for investors' losses.

---

[31] In the case where the defendant is the listed company "Huangshi Dongbei", the Wuhan Intermediate Court recognized the date when a famous Chinese securities newspaper, the Securities Times, reported the misconducts as the revealing date.

In American class action brought under the Rule 10b-5, the damages are calculated with the out-of-pocket model.[32] The investors are entitled to the difference between the "intrinsic value" of and the price paid for the shares. The former is a hypothetical amount, which equals the price absent the securities fraud.[33] However, unlike individual litigation, where the buying and selling prices and the trading volume are easy to obtain, class action pools a large number of plaintiffs, and their exact trading information is impossible to obtain by the class representative. Hence, the total damage is estimated in two steps with theoretical models. First, the per-share loss should be estimated to reflect the proportion of the market price that is ascribed to fraudulent behavior.[34] Normally, the event studies model will be used to construct the theoretical daily return of a given stock at the revealing date, which is the one predicted with the previous daily return and market return.[35] It is the "normal" daily return without the revelation of misconduct. The per-share loss will be the abnormal return on the revealing date, which is the difference between the actual daily return and the theoretical daily return. Second, the aggregate number of shares in the class should be estimated to reflect the amount that is impacted by fraudulent behavior. The difficulty is in the exclusion of frequent traders, who might trade in-and-out within the class period.[36] Several statistical models, such as the proportional trading model and accelerated trading model, were employed to estimate the aggregate number of shares.[37]

6.4   Collective Action Hypothesis, Sample and Identification

As discussed in the previous sections, harmed shareholders suffer from significant institutional obstacles for obtaining judiciary relief. In such "massive torts" cases, the average expected benefits from litigation are limited, although aggregate compensation might be of significant size. It is hence hypothesized that investors tend to suffer from significant collective action problems. This subsection empirically tests the hypothesis using a natural experimental research design.[38] The SPC's 2002 Notice was issued to change its prior position on the tort cases due to misrepresentation, which was stipulated in SPC's 2001 Notice and required that lower courts reject hearing such cases and explicitly allowed private securities suits to be accepted for the first time. Hence, the event that SPC's 2002 Notice was released represents an

---

[32] Alexander [15].

[33] Fischel [16].

[34] Fisch et al. [17].

[35] Gelbach et al. [18].

[36] Unlike in China where shares are held by real-name accounts, shares in the American market are held by brokers in street names. It is consequently impossible to obtain a share-by-share trading record, see Alexander [19].

[37] Koslow [20].

[38] Angrist and Pischke [21].

external shock to the securities investor that they are granted with the *de facto* rights to pursue civil compensation.[39]

A unique institutional setting of the Chinese stock market is that a small percentage of listed companies issued legally identical "twin A/B-shares". SPC's 2002 Notice governs disputes concerning shareholders holding both types of shares. A/B-shares are both ordinary shares with the same voting and dividend rights, but the transactions, dividend payments, trades, and quotes of B-shares are conducted in foreign currencies: Shanghai B-shares are denominated in U.S. dollars, and Shenzhen B-shares are denominated in Hong Kong dollars, which generates an interesting institutional variation that could be employed to test the market responses to the private enforcement system.[40]

Most investors in the A-share market are small retail investors, who hold limited interests in a listed company and adopt a speculative strategy.[41] As shown in the previous subsection, these retail investors suffer from collective action problems and are "rationally apathetic" to bringing private securities litigations, even with administrative sanctions. Given the significant costs, it would be less cost effective for them to pursue compensation than to sell the stock and "vote with their feet". Hence, the right to bring private litigation is likely worthless to retail investors in the A-share market.

In contrast, both foreign and domestic institutional investors have greater stakes at risk in the B-share market. Bohl et al. have noted that "wealthier Chinese are more likely to have the U.S. dollar accounts necessary to engage in B-share trading", and they usually invest in the B-share market through privately managed investment funds.[42] In their study on investors' trading patterns, Chan et al. confirm that stocks in the B-share market are held and traded in larger volumes than those in the A-share market[43] because institutional investors trade in larger sizes in the B-share market.[44] Due to their higher expected return, institutional investors have stronger incentives to overcome the collective action problem and are expected to pursue civil compensation. Of course, they are not bound to use the court system if it is too expensive and could seek alternative mechanisms, such as negotiating settlement

---

[39] The shock-based research design is popular among the empirical law and financial scholarship, see Atanasov and Black [22].

[40] Before February 19, 2001, A/B-share markets were completely segmented. Only domestic investors were permitted to trade on the A-share market, whereas foreign investors were permitted to trade on the B-share market. The restrictions were partially lifted thereafter: Domestic investors could trade on the B-share market, although foreign investors were still prohibited from trading on the A-share market. A popular strategy for domestic investors is to invest through privately managed investment funds, which raise U.S. dollars and Hong Kong dollars from the rich in the grey market.

[41] Mei et al. [23].

[42] Bohl et al. [24].

[43] Kalok Chan et al. [25].

[44] Part of the difference in trading patterns could be ascribed to institutional factors. The minimum trading volume of B-shares is 1000 shares, approximately ten times greater than that of A-shares on the SHSE. However, the minimum trading volume of B-shares is 100 shares, the same as that of A-shares on the SZSE.

agreements with potential defendants. The expected compensation from the court system is important for the bargaining process because it is a reference point for the agreement.

This subsection tests the collective action hypothesis by the returns of the portfolio of B-shares and that of A-shares issued by the same firm during the event windows. It is hypothesized that the former will gain positive abnormal returns relative to the latter because the collective action problem is better handled in the B-share market. The sample employed is mainly a group of listed companies issuing twin A/B-shares. The following algorithm was adopted to select the sample shares. First, we collect data for all A/B-shares listed on the SHSE and SZSE, which undertook their IPOs before December 31, 2001, from Wind Information Co., Ltd., one of the major providers of financial data for listed companies in China.[45] Then, we exclude those stocks that suspended trading on January 15, 2002. Finally, firms issuing only A-shares or B-shares were excluded. As a result, our main dataset includes 162 A/B-shares issued by 81 listed companies. One potential caveat, which could compromise the external validity of our analysis, is that two-thirds of our sample firms are located in Guangdong Province and the city of Shanghai, where the two exchanges are located.

In our natural experimental setup, B-shares expected to be affected significantly by SPC's 2002 Notice are the treatment group, whereas A-shares are the control group, which also serves as the benchmark when estimating the abnormal returns. Hence, a dummy variable TREATMENT is created to indicate whether a given share is a B-share or A-share. If it is a B-share, we set TREATMENT to 1 and 0 otherwise. We use two different event windows, 1 day and 3 days $[-1, 1]$, where Day 0 is January 15th, 2002, to calculate the cumulative return (CR), which is then employed as the dependent variable to test the collective action hypothesis.

To adjust for the differences in pretreatment features, we also controlled for the following set of variables in our multivariate models. First, the A/B-shares issued by the same firm could differ in their liquidity, as a result of which the daily turnover ratio (TURNOVER) averaged over half a year prior to the event date, from July 15, 2001 to January 14, 2002, was included. In addition, given the fixed costs of filing private litigation, only high expected value claims are worth pursuing.[46] Hence, we included the market capitalization (MCAP) of listed companies. Third, firms reporting higher profits in the previous year are more likely to have enough assets to pay for compensation to aggrieved investors. Consequently, we included the earnings per share (EPS) as reported in the 2001 annual report. Fourth, state-owned enterprises might have a particularly large influence on local courts, which should increase the expected costs of private litigation and discourage investors from seeking compensation. We, therefore, included the percentage of shares held by the state in a given firm (STATE).

Sixth, it is found that listed companies having high leverage ratios are more likely to commit financial misrepresentations.[47] Hence, we included the liability to

---

[45] We obtain the data for 1254 listed A/B-shares, among which 114 are B-shares and 1140 are A-shares.

[46] Choi [12].

[47] Firth et al. [26].

Table 6.3 Variable definitions and summary statistics

Variable	N	Mean	Std. dev	Definition
$CR_{(0)}$	162	−1.95	2.31	Raw cumulative share price return on the event day
$CR_{(-1,1)}$	162	−4.19	4.08	Raw cumulative share price return over the 3-day event window
TREATMENT	162	0.50	0.50	Dummy variable (=1 for B-share, 0 otherwise)
TURNOVER	162	0.83	0.40	Average daily turnover ratio over half a year prior to the event date
MCAP	162	3.59	0.22	Logarithm of market capitalization in million RMB as of 14th Jan., 2002
EPS	162	0.10	0.15	Earnings per share as reported in the 2001 semi-annual financial report
STATE	162	35.61	21.94	The percentage of shares held by the government
CE2001	162	7.00	2.42	The regional judiciary efficiency level as reported in Fan and Wang (2003)
LARATIO	162	47.25	20.26	The liability to asset ratio as reported in the 2001 semi-annual financial report
PB	162	5.00	7.54	The price to book ratio as reported in the 2001 semi-annual financial report
ROE	162	0.75	20.97	The return on equity ratio as reported in the 2001 semi-annual financial report

asset ratio (LARATIO), as reported in the half-year report in 2001. Seventh, we also controlled for two financial indicators, the price to book ratio (PB) proxy for growth opportunities and return on equity (ROE), as reported in the 2001 semiannual financial report. Finally, industrial dummies were included to control for possible industry fixed effects. The descriptive statistics and definitions of these variables are reported in Table 6.3.

6.5   Empirical Findings

This section presents the empirical results testing the collective action hypothesis. Table 6.4 reports the OLS regression outputs with CRs as dependent variables utilizing our main sample of 162 stocks. Columns 2–3 present the basic regressions with 1-day and 3-day CRs against TREATMENT, industrial dummies and a constant term. On the event date, the group of B-shares gains approximately 1.21% more in market value compared to that of A-shares, significant at the 1% level, as shown in the second column. The positive treatment effect for B-shares increases to 2.42% when the event window is set to 3 days. The results of basic regressions are consistent with the collective action hypothesis, which states that investors in the

Table 6.4 Regression outputs testing collective action hypothesis

Variable	$CR_{(0)}$	$CR_{(-1,1)}$	$CR_{(0)}$	$CR_{(-1,1)}$	$CR_{(0)}$	$CR_{(-1,1)}$
TREATMENT	1.21***	2.42***	1.30***	2.45***	1.18***	2.08***
	(0.34)	(0.61)	(0.34)	(0.60)	(0.35)	(0.61)
TURNOVER			−1.04*	−0.43	−0.90	0.21
			(0.57)	(0.95)	(0.60)	(0.89)
CE2001			0.013	0.072	0.015	0.089
			(0.084)	(0.16)	(0.082)	(0.15)
EPS			1.15	3.90*	0.54	1.70
			(0.91)	(2.26)	(0.91)	(2.22)
MCAP			1.47*	3.89***	1.53*	3.68***
			(0.78)	(1.24)	(0.82)	(1.30)
STATE			−0.012	−0.014	−0.016*	−0.02
			(0.008)	(0.014)	(0.0086)	(0.014)
LARATIO					0.012	0.021
					(0.011)	(0.018)
PB					−0.034**	−0.11***
					(0.014)	(0.023)
ROE					0.015***	0.048***
					(0.005)	(0.0089)
Constant	−1.57***	−4.32***	−6.37**	−18.91 ***	−6.80**	−18.58***
	(0.42)	(1.02)	(2.88)	(4.72)	(3.11)	(5.08)
Industrial dummies	Included	Included	Included	Included	Included	Included
Observations	162	162	162	162	162	162
R^2	0.1537	0.1397	0.2315	0.2246	0.2528	0.2984

Note (1) The robust standard error is reported in parentheses
(2) *, **, *** indicate 10%, 5%, and 1% levels of significance, respectively

B-share market value the right to seek civil compensation higher than those in the A-share market.

The literature has shown that the potential biases of the estimated treatment effects will be reduced if pre-event features are controlled for.[48] We thus first included the variable TURNOVER proxy for the difference in liquidity between A-shares and B-shares in our model specification.[49] Domestic investors have been allowed to buy and sell B-shares since February 19, 2001, which led to a sharp increase in the trading volume in the B-share market. The average daily turnover ratio for B-shares is 0.87 and that for A-shares is 0.79. Additionally, we included MCAP, EPS, STATE and CE2001 to control for the firm-specific characteristics that could influence the expected costs and benefits of private litigations, the results of which are shown in Columns 4–5.

---

[48] Rubin [27].
[49] Ho et al. [28].

The results are similar to those of the basic regressions. In Column 4, the treatment effect for the group of B-shares increases to approximately 1.30% on the event date and is highly significant (t-stat = 3.82). The variable TURNOVER is shown to have significant negative coefficients, which suggests that more liquid stocks actually gain less on the event date. Furthermore, consistent with the findings of Choi [12], larger firms indeed experience higher treatment effects on the event day, as the coefficient of the MCAP is significant and positive. Although slightly insignificant (p value = 0.138), the STATE variable has a negative coefficient, which is in accordance with the prediction that governmental connections should have negative effects on the expected net profits of private litigations. CE2001 is insignificant and indicates that it does not influence absolute daily returns. In Column 5, the coefficient for TREATMENT is increased to 2.45% during the 3-day event window (t-stat = 4.07). The liquidity proxy, TURNOVER, is no longer significant, but the MCAP proxy for the size of the firm and the EPS proxy for profitability are both significant and positive in magnitude.

Finally, we included controls for additional pre-event financial indicators, LARATIO, PB and ROE, the results of which are reported in Columns 6–7. Generally, the empirical outputs are consistent with those reported in previous columns. The coefficients of TREATMENT are positive and significant but adjusted downwards. The variable MCAP is significant in both columns, which provides strong evidence for the size effects. The coefficients of STATE are negative. The coefficient is significant in Column 5, although the reported p-value in Column 6 is slightly larger than the 10% significance level (p-value = 0.118).

The significant and positive coefficients of the variable TREATMENT confirm the collective action hypothesis, which hypothesizes that the group of B-shares gains a positive treatment effect relative to that of A-shares issued by the same firms. We demonstrate that private enforcement rights are valued higher by investors in the B-share market, where the majority are institutional investors, including foreign institutional investors and privately managed investment funds, which hold and trade in large volumes. In the B-share market, investors face different payoffs from private litigations and have higher expected returns from seeking civil compensation. Thus, they are more likely to exercise the right to seek civil compensation granted by SPC's 2002 Notice and assign higher value to such rights, which was designed primarily to compensate aggrieved investors suffering from misrepresentations by listed companies.

References

1. Pistor, K., & Xu, C. (2005). Governing Stock markets in transition economies: Lessons from China. *American Law and Economics Review, 7*(1), 184–210.
2. Hutchens, W. (2003). Private securities litigation in China: material disclosure about China's legal system. *University of Pennsylvania Journal of International Economic Law, 24*, 599–690.
3. Cox, J. D. (1997). Making securities fraud class actions virtuous. *Arizona Law Review, 39*, 497–524.

4. Choi, S. J. (2004). The evidence on securities class actions. *Vanderbilt Law Review, 57*, 1465–1526.
5. Lu, G. (2003). Private enforcement of securities fraud law in China: A critique of the supreme people's court 2003 provisions concerning private securities litigation. *Pacific Rim Law and Policy Journal, 12*, 781–806.
6. Guo, L., & Ong, A. (2009). The fledgling securities fraud litigation in China. *Hong Kong Law Journal, 39*, 697–718.
7. Huang, R. H. (2013). Private enforcement of securities law in China: A ten-year retrospective and empirical assessment. *American Journal of Comparative Law, 61*(4), 757–798.
8. Layton, M. A. (2008). Is private securities litigation essential for the development of China's stock markets? *New York University Law Review, 83*, 1948–1978.
9. Macey, J., Miller, G., Mitchell, M., & Netter, J. (1991). Lessons from financial economics: Materiality, reliance and extending the reach of *Basic v. Levinson. Faculty Scholarship Series, 77*, 1017–1021.
10. Liu, Z., Wong, T.J., Yi, Y., Zhang, T. (2021). Authoritarian transparency: China's missing cases in court disclosure. *Journal of Comparative Economics*, forthcoming.
11. Armour, J., Black, B., Cheffins, B., & Nolan, R. (2009). Private enforcement of corporate law: An empirical comparison of the United Kingdom and the United States. *Journal of Empirical Legal Studies, 6*(4), 687–722.
12. Choi, S. J. (2007). Do the merits matter less after the private securities litigation reform act? *Journal of Law, Economics, & Organization, 23*(3), 598–626.
13. Bebchuk, L. A. (1988). Suing solely to extract a settlement offer. *The Journal of Legal Studies, 17*, 437–441.
14. Fisch, J. E. (2009). Confronting the circularity problem in private securities litigation. *Wisconsin Law Review, 2009*, 333–350.
15. Alexander, J. C. (1996). Rethinking damages in securities class actions. *Stanford Law Review, 48*, 1487–1537.
16. Fischel, D. R. (1982). Use of modern finance theory in securities fraud cases involving actively traded securities. *The Business Lawyer, 38*, 1–20.
17. Fisch, J. E., Gelbach, J. B., & Klick, J. (2018). The logic and limits of event studies in securities fraud litigation. *Texas Law Review, 2018*, 553–618.
18. Gelbach, J. B., Helland, E., & Klick, J. (2013). Valid inference in single-firm, single-event studies. *American Law and Economics Reviews, 15*, 495–496.
19. Alexander, J. C. (1994). The value of bad news in securities class actions. *UCLA Law Review, 41*, 1421–1470.
20. Koslow, J. (1991). Estimating aggregate damages in class-action litigation under rule l0b–5 for purposes of settlement. *Fordham Law Review, 59*, 811–842.
21. Angrist, J. D., & Pischke, J.-S. (2009). *Mostly harmless econometrics: An empiricist's companion.* Princeton University Press.
22. Atanasov, V. A., & Black, B. S. (2016). Shock-based causal inference in corporate finance and accounting research. *Critical Finance Review, 5*(2), 207–304.
23. Mei, J., Scheinkman, J., & Xiong, W. (2009). Speculative trading and stock prices: Evidence from Chinese A-B share premia. *Annals of Economics and Finance, 10*(2), 225–255.
24. Bohl, M. T., Schuppli, M., & Siklos, P. L. (2010). Stock return seasonalities and investor structure: Evidence from China's B-share markets. *China Economic Review, 21*(1), 190–201.
25. Chan, K., Menkveld, A. J., & Yang, Z. (2008). Information asymmetry and asset prices: Evidence from the China foreign share discount. *Journal of Finance, 63*(1), 159–196.
26. Firth, M., Rui, O. M., & Wu, W. (2011). Cooking the books: Recipes and costs of falsified financial statements in China. *Journal of Corporate Finance, 17*(2), 371–390.
27. Rubin, D. B. (1973). The use of matched sampling and regression adjustment to remove bias in observational studies. *Biometrics, 29*(1), 185–203.
28. Ho, D. E., Imai, K., King, G., & Stuart, E. A. (2007). Matching as nonparametric preprocessing for reducing model dependence in parametric causal inference. *Political Analysis, 15*, 199–236.

Chapter 7
Securities Law of 2019 and the Enhanced Private Enforcement Regime

From the perspective of the "rule on the book", the Securities Law of 2019 has significantly changed the landscape of private enforcement in China and improved the efficiency concerning securities litigation. After the Securities Law of 2019, a multidimensional securities litigation system was formed, which comprises individual litigation, "opt-in" regular representative litigation and "opt-out" special representative litigation. The last one is also called "Chinese class action". This chapter examines the institutional innovations of the Securities Law of 2019, the typical cases adjudicated thereafter, and the market response to both the new rules and judgments.

7.1 Securities Law of 2019 and Multidimensional Securities Litigation System

The Securities Law of 2019 was amended against the background of registration reform, which tries to increase market efficiency in allocating securities resources. The registration reform was proposed on 12 November 2014, when the Third Plenary Session of the 18th CPC Central Committee issued the Decision on the Major Issues concerning Comprehensively Deepening Reform.[1] The Decision for the first time incorporates the registration reform in the party policy document and provides strong political support for the reform. But there was no consensus on the content of registration reform, which leads to a heated academic debate. The concept of IPO registration system was borrowed from the U.S. securities market, and the removal of entry regulation was placed at the central of the discussion. It is argued that the securities regulators should only focus on the completeness of the application materials, and pay no attention to their merits. But the securities market went through a stock

---

[1] See Zhonggong Zhongyang Guanyu Quanmian Shenhua Gaige Ruogan Zhongda Wenti De Jueding, available at http://www.beijingreview.com.cn/2009news/wenujian/2014-01/24/content_5 92979.htm (Last accessed 31 October, 2021).

© The Author(s), under exclusive license to Springer Nature Singapore Pte Ltd. 2022
W. Xu, *The Enforcement of Securities Law in China*,
https://doi.org/10.1007/978-981-19-0904-7_7

market crash in 2015, and the legislature was alerted to the devastated securities market. Consequently, the final revision was a balance between the risks and benefits of financial liberalization.[2]

The Securities Law of 2019 established a separate new chapter titled "Investor Protection". In this section, Article 95 lays down the foundation for a multidimensional securities litigation system and systematically increases its efficiency. Section 1 specifies that for civil litigation against the same securities fraud misconduct, if there are many plaintiffs and/or defendants, the case could be adjudicated by way of representative litigation. Section 2 stipulates that if the representative litigation has potential plaintiffs, who have been harmed by securities misconduct and with similar appeals for civil compensation, the courts could make public announcements and explain the case information and notify investors to register and participate in the representative litigation. The judgements and rulings made in the case are binding for registered investors. Section 3 further lays down the foundation for the "Chinese class action" and states that the investor protection agency, which has obtained the authorization of more than 50 investors, could serve as the representative in the representative litigation, as stipulated in Section 2. This investor protection agency could obtain a list of qualified plaintiffs from securities registration and clearing institutions. Those investors failing to explicitly quit the representative class are deemed to automatically join the representative litigation.

SPC later issued SPC's 2020 Provisions and stipulated details about the multidimensional securities litigation system, which significantly revised the framework-established SPC's 2003 Provisions. Article 1 of SPC's 2020 Provisions expands the scope of qualified investors and includes those investors harmed by misrepresentation, insider trading and market manipulation. It further divides representative litigation into regular representative litigation, which is governed by Article 53 and Article 54 of the Law of Civil Procedure and Section 1 and Section 2 of Article 95 of the Securities Law of 2019, and special representative litigation, which is governed by Section 3 of Article 95 of the Securities Law of 2019. The former could be further divided into two types of proceedings, i.e. the one with a determined number of plaintiffs and the one with an indetermined number of plaintiffs at the stage of filing the lawsuits.

For the jurisdiction of securities litigation, Article 2 makes a significant change concerning special representative litigation, which should be heard by intermediate courts or specialized financial courts in the regions where securities exchanges or securities trading venues approved by the State Council that trade the concerned securities are located. Hence, only the intermediate court or specialized financial court in Beijing, Guangzhou and Shanghai enjoy the jurisdiction over the special representative litigation. The institutional reform responds to the criticism that the court system in certain regions lacks the expertise to adjudicate civil litigations concerning securities fraud misconduct and might be subject to governmental influence and hence

---

[2] See The Report of the Law Committee of the National People's Congress on the Revision of the Securities Law (Draft Amendment), available at http://www.npc.gov.cn/npc/c30834/202001/f80cb744b0964ab8aafd0e1a8142d99f.shtml (Last accessed 31 October, 2021).

biased against harmed investors. The new jurisdictional rules set by the SPC's 2020 Provisions centralize the jurisdictions of those cases with the largest stakes and mitigate local protectionism. The courts in these regions also have the highest expertise in resolving financial disputes. It is expected that the reform could significantly improve the efficiency of harmed investors for obtaining judiciary relief.

Article 5 of the SPC's 2020 Provisions further specifies the requirements for applying the representative litigation.[3] First, there should be more than 10 plaintiffs or defendants, and the pleadings should be qualified for Article 119 of the Law of Civil Procedure and the criteria for joint suits. Second, the statement of charges should explicitly name 2 to 5 representatives, which qualify for the criteria set by Article 12 of the SPC's 2020 Provisions. Third, the plaintiffs should submit with the statement of charges together with the administrative sanction decisions, criminal judgements, disciplinary or self-regulatory sanctions issued by the stock exchanges and securities trading venues approved by the State Council against the defendants, or self-pleading material of the defendants as the preliminary evidence for the existence of securities misconducts. This is a significant leap forwards in the satisfaction of litigation prerequisites compared to those stipulated in the SPC's 2003 Provisions, which only admits administrative sanctions and criminal judgements. As shown in the previous sections, the CSRC and its ROs and stock exchanges have issued hundreds of sanctions each year, which significantly increases the scope of private enforcement. If the aforementioned criteria are not satisfied, the court should not adjudicate the case with representative litigation but individual litigation.

The court has played an active monitoring role in representative litigation. Article 6 of the SPC's 2020 Provisions specifies the rules governing the identification of the plaintiffs in those cases with indetermined plaintiffs at the pleading stage. The adjudicating court has the authority to read case documents, investigate and assemble hearings to review the nature and facts of tortious misconduct, and delineate the scope of the individuals with the right to litigate by way of ruling within 30 days after it accepts the case before it makes the announcement for plaintiff registration. Those having disputes about the ruling should appeal to the upper court within 10 days after receiving the ruling, and the upper court should rule within 15 days after receiving the appeal. Article 9 furthermore grants the court the authority to review the qualification of the registered rightsholder and could reject to confirm its plaintiff status.

Furthermore, the selection of representatives is correlated with the incentives and qualification of the plaintiffs. Article 12 emphasizes that representatives should have significant stakes and that they or their lawyers should have the competence and expertise to participate in litigation. However, investor protection agencies and their staff or agents assigned by such agencies to help investors participate in the trial can be appointed as representatives without satisfying the aforementioned conditions. The selection of the representatives follows the principle of "one plaintiff one vote", and the selected representative should obtain more than 50% of the plaintiffs participating

---

[3] Compared to the previous judiciary practice, Chinese courts are uncertain about the application of the representative litigation and might be reluctant to transfer individual suits to representative litigation in afraid that the litigation might turn into a mass event.

in the voting. If all candidates fail to obtain such a quota, the second selection should be carried out with the candidates who have obtained the top five votes in the first selection. If the plaintiff class cannot choose the representatives, the court could appoint the representative. After the selection of the representative, the court should announce the results, and plaintiffs could actively quit the litigation and bring the suit independently.[4]

In calculating the losses, Article 24 states that with the application of litigants, the court could consult with a professional institution, which is randomly selected or appointed by both parties, to estimate the investment losses and losses due to factors other than securities misconduct. If litigants do not apply, but the court thinks that it is necessary and could randomly select professional institutions to provide consulting services. The opinions issued by professional institutions should be subjected to the debates of both parties.

The Third Part of SPC's 2020 Provisions stipulates the rules governing special representative litigation. Article 32 stipulates that regular representative litigation is transformed to special representative litigation if the investor protection agency has successfully obtained authorization from more than 50 investors during the announcement period for rightsholder registration. The CSRC also issued the Notice on the Participation of Investor Protection Agencies in Special Representatives Litigation (Henceforth Notice on the Participation of Investor Protection Agencies) in July 2021.[5] The Notice on the Participation of Investor Protection Agencies explicitly assigns the China Securities Investor Services Centre and China Securities Investor Protection Fund, both of which are nonprofit organizations and under the direct administration of the CSRC, as the agency to participate in special representative litigation.[6] In practice, the China Securities Investor Services Centre seems to assume a more active role. Because the investor protection agency has discretion over the acceptance of authorization from harmed investors, Article 4 of the Notice provides some principles guiding its choice. It should select those cases with significant national adverse impacts, and at the same time, the defendants should have the ability to pay civil compensation and sanctioned administratively or criminally. Because the special representative follows different jurisdictional rules, the court first accepting the case could have no jurisdiction over special representative litigation and hence should transfer it to the one with jurisdiction or to the one designated by the SPC.

The procedure to confirm the plaintiff class is different from the regular one and adopts the "opt-out" rule. The adjudicating court should announce the details of the investor protection agency in addition to those required by Article 7 of the SPC's 2020 Provisions. The announcement should also notice investors about the consequence of failing to opt out litigation. Article 34 specifies that investors who would not like

---

[4] Article 16 of SPC's 2020 Provisions.

[5] See Guanyu Zuohao Touzizhe Baohu Jigou Canjia Zhengquan Jiufen Tebie Daibiaoren Susong Xiangguan Gongzuo De Tongzhi, available at http://www.csrc.gov.cn/newsite/zjhxwfb/xwdd/202 007/t20200731_380952.html (Last accessed 31 October, 2021).

[6] Article 2 of the Notice on the Participation of Investor Protection Agencies.

to participate in the representative litigation should submit quit statements within 15 days after the expiration of the announcement period. Otherwise, they are regarded as agreeing to participate in litigation.

The special representative litigations at least have the following two special features. First, the investor protection agency could obtain the list of qualified rightsholders according to the scope decided by the adjudicating court from the China Securities Depository and Clearing Corporation LTD,[7] which is also disclosed to the general public. The court should register these rightsholders as the plaintiffs of the cases and inform them. The obvious advantage of such a rule is the precision of the compensation, in the sense that if the plaintiffs are granted the right to civil compensation, the court could decide the exact amount of compensation for each of the members in the plaintiff class. This is because, on the one hand, Chinese securities law requires that securities accounts be held under the real name, which could be individuals or organizations; on the other hand, their trading information is transparent to the court, and hence, their losses could be calculated according to the rules set by SPC's 2003 Provisions.

The disadvantage of such a rule is also obvious. If the court mistakes the scope for rightsholders, the investor protection agency obtains an incorrect list of harmed investors. This matters when the defendants have enjoyed strong political protection, and the court is subject to the influence of local government. It is likely that the court will delineate a scope with a small expected civil compensation and exclude certain investors from the civil compensation. Although in theory these investors still have the rights to bring about individual suits, the court is unlikely to grant them civil compensation considering that they are excluded from the qualified plaintiffs in its prior ruling.

Second, in the special representative litigation, the parties are exempted from paying the court fee in advance. If the plaintiffs completely or partially lose the case and have to pay court fees, they could apply for a reduction or exemption of such fees. The court will consider the application based on the financial conditions of the plaintiffs in accordance with the Measures for Payment of Litigation Costs.[8] This treatment considers the "opt-out" feature of the special representative litigation. On the one hand, some of the plaintiffs are automatically included in the plaintiff class, and it would be difficult to charge them with the court fee; on the other hand, if only those active investors are charged with the court fee, they are likely to be discouraged from bringing the suit in the first place and waiting for other investors to act first. The free-rider problem might compromise institutional innovation and reduce the frequency of special representative litigation.

---

[7] Article 10 of the Notice on the Participation of Investor Protection Agencies.

[8] Article 39 of SPC's 2020 Provisions.

7.2   Regular Representative Litigation: Wuyang Case

The importance of private enforcement has been emphasized after the promulgation of the Securities Law for its function of deterrence and compensation. Policymakers have repeatedly stressed that investor protection is among the primary goals of securities regulation, and civil litigation is an instrument for compensating harmed investors and making violators pay for their misconduct. This subsection discusses one case litigated with regular representative litigation.

7.2.1   *The Corporate Bond Sector and Wu Yang Misrepresentation Case*

The bond market has been growing exponentially post the Subprime Mortgage Crisis and reached the second largest in the world in 2019. Its fast growth has accumulated significant credit risks. The first default of the corporate bond only occurred in 2014, and a total of 696 corporate bonds were in default until the end of 2020.[9] Civil compensation matters little to investors when default bonds will be bailed out but maters significantly for investors when they will not be able to be paid fully by the issuers.

Wuyang Construction Group Co. LTD (henceforth Wuyang) is a private company in the real estate construction industry. On 10 August 2015, Wuyang announced the prospectus for the public issuance of company bonds to qualified investors. It issued two company bonds, the "15 Wuyang" (122423. SH) of 800 million RMB matured in three years with an interest rate of 7.48% on 14 August 2015, and the other one "15 Wuyang02" (122454. SH) of 560 million RMB matured in five years with an interest rate of 7.8% on 11 September 2015. Both bonds are listed on SHSE.

In the prospectus, net asset of Wuyang is estimated to be 3.7 billion RMB, and the net profit for the last three consecutive years are 145 million RMB, 187 million RMB and 199 million RMB, which is more than twice of the interests of the bond. Wuyang and its bonds are both rated AA by the Dagong Credit Rating Agency. Interest was regularly paid until Wuyang declared that it was unable to pay its debt on 14 August 2017. The issuer and related parties were investigated by the CSRC in August 2017, and on 6 July 2018, Wuyang and its controllers and other related individuals were sanctioned by the CSRC administratively.

It becomes the first company bond issuer that its bond is in default and at the same time sanctioned administratively by the CSRC. As disclosed in the administrative sanction, Wuyang conducted the following misconducts. First, it falsified its financial statements to defraud regulators to obtain entry to issue company bonds. Its distributable profits in the most recent three years were not enough to pay the

---

[9] The Chinese bond market has a tradition of offering implicit guarantee and the defaulted bonds are all fully paid before 2014 by either the shareholders of the issuers, the underwriters or the local governments, see Livingston [1].

interests in the first year and hence are not qualified for company bond issuance, as stipulated in Article 16 of the Securities Law of 2014. However, Wuyang offset the account payables and account receivables of the construction projects and hence reduced the size of the bad debt provision to increase its profits.

The case was brought to the Hangzhou Intermediate Court and pleaded that the issuers and its controllers pay the damages for misrepresentation in the issuance process and required that the financial intermediaries, including Debang Securities Firm, Daxin Accounting Firm, Jintiancheng Law Firm and Dagong Credit Rating Agency, assume joint and several obligations. The Hangzhou Intermediate Court issued the judgement of the First Instance at the end of 2020 and ruled that the issuers and its controllers should repay the principle and unpaid interests, the underwriter and the accounting firm assume the full joint and several obligation of the said liability, and the law firm and the credit rating agency assume the joint and several obligation of the said liability in the ranges of 5% and 10%, respectively.[10] The defendants of the First Instance all appealed to the Higher People's Court of Zhejiang Province, and the case was accepted on 3 March 2021. The judgement was made on 22 September 2021, and the decision made at the First Instance was upheld. According to the Civil Procedural Law, the decision of the Second Instance is final, although the losing parties could appeal to the SPC for a retrial.

7.2.2 The Debatable Elements About the Compensation Awarded

The standings taken by Chinese courts in the Wuyang case experience a U-turn and seem to be extremely investor friendly, and nearly all major parties participating in the bond issuance are required to bail investors out. Judiciary attitudes are understandable considering the national policy to develop securities markets and promote investor protection. In particular, the Opinions on Cracking down on Securities Misconducts was jointly issued by the General Office of the CPC Central Committee and that of the State Council in July 2021. In the substantive dimension, the case is adjudicated according to the Securities Law of 2014 because misconduct was performed before the most recent revision of the Securities Law in 2019; however, in the procedural dimension, the case is adjudicated with the representative litigation specified in Article 95 of the Securities Law of 2019. The Hangzhou Intermediate Court applied the procedure of representative litigation as specified and called for qualified harmed investors to join the suit on 13 March 2020. Because the bond is offered to qualified individual and institutional investors, who hold significantly higher stakes than those retail investors in the stock market, the collective action problem is not that severe. The representatives are selected on 30 June 2020, and the case was accepted on 13

---

[10] An interesting observation is that both Civil Code and Securities Law do not specify proportional joint and several obligations, but the Article 24 of the SPC's 2003 Provisions stipulates that the culpable should assume the liability according to the magnitude of its fault.

July 2020 with a plaintiff class size of 488 investors. According to the judgement released, the plaintiffs want the defendants to repay the principle and three times the unpaid interests calculated with the formulae specified in the debt contract, which amount to a civil compensation of more than 700 million RMB.

Article 69 of the Securities Law of 2014 specifies the strict liability for the issuers undertaking misrepresentations in the issuance process and requires that the losses due to the misrepresentation should be paid by the issuers; the controllers of the issuers should assume the joint and several obligations for the said tortious liability if they fail to prove that they have no faults.[11] Similarly, Article 173 of the Securities Law of 2019 specifies the joint and several obligations for the financial intermediaries that provide service in the securities issuance, listing and transaction and requires that they should assume joint and several obligations for the tortious liability assumed by the issuers should they fail to prove that they have no faults.[12]

The decision in the First Instance is made according to the Notes on the National Symposium for the Adjudication of Cases Concerning Bond Disputes (henceforth Notes on Bond Disputes),[13] which was issued by SPC to guide the adjudication of the cases concerning bond market disputes. However, the decision of the Wuyang case mistakes the breach of contractual obligations and the tortious liability of the issuer. The misrepresentations committed by Wuyang in the offering documents breached the contractual obligations and simultaneously resulted in a tortious liability to harm investors. According to Article 21 of the Notes on Bond Disputes, issuers and their controllers should repay the principal and unpaid interests as a contractual remedy to investors. On the one hand, Article 3 of the Notes on Bond Disputes has clarified that issuers conducting fraudulent issuance should assume tortious liability. Article 31 further delineates that financial intermediaries assisting issuance should assume joint and several obligations of tortious compensation to the limit proportional to their fault.

It is relatively less debatable that the issuer and its controllers have committed the misrepresentation, considering that they have already been sanctioned by the CSRC, but the calculation of the monetary damages and the allocation of the joint and several obligations disclosed in the judgements are worthy of further discussion. In the decision of the First Instance, the Hangzhou Intermediate Court mandated that the issuer and its controllers pay the principal and unpaid interests, and the amount is also used as the basis to calculate the joint and several obligations for the financial intermediaries. As discussed in the previous paragraphs, the issuer is in the bankruptcy procedure, and the plaintiffs are highly unlikely to recover much from the issuer and its controllers. Financial intermediaries will be the major sources of investor compensation. However, the contractual liability that the issuer and its controllers should pay for the principal and unpaid interests is not a proper basis

---

[11] This is now specified in the Article 85 of the Securities Law of 2019.

[12] This is now specified in the Article 163 of the Securities Law of 2019.

[13] See Quanguo Fayuan Shenli Zhaiquan Jiufen Anjian Zuotanhui Jiyao, available at http://www.court.gov.cn/zixun-xiangqing-241671.html (Last accessed 31 October, 2021).

to determine the joint and several obligations of financial intermediaries, which are only jointly responsible for tortious liability due to misrepresentation.

Hence, it is important to clarify the estimation of the tortious losses due to financial misrepresentations, which, according to the out-of-pocket model, is the difference between the "intrinsic value" of the bond and the price paid by investors. Because the defendant has conducted fraudulent issuance, the implementation date is straightforward and is chosen by the adjudicating court to be the issuance date of the bond. However, the identification of the revealing date should be subject to careful deliberation. In the decision of the First Instance, the date of 19 January 2018 is selected as the revealing date, when the CSRC issued the preliminary sanction decision. Considering that trading of both bonds issued by Wuyang was suspended in August 2017, those investors buying both company bonds prior to this date and holding them after the suspension are all regarded as qualified plaintiffs.

However, such selection of the revealing date by the adjudicating court is not without any questions. As specified in the SPC's 2003 Provisions, the revealing date is the first time when the market learns about misconduct. Hence, the selection should be based on the market information mix and the changes in the bond price. Figure 7.1 presents the daily return of the "15 Wuyang" and "15 Wuyang02" company bonds between 1 July 2016 and 10 August 2017, when the two bonds are permanently in the trading halt. It should be noted that the CSRC announced an administrative investigation on 11 August 2017. The administrative investigation is comparatively lengthy, and it is likely that the market information mix has already reflected the information.

By checking the announcements made by the issuers, it is found that prior to the selected revealing date, there exist multiple announcements and sanctions issued by SHSE that could warn the market about potential misconduct. On 27 April 2016, SHSE publicly criticized the issuer for a part of its fraudulent misconduct. The first is the inappropriate use of the fund raised. Wuyang transferred 1.048 billion RMB raised through bond issuance to an unrelated company, which later transferred the money to another company controlled by the controller of Wuyang, who used it to pay other debts. The second is the incomplete disclosure of ongoing litigations.

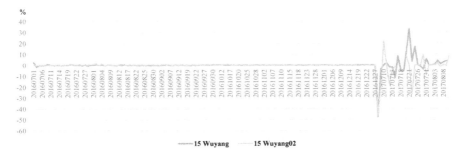

Fig. 7.1 The daily return of "15 Wuyang" and "15 Wuyang02" company bonds. *Source* Choice Information

The subsidiary of Wuyang was a defendant in one ongoing case, which could lead to an expected liability of more than 140 million RMB. However, in the issuance document, the size of restricted assets and contingent liability was only estimated to be 47.6 million RMB. Later, on 12 May 2016, Wuyang disclosed the receipt of the Disciplinary Decision issued by the SHSE, the content of which is the same as that in the public criticism.

Between 28 December 2016 and 6 July 2017, both bonds issued by Wuyang stopped trading, and a series of events that concern the fraudulent behaviors of the issuer and might influence its solvency were disclosed to the market. On 1 June 2017, the issuer disclosed that the stakes at Wuzhou Commercial Plaza Development Co., LTD, which held a valuable commercial real estate project, were disposed of. In addition, Debang Securities issued a warning letter documenting 16 risky events that might increase the credit risks of the issuer. For example, first, the issuer has not arranged sufficient fund to repay the company bond, and there is significant uncertainty concerning the payment of the principal and interests; second, individual investors could only sell and could not buy the company bond after it started trading again; third, the annual report of 2016 could not be disclosed; fourth, the issuer was on the Credit-broken Entity List of the National Court System, which discloses those entities failing to honor the judiciary judgements; fourth, the credit rating of the bond was adjusted downwards to AA- by Dagong credit rating agency, which also expressed concerns about the credit risks of the issuer.[14]

The bond price movement also supports that the market has already learned about potential misrepresentation. The market price has maintained a relatively stable movement, and the daily change has been within the range of 3% between the issuance of the bond and the date of 28 December 2016 when both bonds were stopped trading temporarily. For example, "15 Wuyang" was traded at 98.65 RMB on 27 December 2016, the last trading day before the suspension. However, on the first trading day after the temporary suspension, the market prices of "15 Wuyang" and "15 Wuyang02" declined by −47.29% and −46.75%, respectively, on 6 July 2017. It should be compelling evidence that the market has learned about the potential credit inflation of issuers and adjusted the market price to incorporate new information. It would be better justified if the revealing date is chosen to be the first trading date (6 July 2017) after the temporary suspension.

---

[14] The credit rating in Chinese bond market is highly coarse and 95% of the bond issued are rated AA and above, which is partly due to regulatory reliance on credit rating. The majority of the institutional buyers in the bond market prefer to invest in bond rated AA and above due to regulatory limits. In addition, Chinese credit rating industry has been criticized to be issuer friendly, and seldom adjusts credit ratings downward. Hence, from the market perspective, the negative rating adjustment is a big warning, see Xu and Liu [2].

7.3 Special Representative Litigation

SPC's 2020 Provisions have established two prominent institutional innovations of the special representative litigation. First, the China Securities Investor Services Centre is assigned with the role of lead plaintiff and has got the authority to decide whether the special representative litigation should be launched. Second, a unique jurisdictional rule is applied to the special representative litigation, which should be adjudicated by the financial courts or intermediate courts in the regions where the stock exchanges or national trading venues authorized by the State Council listing the concerned securities are located.

7.3.1 China Securities Investor Services Centre

China Securities Investor Services Centre was established in 2017 as a public agency under the supervision of the CSRC. The agency holds small stakes in all listed companies and is designed as an active player of corporate governance. It could improve the corporate governance and protect shareholder interests via both internal and external mechanisms. First, internally, Article 82 of the Guidelines for Corporate Governance of Listed Companies of 2018 stipulates that China Securities Investor Services Centre should use the shareholder rights to protect the interests of minority shareholders. On one hand, it could participate the annual shareholder conference and other shareholder meetings, and express independent opinions. According to the Article 90 of the Securities Law of 2019, the China Securities Investor Services Centre could publicly solicit proxy voting, and attend annual conference and vote on behalf of those investors. In 2018, it is reported that China Securities Investor Services Centre attended more than 100 annual conferences of listed companies.[15] Second, it can also use the shareholder inquiry rights and inspection rights as stipulated by the Company Law to uncover potential misconducts.

Second, externally, China Securities Investor Services Centre also actively or passively participates in litigations against various misconducts. On one hand, it could actively bring litigations against misconducts committed by listed companies or the controllers. Article 94 of the Securities Law of 2019 provides a special rule governing the derivative action initiated by China Securities Investor Services Centre, and stipulates that if the directors, supervisors, senior management or controllers have infringed legitimate interests of listed companies, China Securities Investor Services Centre could bring litigation against these culpable without satisfying the conditions specified by the Company Law.[16] For example, Haili Shengwu (SH: 603718), which is a listed company specializing in researching and producing veterinary drugs, was

---

[15] See China Securities Investor Services Centre Speaking for Minority Investors, available at http://www.gov.cn/xinwen/2019-03/13/content_5373424.htm (Last accessed 31 October, 2021).

[16] Article 151 of the Company Law requires that the plaintiffs of such litigations should hold at least 1% of total share for more than 180 days.

sued by the China Securities Investor Services Centre for misappropriately amending its charter and incorporate articles restricting the shareholder right to nominate directors. Shanghai Intermediate Court upheld the pleadings of the plaintiff and decided that the amendment was void in 2018.[17] On the other, it is specified by the Securities Law of 2019 as the "gatekeeper" of special representative litigation. China Securities Investor Services Centre has got the authority to transform certain regular representative litigations to special representative litigations, and serves as the statutory lead plaintiff.

The "gatekeeper" role of China Securities Investor Services Centre is mainly intended to contain the potential agency costs of American securities class action, which is accused of undermining the competitive advantage of the American securities market.[18] The controversy in such model is also manifested by the recent U.S. legislative proposals. The bill of Forced Arbitration Injustice Repeal Act, which was passed by the Democratic-controlled House of Representatives in 2019, would like to make any contractual agreements on barring class actions unenforceable and remove the most significant barrier for its application, whereas the bill of Fairness in Class Action Litigation Act aims to restrict the scope of class action.[19] The significant costs of American securities class action are caused by the agency relationship between shareholders and securities lawyers, which act as the "bounty hunter" and control the litigation.[20] The problem of incompatible incentives compromises the efficiency of such model. Securities lawyers tend to pursue their private total income, instead of maximizing compensation for shareholder class.

The cure proposed by PSLRA for the "run-away" securities class action is to reform the lead plaintiff rule, which requires the investors holding the largest stakes to serve as the lead plaintiff to control the litigation.[21] The shareholders holding the largest stakes are normally institutional shareholders, which are deemed to have sufficient incentives to participate the litigation. However, empirical studies find that the effects of the reform are at best mixed. With both court and lead plaintiff monitoring, the lawyers still tend to over bill their clients.[22] The institutional investors serving the lead plaintiffs rarely negotiate *ex ante* fee agreements with their counsel,[23] neither do they successfully control the size of lawyer fees *ex post*.[24] In addition, the litigation outcomes for plaintiffs do not seem to improve. Those innovative firms are subjective to higher litigation risks, which in turn tend to repress their innovative activities. But these activities are most beneficial to the long-term value of listed

---

[17] See China Securities Investor Services Centre Has Won the Case Against Haili Shengwu, available at https://www.163.com/money/article/DHFQSVBH00259ARN.html (Last accessed 31 October, 2021).

[18] Atkins [3].

[19] Faisman [4].

[20] Rubenstein [5].

[21] See S. REP. NO. 104-98 (1995).

[22] Choi et al. [6].

[23] Baker et al. [7].

[24] Choi et al. [8].

companies.[25] The securities lawyers also try to reach low-value settlements with defendant as fast as possible, which are not in the best interests of shareholder class.[26]

Weighing the costs and benefits of American class action, China takes a different model of controlled class action adopted by EU, and other jurisdictions.[27] For example, the European Union promulgated the rule of collective redress mechanism in 2020,[28] and allowed qualified entities instead of lawyers to bring representative litigation on behalf of harmed consumers. China modifies the model and forms the special representative litigation by replacing the non-profit organization with China Securities Investor Services Centre, a public agency approved and supervised by CSRC. The strategy takes the benefits of the American opt-out regime, which realizes the economy of scale to address mass tort case and maintains the consistency among the judgments awarded to different plaintiffs, and also avoids the costs of frivolous suits and the failure of damage distribution. But it also increases the connection between lead plaintiffs and the governmental agencies, and might compromises the independence of special representative litigation.

7.3.2 The Specialized Financial Court

The judiciary reform in the field of specialized court also improves the efficiency of representative litigation. The specialized court is regarded as one of the most important institutional innovations in the judiciary system.[29] The specialized courts have been established in various fields, including martial courts, intellectual property courts and others. Article 15 of the Law of the Court Organization, which was revised in 2018 to incorporate the recent reform in specialized courts, recognizes the legal status of financial courts as a type of specialized courts. The financial court is mainly built for the following reasons. First, financial disputes are highly specialized and adjudicating judges need to have relatively in-depth knowledge of financial markets and products. Second, the specialized financial court would help to accumulate specialized human resource, which will in turn increase the efficiency and fairness of disputes resolution.

The first specialized financial court could be dated back to 2008, when the Pudong District Court in Shanghai set up the financial tribunal to adjudicate financial disputes. After the Fifth National Financial Work Conference, SPC released Opinions on Further Strengthening Financial Adjudication in 2017, and encouraged lower courts

---

[25] Kempf and Spalt [9].

[26] Cooper [10].

[27] Lin and Xiang [11].

[28] See Directive (EU) 2020/1828 of the European Parliament and of the Council on Representative Actions for the Protection of the Collective Interests of Consumers.

[29] See SPC's Opinions on Deepening the Comprehensive Reform of the Judicial System (2019–2023), available at http://www.court.gov.cn/zixun-xiangqing-144202.html (Last accessed 31 October, 2021).

to set up specialized organizations to adjudicate financial disputes.[30] There are two main types of specialized organization for adjudicating financial disputes, one is financial tribunal, the other is financial court. The formal is set up in general courts, such as lower or intermediate courts, and is responsible for hearing financial disputes within the court's jurisdiction. For example, both Guangzhou Intermediate Court and Shenzhen Intermediate Court have set up financial tribunal as an independent internal division. The latter is a recent institutional innovation, and only includes Shanghai Financial Court and Beijing Financial Court. The formal is the first one of this type and was set up in March 2018 and its jurisdiction is increased to cover all financial disputes within that of the intermediate court in Shanghai. Beijing Financial Court was set up in March 2021. Until the end of 2018, the number of specialized financial courts and tribunals has reached nearly 300.[31]

Article 2 of the SPC's 2020 Provisions in addition offers a unique jurisdictional rule for special representative litigation, which should be adjudicated by the intermediate courts or specialized financial courts in the region where stock exchanges and national trading venues authorized by the State Council are located. Considering the locations of the stock exchanges and national trading venues, the special representative litigation will be heard by the Shanghai Financial Court, Beijing Financial Court and the financial tribunal of Guangzhou Intermediate Court and Shenzhen Intermediate Court. The arrangement significantly reduces the potential rent seeking behaviours which might compromise the independence of the court decision. The previous studies have argued that because listed companies are crucial to local economic development and have strong political ties, the adjudicating courts will be subject to strong external influence and deliver favorable judgments for defendants.[32] The specialized financial court and centralized jurisdictional rule together improve the efficiency and fairness of the securities private enforcement regime.

7.3.3 Kangmei Case

Because the Securities Law of 2019 was recently promulgated, the civil case against Kangmei Pharmaceutical Co., LTD (Henceforth Kangmei) is the first one adjudicated with the special representative litigation procedure. Kangmei (600518. SH), founded in 1997, is a private company specializing in the pharmaceutical industry. It successfully got listed on SHSE in 2001. Kangmei announced being under the investigation of the CSRC for its informational infractions on 29 December 2018. The CSRC issued the final sanction decision in May 2020 after holding a hearing according to the application of Kangmei on 22 April 2020. The CSRC sanctioned Kangmei for its misrepresentation in the annual reports released in 2016, 2017 and

---

[30] See Guanyu Jinyibu Jiaqiang Jinrong Shenpan Gongzuo De Ruogan Yijian, available at https://www.sohu.com/a/191296672_465600 (Last accessed 31 October, 2021).

[31] Li [12].

[32] Huang [13].

2018. First, it overstates annual sales of 9 billion RMB and net profits of 660 million RMB in the annual report of 2016; it further inflates annual sales of over 10 billion RMB and net profits of 1.3 billion RMB in the annual report of 2017; and it overstates annual sales of over 1.6 billion RMB and net profits of 165 million RMB in the annual report of 2018. Second, it also inflates the cash flow for a total of 88.6 billion RMB in the annual reports between 2016 and 2018. Third, fixed assets and real estate assets were inflated by 3.6 billion RMB and 2 billion RMB, respectively, in 2018. Finally, the size of related-party transactions was understated to be 11 billion RMB between 2016 and 2018. Kangmei and 22 affiliated individuals are sanctioned administratively.

The Guangzhou Intermediate Court accepted the pleadings of 11 investors against Kangmei and other related individuals on 31 December 2020. On 26 March 2021, the Guangzhou Intermediate Court announced the notice for the registration of litigation rights in regular representative litigation, and on the same day, the China Securities Investor Services Centre released the announcement for acceptance of special authorization from harmed investors in the Kangmei case.[33] Guangzhou Intermediate Court announced that the 11 plaintiffs first raising the case proposes the implementation date to be 20 April 2017, which is the date when Kangmei released its annual report of 2016, and the revealing date to be 16 October 2018, when the internet media has widely reported the misrepresentation of Kangmei.

The Guangzhou Intermediate Court regards investors buying the stock of Kangmei between 20 April 2017 and 15 October 2018 and holding the shares after 15 October 2018 to be the scope of qualified investors. The Court even designs an app named "Guangzhou Weifayuan" powered by WeChat, which is widely used, to reduce participation costs. The aforementioned period is also employed by the China Securities Investor Services Centre to delineate qualified investors in its announcement for soliciting investors' authorization.[34] Until 7 April 2021, the China Securities Investor Services Centre had received authorization from nearly 500 investors, and more than 300 investors met the preliminary selection criteria. Because the China Securities Investor Services Centre has successfully obtained authorizations from more than 50 investors, regular representative litigation is transformed to special representative litigation according to Section 3 of Article 95 of the Securities Law of 2019.

On 16 April 2021, the Guangzhou Intermediate Court issued an announcement for the registration of litigation rights in special representative litigation against Kangmei after the China Securities Investor Services Centre submitted the application for transforming regular representative litigation to special representative litigation on 8 April 2021. The China Securities Investor Services Centre later resorted to the China Securities Depository and Clearing Corporation for the list of qualified investors

---

[33] See Guangzhou Intermediate Court Has Announced the Registration for Regular Representative Litigation, available at https://www.investor.org.cn/rights_interests_protection/rights_protection_s ervice/repre_action/xxxaction/202103/t20210326_484901.shtml (Last accessed 31 October, 2021).

[34] See Explanations of China Securities Investor Services Centre on Soliciting Authorization from Harmed Investors in Kangmei, available at https://www.investor.org.cn/rights_interests_pro tection/rights_protection_service/repre_action/xxxaction/202103/t20210326_484900.shtml (Last accessed 31 October, 2021).

based on the period determined by the Guangzhou Intermediate Court. On 30 April 2021, the China Securities Investor Services Centre submitted the list of qualified investors.[35] The pretrial hearing was carried out on 28 May 2021, and the first trial was on 27 July 2021. The judgment of the first instance was delivered on November 12, 2021, and the plaintiffs were awarded a civil compensation of more than 2.45 billion RMB.

From the case of Kangmei, special representative litigation is an obvious improvement compared to previous individual litigation. The underlying logic is straightforward and to achieve the maximization of the costs to obtain civil compensation. The special representative litigation combines the "opt-in" design and the assignment of public agencies as the representative plaintiff. It takes advantage of class action to maximize the participating plaintiffs and hence improve the quality of investor compensation and assigns the China Securities Investor Services Centre to monitor and control the litigation process, which minimizes the potential costs due to frivolous suits and strike suits. Another unique advantage of the special representative litigation is that the China Securities Investor Services Centre could resort to the China Securities Depository and Clearing Corporation and obtain the list of qualified plaintiffs according to the period confirmed by the adjudicating courts. Such an arrangement improves the precision of investor compensation.

However, special representative litigation is at least subject to the following two debatable aspects. First, the identification of qualified plaintiffs is determined without going through a court trial. On the one hand, the SPC's 2020 Provisions have set a prerequisite that plaintiffs should provide preliminary evidence, which is the precondition for special representative litigation, so that the court will start regular representative litigation; on the other hand, the adjudicating court has already delineated the time period for the identification of harmed investors in the stage of the announcement for the registration of litigation rights in regular representative litigation. Because the implementation date and revealing date are the crucial elements for the identification of qualified plaintiffs and the scope of tortious loss, investor compensation is largely determined in this stage. Hence, special representative litigation is more likely to function as a centralized compensation determination and distribution process.

Second, the China Securities Investor Services Centre will have difficulty selecting the appropriate cases to initiate special representative litigation. Considering the cost effectiveness, it is impossible for the China Securities Investor Services Centre to participate in every case where more than 50 investors decide to authorize it to participate. As discussed in the previous chapters, the number of cases satisfying the admitting criteria of the representative litigations increases significantly because the SPC's 2020 Provisions has lowered the prerequisites and included those with disciplinary or self-regulatory sanctions and self-pleading materials, in addition to administrative sanctions and criminal judgements. Hence, there is likely to be political influence to

---

[35] See The China Securities Investor Services Centre Submitting the List of Qualified Investors of Kangmei Case to Guangzhou Intermediate Court, available at https://www.investor.org.cn/rights_interests_protection/rights_protection_service/repre_action/xxxaction/202105/t20210514_493692.shtml (Last accessed 31 October, 2021).

persuade the China Securities Investor Services Centre from accepting the authorization and hence left investors insufficiently compensated. This problem is a general problem concerning the compensation process dominated by public agencies.

7.4 Stock Market Reactions to the Private Enforcement Reform

7.4.1 The Hypothesis, Identification Strategy and Sample

7.4.1.1 The Hypothesis

A large empirical and theoretical literature have been devoted into the discussion of "Law matters hypothesis" and "Enforcement matters hypothesis". For example, La Porta et al. argue that securities law on the book is the main determinant of the stock market,[36] but in contrast, prove that the actual enforcement outputs have the most significant effects.[37] This subsection aims to employ the exogenous shocks brought about by the recent reforms in the securities representative litigation and judgments made post the reform, and tests the aforementioned hypotheses by measuring the stock market price reactions with event studies. Post the promulgation of the Securities Law of 2019, there are three major events concerning the "on the book" and "in action" securities law, which are the promulgation of SPC's 2020 Provisions, and the judgments of "Wuyang Case" and "Kangmei Case" respectively.

SPC's 2020 Provisions provides a detail guidance on the securities representative litigation as is stipulated in the Article 95 of the Securities Law of 2019. The institutional innovations significantly increase the intensity of "on the book" deterrence to potential securities misconducts. Based on the "Law matters hypothesis", it is hypothesized that the stock market will incorporate this new information on the increased costs, and Hypothesis 7.1 is proposed as follows.

Hypothesis 7.1: Those stocks issued by firms having committed securities misconducts should suffer abnormal return when SPC's 2020 Provisions are disclosed.

The judgment of "Wuyang Case" is the first one with the procedure of representative litigation delivered by Chinese courts post the Securities Law of 2019, and the judgment of "Kangmei Case" is the first with the procedure of special representative litigation. The size of the damages awarded to the plaintiffs in these two judgments is of historical record. Hence, the judgments should renew the market perception about the expected costs of securities misconducts. Based on the "Enforcement matters

---

[36] La Porta et al. [14].

[37] Bhattacharya and Daouk [15].

hypothesis", it is hypothesized that the stock market will readjust the expectation on the costs of securities misconducts, and Hypothesis 7.2 is proposed as follows.

> Hypothesis 7.2: Those stocks issued by firms having committed securities misconducts should suffer abnormal return when the judgments of "Wuyang Case" and "Kangmei Case" are disclosed.

7.4.1.2   The Identification Strategy and Sample

We follow the shock-based approach and adopt a difference-in-difference research design to test the aforementioned two hypotheses.[38] SPC's 2020 Provisions and the two judgments are the sources of exogenous shocks, which in theory should bring external shocks to the expectations of stock market participants on the expected costs for securities misconducts. The event studies are used to estimate the abnormal return of the sample stocks on different event dates, which use the market return as the benchmark. The estimated abnormal returns are proxies for the market expectation of the magnitude and significance of the effects on the costs of securities misconducts due to the increase intensity of private securities litigation.

To control for the potential self-selection bias, the sample selection algorithm adopts the "straddle approach", which is designed to tackle the selection problem due to strategical adjustment of listed companies to the changes in the behavior of courts.[39] In its original application, the researcher only includes cases filed before the event and compare the outcomes of those cases decided before the event to those after the event. Hence, it is employed here to minimize the bias introduced by the fact that listed companies may self-select into the commitment of the securities misconducts based on the anticipated costs and benefits of private litigations. Following the spirit of this approach, our sample only includes the shares issued by those listed companies that disclose the Investigation Announcement and/or Preliminary Announcement within one year prior to the event, and excludes those disclosing Sanction Announcement. Recalling the discussions in Chap. 4, those listed companies committing securities misconducts will mainly go through three stages and should make separate announcements in the securities market. Hence, our sample selection algorithm makes sure that the included companies are those having committed misconducts but not been suited by harmed investors. The securities market participants should learn that our sample companies have committed misconducts, and the marginal changes in the costs due to private securities litigation are likely to be incorporated in the stock prices around the event dates.

---

[38] Atanasov and Black [16].

[39] Hubbard [17].

Table 7.1 Stock price reactions to SPC's 2020 provisions

Trading day	Sample size	Mean AR (%)	Median AR (%)	"z value", Wilcoxon Sign-rank Test
7	9	−0.66	0.00	−0.296
6	9	0.06	−0.46	−0.178
5	9	0.64	0.29	0.415
4	9	−0.18	−1.03	−0.652
3	9	1.37	0.35	0.652
2	9	2.02	1.68	1.955*
1	9	3.74	5.16	2.073*
0	9	1.75	1.28	1.955*
−1	9	0.05	0.13	0.059
−2	9	−0.03	−0.64	−0.059
−3	9	0.71	−0.02	0.415
−4	9	1.24	0.75	0.770
−5	9	0.66	−0.60	0.178
−6	9	1.46	1.55	1.125
−7	9	−0.03	−0.72	−0.296

Note (1) *, **, *** represent 10%, 5% and 1% significance levels
(2) The "z value" of the Wilcoxon sign-rank test with the null hypothesis that the median is zero is reported in the last column

7.4.2 Market Responses to SPC's 2020 Provisions

SPC's 2020 Provisions were disclosed to the market on July 31, 2020, and the first trading date post the event is August 3, 2020, which is chosen as the event date for our study. The sample includes 9 listed companies making the Investigation Announcement and/or Preliminary Announcement between August 1, 2019, and July 31, 2020.[40] The information about the dates of the announcements is obtained from the CNINF, and the trading data is obtained from CSMAR. The abnormal return is estimated with the event studies model, and the parameters are estimated over a period of 150 trading days prior to the event window.

According to the "Law matters hypothesis", the stock market should respond to SPC's 2020 Provisions, because "on the book" reform in the private securities litigation has significantly increased the private enforcement intensity. Hence, the stock prices should experience significant and negative abnormal return, which reflects the increased expected damages that should be paid by the listed companies. Table 7.1 reports the empirical results. The sample stock portfolio experienced significant and positive abnormal return over the [0, 2] event window, the mean of cumulative

---

[40] We manage to obtain a sample of 17 listed companies from CNINF, and drop 8 of them because they have no trading records around the event date.

abnormal return is around 7.51% and the median is around 8.12%. Such effect could be ascribed to the improvement brought about by SPC's 2020 Provisions, but it is difficult to interpret it meaningfully because of the limited sample size.

7.4.3 Market Responses to Wuyang Case and Kangmei Case

7.4.3.1 Wuyang Case

The judgment of Wuyang Case was disclosed to the market on December 31, 2020, and the first trading date post the event is January 4, 2021, which is chosen as the event date for our study. The sample includes 62 listed companies making the Investigation Announcement and/or Preliminary Announcement between January 1, 2020, and December 31, 2020.[41] The information about the dates of the announcements is obtained from the CNINF, and the trading data is obtained from CSMAR. The abnormal return is estimated with the event studies model, and the parameters are estimated over a period of 150 trading days prior to the event window.

According to the "Law matters hypothesis", the stock market should not respond to the judgment of Wuyang Case, because "on the book" reform in the private securities litigation has already been learned by the market participants. Hence, the judgment should reveal no additional information concerning the private enforcement costs, and stock prices should not respond to the event. In contrast, the "Enforcement matters hypothesis" proposes that the enforcement outcomes will deliver additional information and increase the marginal deterrence to securities misconducts. Table 7.2 reports the empirical results. The sample stock portfolio experienced significant and negative abnormal return over the $[-2, 3]$ event window, the mean of cumulative abnormal return is around -12.64% and the median is around -13.28%. The empirical results provide supporting evidence for the "Enforcement matters hypothesis".

7.4.3.2 Kangmei Case

The judgment of Kangmei Case was disclosed to the market on November 12, 2021, and the first trading date post the event is November 15, 2021, which is chosen as the event date for our study. The sample includes 43 listed companies making the Investigation Announcement and/or Preliminary Announcement between November 11, 2020, and November 12, 2021.[42] The information about the dates of the announcements is obtained from the CNINF, and the trading data is obtained from CSMAR.

---

[41] We manage to obtain a sample of 70 listed companies from CNINF, and drop 8 of them because they have no trading records around the event date.

[42] We manage to obtain a sample of 47 listed companies from CNINF, and drop 4 of them because they have no trading records around the event date.

Table 7.2 Stock price reactions to the judgment of Wuyang Case

Trading day	Sample size	Mean AR (%)	Median AR (%)	"z value", Wilcoxon Sign-rank Test
7	62	−1.23	−1.74	−3.327***
6	62	−1.72	−2.16	−3.937***
5	62	−1.88	−2.81	−4.336***
4	62	0.23	−0.21	0.060
3	62	−4.09	−4.84	−6.040***
2	62	−2.13	−2.67	−4.841***
1	62	−2.95	−2.87	−5.360***
0	62	−0.72	−0.56	−1.805*
−1	62	−1.24	−1.17	−4.399***
−2	62	−1.51	−1.17	−4.673***
−3	62	0.33	0.25	0.592
−4	62	−0.56	−1.27	−1.967**
−5	62	0.89	0.76	2.647***
−6	62	−1.13	−1.75	−2.969***
−7	62	−0.25	−0.42	−1.153

Note (1) *, **, *** represent 10%, 5% and 1% significance levels
(2) The "z value" of the Wilcoxon sign-rank test with the null hypothesis that the median is zero is reported in the last column

The abnormal return is estimated with the event studies model, and the parameters are estimated over a period of 150 trading days prior to the event window.

Though the judgment is not the first representative judgment made post the Securities Law of 2019, it is the first special representative judgment. Hence, according to the "Enforcement matters hypothesis", the actual enforcement of a special institutional innovation in private securities litigation should trigger the securities market to respond to the changes in the private enforcement intensity. Table 7.3 reports the empirical results. The sample stock portfolio experienced insignificant abnormal return over the event window, which is likely to be ascribed to the fact that market participants have already fully anticipated the changes in the intensity of private enforcement when the judgment of Wuyang Case is disclosed.

7.5   Alternative Dispute Resolution for Securities Fraudulent Misconducts

One of the major features of China's securities market is that retail investors have played a dominant role. By the end of August 2021, the number of individual investors surpassed 190 million, and 97% of these investors held less than 0.5 million RMB in

Table 7.3 Stock price reactions to the judgment of Kangmei Case

Trading day	Sample size	Mean AR (%)	Median AR (%)	"z value", Wilcoxon sign-rank test
7	43	−0.27	−0.38	−1.594
6	43	0.01	0.01	2.717***
5	43	−0.01	0.09	−3.502***
4	43	−0.18	0.09	−0.229
3	43	−0.57	−0.57	−2.318**
2	43	1.26	0.90	2.475***
1	43	−0.30	−0.28	−1.389
0	43	0.07	0.58	0.290
−1	43	0.01	0.03	−0.097
−2	43	0.24	0.72	0.749
−3	43	0.14	0.32	0.254
−4	43	1.55	1.00	3.260***
−5	43	0.84	0.73	2.222**
−6	43	−0.51	−0.67	−0.966
−7	43	0.23	0.10	−0.060

Note (1) *, **, *** represent 10%, 5% and 1% significance levels
(2) The "z value" of the Wilcoxon sign-rank test with the null hypothesis that the median is zero is reported in the last column

their accounts.[43] Hence, a large percentage of securities disputes are concerned with small stakes, and it is not economical for both the concerned parties and society as a whole if such disputes are all settled in the court system. Hence, private enforcement in China also comprises multiple alternative dispute resolution mechanisms, which mainly include securities mediation and arbitration. China's general judiciary reform also highlights the solution mechanisms outside the court room. As early as June 2019, the SPC and CSRC jointly released the Opinions on Comprehensively Promoting the Alternative Disputes Resolution for Resolving the Securities Disputes[44] and established the coordination between the mediation procedures administered by the CSRC and judiciary hearing. Article 7 of the Opinions on Cracking down on Securities Misconducts has furthermore emphasized employing securities arbitration to facilitate investor compensation.

There are two main alternative dispute resolutions for securities disputes administered by the CSRC. The first is the mediation procedure administered by the China Securities Investor Services Centre. Article 94 of the Securities Law of 2019 delegated the China Securities Investor Services Centre to act as the mediator to settle

---

[43] See The Number of Individual Surpassed 190 million, available at https://wallstreetcn.com/art icles/3640962 (Last accessed 31 October, 2021).

[44] See Guanyu Quanmian Tuijin Zhengquan Qihuo Jiufen Duoyuan Huajie Jizhi Jianshe De Yijian, available at http://www.csrc.gov.cn/newsite/flb/flfg/sfjs_8249/201906/t20190627_358081. html (Last accessed 31 October, 2021).

securities disputes. It mandates that both parties in the disputes between investors and issuers and/or securities firms could apply for securities mediation administered by the China Securities Investor Services Centre; and in disputes between retail investors and securities firms, if the former decide to file for mediation, the securities firms could not deny and should participate.

The China Securities Investor Services Centre has cooperated with local securities regulators to establish securities mediation hubs. Until March 2019, there were 35 mediation hubs across the nation.[45] Such hubs are designed to be investor friendly and to reduce their costs for obtaining relief. According to Article 8 of the Mediation Rules of the China Securities Investor Services Centre, the process could be divided into a regular mediation procedure and a simplified mediation procedure. In the regular process, the China Securities Investor Services Centre shall seek opinions from the respondent within 7 days, and the process shall conclude within 30 days. In the simplified process, the case should be concluded within 20 days and could be adjudicated in written form or through the internet. The mediation decision has binding power, and the CSRC will employ reputational sanctions for those disobeying the decision. Such an arrangement significantly reduces the time costs for investors compared to securities litigations. Until early 2019, the China Securities Investor Services Centre registered over 8000 applications and accepted more than 6000 cases, among which over 4300 cases were concluded and investors received compensation for nearly 1 billion RMB.[46]

The second is the mediation procedure administered by the Securities Association of China, which is based on the authorization from Section 7 of Article 166 of the Securities Law of 2019. The Securities Association of China has promulgated the Measures for Administrating Securities Mediation and the Rules for Administrating Securities Mediation.[47] According to Article 11 of the Measures for the Administrating Securities Mediation, three types of disputes could be submitted to the Securities Association of China for resolution, which include those between investors and the members, those between members and those between members and other stakeholders. The mediators are selected from member organizations, regulatory agencies, professional mediators, retired judges and governmental officials and academic staff.[48] According to the data released by the Securities Association of China in October 2020, it has hired 294 mediators nationwide, among which those from securities firms and from regulatory agencies account for 43% and 25%, respectively.[49] Between 2012 and 2020, the mediation hub of the Securities Association

---

[45] See Securities Dispute Mediation Hubs, available at http://www.isc.com.cn/html/djgzz/ (Last accessed 31 October, 2021).

[46] See Introduction to the Mediation Hubs of China Securities Investor Services Centre, available at https://www.sohu.com/a/304029209_115124 (Last accessed 31 October, 2021).

[47] See Zhengquan Jiufen Tiaojie Gongzuo Guanli Banfa and Zhengquan Jiufen Tiaojie Guize, available at https://www.sac.net.cn/hyfw/zqjftj/tjgz/ (Last accessed 31 October, 2021).

[48] See Article 13 of the Measures for the Administrating Securities Mediation.

[49] See Introduction to the Mediation of the Securities Association of China, available at https://tzz.sac.net.cn/zqzsjs/zqjftj/tjgzjs/202010/t20201016_144381.html (Last accessed 31 October, 2021).

of China received 2364 applications, of which 1724 were successfully settled and investors received 335 million RMB.[50]

References

1. Livingston, M., Poon, W. P. H., & Zhou, L. (2018). Are Chinese credit ratings relevant? A study of the Chinese bond market and credit rating industry. *Journal of Banking & Finance, 87*, 216–232.
2. Xu, W., & Liu, Y. (2021). Does reputational capital affect credit rating agencies? Empirical evidence from a natural experiment in China. *European Journal of Law and Economics, 51*(3), 433–468.
3. Atkins, P. S. (2007). Speech by SEC commissioner: Is excessive regulation and litigation eroding U.S. financial competitiveness? Available at https://www.sec.gov/news/speech/2007/spch042007psa.htm. Last accessed 31 Oct 2021
4. Faisman, A. (2021). The goals of class actions. *Columbia Law Review, 121*(7), 2157–2202.
5. Rubenstein, W. B. (2006). Why enable litigation? A positive externalities theory of the small claims class action. *UMKC Law Review, 74*, 709–722.
6. Choi, S. J., Erickson, J., & Pritchard, A. C. (2020). Working hard or making work? Plaintiffs' attorney fees in securities fraud class actions. *Journal of Empirical Legal Studies, 17*(3), 438–465.
7. Baker, L. A., Perino, M., & Silver, C. (2015). Is the price right? An empirical study of fee-setting in securities class actions. *Columbia Law Review, 115*, 1371–1452.
8. Choi, S. J., Pritchard, A. C., & Fisch, J. E. (2005). Do institutions matter? The impact of the lead plaintiff provision of the private securities litigation reform act. *Washington University Law Quarterly, 83*, 869–905.
9. Kempf, E., & Spalt, O. (2019). Litigating innovation: Evidence from securities class action lawsuits. *SSRN Finance Working Paper NO. 614/2019.* Available at http://ssrn.com/abstract_id=3143690
10. Cooper, A. J. (1991). Do the merits matter? A study of settlements in securities class actions. *Stanford Law Review, 43*, 497–598.
11. Lin, Y.-H. L., & Xiang, Y. (2022). The rise of non-profit organizations in global securities class action: A new hybrid model in China. *Columbia Journal of Transnational Law, 60*, Forthcoming.
12. Li, Y. (2018). *China financial judiciary report*. People's Court Press.
13. Huang, R. H. (2013). Private enforcement of securities law in China: A ten-year retrospective and empirical assessment. *American Journal of Comparative Law, 61*(4), 757–798.
14. La Porta, R., Lopez-de-Silanes, F., & Shleifer, A. (2008). The economic consequences of legal origins. *Journal of Economic Literature, 46*(2), 285–332.
15. Bhattacharya, U., & Daouk, H. (2002). The world price of insider trading. *Journal of Finance, 57*, 75–108.
16. Atanasov, V. A., & Black, B. S. (2016). Shock-based causal inference in corporate finance and accounting research. *Critical Finance Review, 5*(2), 207–304.
17. Hubbard, W. (2017). The effects of Twombly and Iqbal. *Journal of Empirical Legal Studies, 14*, 474–526.

---

[50] See Introduction to the Securities Mediation, available at https://tzz.sac.net.cn/zqzsjs/zqjftj/tjgzjs/ (Last accessed 31 October, 2021).

Chapter 8
Conclusion

This book follows the law-and-economic pathway to investigate securities law enforcement in China and adopts the perspective of functional analysis to examine the efficiency of the enforcement regime in compensating investors and deterring securities misconduct. Law enforcement in this book is broadly defined as the proceedings through which legal liabilities are imposed on those committing securities misconduct, which could be mainly divided into private enforcement and public enforcement based on the identity of the entities initiating the enforcement proceedings. Both enforcement strategies have advantages and disadvantages. Private enforcement has obtained the right incentive structure, informational advantage concerning certain misconduct and impetus for enforcement innovation, whereas it also suffers from the collective action problem and significant costs of frivolous litigation. In contrast, public enforcement has enjoyed professionalism and the economy of scale but is subjected to problems of insufficient incentives and selective enforcement.

The rise of law and finance scholarship has vitalized the empirical analysis on securities law enforcement since the early 2000s. The "Law Matters" scholarship has received extensive criticisms from the "Enforcement matters" scholarship, which argues that the effects of law enforcement dominate those of the "law on the book" in both cross-jurisdictional and single-country contexts. Currently, a mixed enforcement regime has become the dominant model across the world, although different jurisdictions vary in their reliance on public or private enforcement of securities law. A potential bias in the existing literature is that the majority of attention has been devoted to the enforcement regime in developed markets, and that in emerging nations, such as Chinese securities law enforcement, have received insufficient academic examination. China's enforcement regime adopts a centralized model, which is in sharp contrast to the American decentralized model. An analysis of the former model will offer a completely different picture and an interesting case study on the advantages and disadvantage of competing models.

This book hence tries to fill the gap in the literature and provides the empirical analysis on the securities law enforcement regime in China with the most updated data. Empirical studies in the early twenty-first century find that securities law enforcement

© The Author(s), under exclusive license to Springer Nature Singapore Pte Ltd. 2022   145
W. Xu, *The Enforcement of Securities Law in China*,
https://doi.org/10.1007/978-981-19-0904-7_8

in China used to be extremely weak. Such findings are not unexpected considering that the stock market has a history of less than a decade, and the first Securities Law was promulgated in 1998. At that time, the Chinese stock market still emphasized entry regulation and was in the shadow of a quota system, which allocates the IPO quota based on the prior performance of the listed companies recommended by the ministerial governmental agencies. SOEs are primary candidate companies for listing, and financial scandals frequently occur. Although merit regulation was instituted to replace the quota system and increased the reliance on the market-based mechanism, the administrative authorities had relatively strong influences on the market.

However, the static view that securities law enforcement does not matter in China is questionable, considering that securities regulations have been undergoing drastic reform and that the efficiency of enforcement regimes has been repeatedly emphasized by securities regulators. In particular, the pilot project initiated by the CSRC to delegate the enforcement authority to impose administrative sanctions on ROs in Shanghai, Guangdong and Shenzhen in 2011 represents an important effort for improving public enforcement efficiency. In October 2013, all ROs obtained such authority and were responsible for investigating and sanctioning minor cases within their jurisdictions. The governance structure is similar to China's authoritarian political regime, which is named the RDA model. It centralizes the political and personnel governance structure and decentralizes the considerable enforcement authority to ROs, which enjoy strong incentives to compete with each other in the dimension of enforcement outputs.

The systematic reform of the private enforcement regime in China was brought about by the revised Securities Law in 2019. Prior to this revision, SPC's 2003 Provisions was the governing rules for private litigations, which adopted an "opt-in" design. Consequently, investors need to assume high litigation costs and are poorly compensated because of collective action problems. The IPO registration reform launched in 2014, which reduces the reliance on entry regulation and increases that on market forces, calls for an improvement in investor protection and compensation. The Securities Law of 2019 specifies a multilayered securities private litigation regime, which includes Chinese-style class action adopting the American "opt-out" design to solve the collective action problem.

Both reform measures are expected to increase the enforcement intensity, and our empirical analysis with the most updated data confirms the predictions. In the public enforcement domain, which mainly assumes the responsibility of deterring securities misconduct, the CSRC and its 38 ROs, SHSE and SZSE, and securities self-regulatory organizations all enforce securities law and sanction violators. Article 170 of the Securities Law of 2019 lists a broad range of enforcement instruments that could be employed by the CSRC. The first group is administrative sanctions, including warnings, administrative fines, disgorgement, correction, disqualification and closedown. The administrative enforcement proceedings initiated by the CSRC and its 38 ROs follow strict procedure requirements because of its severe impacts on those sanctioned. The enforcement proceeding can be further divided into the stages of informal investigation, filing and registering the case, formal investigation and case closing. If the CSRC decides to register the case after informal investigation, it should send Notice Letter of Investigation to the investigated parties so that they are aware of the ongoing investigation. Administrative sanctions also cause significant derivative costs. First, those sanctioned administratively will be exposed to the risk of private litigations, according to the SPC's 2003 Provisions. Second, those listed companies and their affiliated will be disqualified for favorable regulatory treatment and be subject to restrictions in certain transactions.

The second group is non-administrative sanction. According to Article 2 of the Measures for Implementing the Non-administrative Sanctions in the Securities and Futures Market (Draft for Soliciting Comments), there are a total of sixteen types of non-administrative sanctions. The indirect costs to the sanctioned, particularly the listed companies, are increased after SPC's 2020 Provisions, which stipulates that non-administrative sanctions could be used as the preliminary proofs for misconducts and requires lower courts to accept the pleadings with such proofs in the form of representative litigation. Consequently, entities sanctioned by the CSRC and its ROs nonadministratively are also exposed to the risks of private litigation.

The inputs of public enforcement are limited. The data show that the annual budget and staffing number of the CSRC and its ROs between 2011 and 2019 are small in magnitude. The resource constraint seems to be exacerbated after the registration reform, which increases the number of listed companies at an accelerated pace. Public enforcement outputs have remained at a relatively low level. However, from a time-series perspective, the situation changed after the reform of the public enforcement regime in 2011, and the enforcement outputs had grown at a higher rate. The outputs at the commission level have been approximately 80 sanctions and have maintained a steady growth rate of approximately 7% in recent years. The monetary sanctions imposed by the CSRC even increase exponentially and reach a peak of 10.6 billion RMB in 2018, which is approximately 80 times of the size in 2011. The enforcement outputs at the RO level maintained a fast growth rate between 2011 and 2019 and reached a total of 1472 sanctions. The actions initiated by ROs are mainly non-administrative and against informational infractions. The RDA model successfully improved the enforcement intensity at the regional level.

Public enforcement is often criticized for selectively targeting certain market participants. The selective enforcement hypothesis is tested using sanctions against listed companies, which are further divided into CGCFs, PGCF, MGCF and PF. The CGCFs enjoyed significant favorable treatment and faced the lowest probability of receiving public sanctions before 2010. However, the difference in the probability of receiving public sanctions among the four groups has converged since then, which is due to the increase in the number of PF and the active participation of ROs in the enforcement actions. Nevertheless, CGCFs have the lowest likelihood of becoming sanctioned and the highest likelihood of receiving non-administrative sanctions.

Another often-cited criticism is that public enforcement only leads to a weak price reaction, which suggests that it does not matter for market participants. However, it is shown that such conclusions are mainly due to mistakes in the understanding of the institutional features of Chinese public enforcement proceedings. There is a procedural difference between administrative and non-administrative proceedings.

The former can be divided into three stages, which are correlated with three separate disclosure announcements. Event studies are applied separately on the investigation announcement date, preliminary announcement date and sanction announcement date. It is found that the portfolio of stocks sanctioned administratively has experienced a significant and negative cumulative AR of -12.03% over the $(-1, 5)$ event window, which is much higher than those estimated by previous studies. Hence, it is argued that the administrative sanctions issued by the CSRC and its ROs are not toothless, as claimed in previous empirical studies.

Because the enforcement proceedings initiated by the CSRC and its ROs are deterrence oriented and the compensation function is overlooked, the CSRC has experimented with two alternative enforcement proceedings, i.e., the prioritized compensation scheme and administrative settlement, which are compensation oriented. The violators are offered with an opportunity to compensate harmed investors in exchange for lenient administrative sanctions in both mechanisms. However, because the expected benefits of market participants from both procedures are limited, the results of the pilot projects are far from satisfactory.

In addition to the enforcement efforts of the CSRC and its ROs, multiple public agencies participate in public enforcement actions. One important public enforcer is the stock exchange. Article 96 of the Securities Law of 2019 specifies that SHSE and SZSE are the self-regulatory organizations of the securities market and assumes the responsibilities of direct market supervision and self-regulation. Stock exchanges are not equipped with the authority to impose administrative sanctions but could impose self-regulatory penalties. The enforcement proceedings of stock exchanges take a relatively short time and would be highly responsive to discovered misconduct. Between 2010 and 2019, the two stock exchanges imposed a total of 1932 sanctions.

Another interesting question concerning the public enforcement regime is whether it is responsive, which tends to adopt a "tit-for-tat strategy" and a dynamic relationship of "deterrence-cooperation" between the public regulators and the regulated regulators. Using a sample of enforcement outputs of the CSRC and two stock exchanges issued between 2009 and 2020, the sanctions are classified into five categories according to the degree of punitiveness, including "Strong-punitive administrative sanction", "Weak-punitive administrative sanction", "Strong-punitive nonadministrative sanction", "Weak-punitive nonadministrative sanction" and "Cooperative nonadministrative sanction". Public enforcement outputs exhibited a pyramidal distribution, and "weak-punitive nonadministrative sanction" had the highest percentage. In addition, public sanctions also become more severe for repeated offenders. Those companies sanctioned before are more likely to be sanctioned with punitive sanctions.

In the private enforcement domain, the governing rules of securities private litigation used to be SPC's 2003 Provisions, but the situation changed after the Securities Law was revised in 2019 and a multidimensional securities litigation system was established. SPC's 2003 Provisions is investor unfriendly and sets a significant obstacle for investors to obtain judiciary relief. First, the provisions restricted the scope of qualified plaintiffs to investors suffering from losses due to misrepresentation, and those due to insider trading and market manipulation were excluded. Second, the intermediate-level courts at the place where the defendant firms are located have territorial jurisdiction. Third, investors need to satisfy administrative prerequisites that defendants are sanctioned administratively or criminally so that courts will admit the pleadings. Finally, investors could only bring individual or joint suits instead of U.S.-style class actions, which causes the collective action problem.

Using the judgements disclosed in the China Judgements Online between 2013 and 2016, it is found that the intensity of private enforcement is extremely weak. Only 40 informational violators are named defendants, and only 7 listed companies paid more than 1 million RMB for investor compensation. The percentage of shareholders actually seeking compensation ranges between 1.25% and 0.07%, and the average of our sampled case is approximately 0.22%. A large number of potentially harmed investors are "rationally apathetic" to the right to seek compensation from violators. In addition, the calculation of tortious compensation is inconsistent among adjudicating courts. Generally, the losses due to misrepresentation are the difference between buying and selling prices multiplied by the qualified trading volume, excluding those due to systematic risk. Investor compensation is hence determined by the "Implementation date" and "Revealing date", which jointly determine the buying price, selling price and qualified trading volume, and the "calculation of systematic risk", which determine losses unrelated to misrepresentation.

The inconsistency in calculating civil compensation is mainly due to the following two factors. First, adjudicating courts have different opinions about the "Revealing date" of misconduct. Based on SPC's 2003 Provisions, it is the first time that misrepresented information is corrected and learned by the market. The following dates, including the media coverage day, the announcement day of non-administrative sanction, investigation announcement day, preliminary sanction day and final sanction day, were chosen to be the "Revealing dates". From the perspective of the efficient market hypothesis, the choice of the "Revealing date" should be no later than the investigation announcement day. Second, the "Calculation of systematic risk" varies among different courts. SPC regards that civil compensation for misrepresentation is tortious in nature and hence needs to exclude losses unrelated to misconduct. Hence, it is important to estimate the price variation due to systematic risk. Different market indices, such as the SZSE index and industrial index, are chosen as proxies for systematic factors, and their variation between "Implementation date" and "Revealing date" is directly excluded from the estimated per share losses of the plaintiffs.

To estimate the impact of the collective action problem on the private enforcement regime, a shock-based research design using the SPC's 2002 Notice as a natural experiment is employed. The empirical analysis takes advantage of a unique institutional setting in which some listed companies issued legally identical "twin A/B-shares". A-share is mainly held by retail investors, which suffer from collective action problems and are "rationally apathetic" to the right to bring private litigations; in contrast, B-share is held by wealthy individual investors and institutional investors, which have higher stakes and value higher the right to bring private litigations. The sample hence includes 162 A/B-shares issued by 81 listed firms. A significant positive abnormal return for B-shares relative to A-shares is documented, which is approximately 2.08% over the 3-day event window after controlling for the market liquidity proxy, firm-specific characteristics and industrial dummies. It is shown that the collective action problem significantly reduces the efficiency of securities litigation in protecting securities investors.

The collective action problem is addressed by the Securities Law of 2019, which significantly changes the landscape of private enforcement in China. Article 95 lays down and establishes a multidimensional securities litigation system comprising individual suits, "opt-in" regular representative litigation and "opt-out" special representative litigation. In particular, "opt-out" special representative litigation is also called "Chinese class action", which combines the "opt-out" design of class action and appointment of nonprofit investor protection agencies as the lead plaintiff. Institutions balance the economic benefits of scale in solving massive securities torts and the costs due to frivolous litigation. SPC's 2020 Provisions was issued later to provide detailed guidance on both regular and special representative litigation.

A case study on the regular representative litigation brought about by harmed investors against Wuyang for its fraudulent issuance on the company bond market has revealed several interesting findings. First, the adjudicating court shows a U-turn and seems to be extremely investor friendly, and investors are awarded with the full compensation of the principal and interests, with all major parties participating in the bond issuance assuming the joint and several obligations for the civil liabilities. However, such a judgement is inappropriate because financial intermediaries are required to jointly assume the liability for breach of contractual terms instead of tortious liabilities. Second, the "Revealing date" is chosen to be the one when the CSRC issued the preliminary sanction decision, which seems to be too late. Taking into consideration the announcement made and the price movement of the listed company bond, the "Revealing date" should be much earlier and the one when both bonds were stopped trading temporarily.

The analysis of the special representative litigation brought about by harmed investors against Kangmei for its fraudulent issuance on the stock market also generates inspiring findings. On the one hand, special representative litigation maximizes the number of plaintiffs and hence reduces the average litigation costs. Second, the China Securities Investor Services Centre could obtain the list of qualified investors from the Securities Depository and Clearing Corporation with reference to the period determined by the adjudicating court. The arrangement significantly increases the precision of investor compensation. Finally, the case is adjudicated with a much shorter time compared with the previous cases. On the other hand, special representative litigation has been controversial. First, the boundary of the qualified plaintiffs is determined without going through a court trial, which means that the scope of civil compensation is largely determined. Second, the China Securities Investor Services Centre will have difficulties selecting the appropriate cases to initiate special representative litigation and might suffer from political influences.

In addition to the formal procedure of civil litigation, alternative dispute resolution also facilitates investor compensation. The securities mediation procedure administered by the China Securities Investor Services Centre and the Securities Association of China is the primary venue. The former mainly solves the disputes between investors and issuers and/or securities firms; the latter mainly solves those between investors and the affiliated members. Both procedures have settled thousands of disputes in the last ten years and obtained significant compensation for harmed investors.

In sum, if a dynamic view is taken to evaluate the enforcement regime of securities law in China, it is not difficult to see that both investor protection and sanctions of misconduct have been significantly improved compared to the situation in the early twenty-first century. The intensity of public enforcement is heightened due to the RDA model, and ROs become major enforcers; the collective action problem is addressed by the newly revised Securities Law in 2019, and the analysis of recent cases shows that investor compensation is substantially increased. However, there are several obvious drawbacks concerning the enforcement regime. It is mainly controlled by public agencies and hence subject to potential caveats of public enforcement, for example, selective enforcement and underenforcement. The improvement of the enforcement regime of securities law is far from the end, but needs ongoing attentions from academics, professionals and politicians.

Ingram Content Group UK Ltd.
Milton Keynes UK
UKHW010651210323
418913UK00006B/400